WES ANDERSON
ALL THE FILMS

WES ANDERSON

ALL THE FILMS

THE STORY BEHIND EVERY MOVIE, EPISODE, AND SHORT

Christophe Narbonne

BLACK DOG
& LEVENTHAL
PUBLISHERS
NEW YORK

CONTENTS

BEFORE YOU BEGIN

Wes Anderson's filmography is presented chronologically. Each film or short is introduced by a fact sheet. For reasons of space, the cast is not exhaustive, and for consistency, the nationalities listed correspond to the production companies and co-producing studios. Data that cannot be found is indicated by a question mark.

FOREWORD

The last time I saw Wes Anderson was in Lyon, during the winter of 2024. He was on vacation with his family and traveling around Europe in his bus. He had come from Spain, was going up the Rhône valley but was stopped in a traffic jam in Lyon. We went to a local restaurant and, as usual, he proved to be a generous and curious guest, not hesitating to inquire about the name and composition of the dishes in his quirky French. This might contrast with the image we have of him through his films, but let's make no mistake: He was enjoying the andouillette gratin with his customary elegance.

I looked at him. I felt a certain pride in having welcomed him several times at the Cannes Film Festival and, even, in considering him a friend. Wes always arrives in a group, assembling a tribe of people happy to be from his world—an "Andersonian consulate" he watches over, away from everything.

Paradoxically, Wes Anderson does not come from space, but from Texas, from real America. And from the depths of the United States, he emerged at the turn of the 2000s as a screenwriter and director to regenerate world cinema, from the seabed of *The Life Aquatic* to the India traveled in *The Darjeeling Limited* to the European hub of *The Grand Budapest Hotel*. Wes Anderson is someone who lives comfortably both inside and outside the system and who explores territories that clearly escape the Hollywood norm.

And when he seems to return home, as in the very moving *Asteroid City*, after having traveled the world, it is to explore in his own way, as through a book of pictures, a fragment of Americana, a skein of American mythologies, the desert, the extraterrestrial threat, the melancholy of movie stars... Because the central star of his solar system is indeed cinema, whose history he devours with relish, from high-energy American thrillers of the early 1930s to the restless humanism of Indian filmmaker Satyajit Ray. [As a guest of honor at the 2023 Lumière Festival, Wes Anderson gave a memorable presentation of Ray's Apu trilogy.] He builds his works as a smiling observer, and nothing really distinguishes his animated films, like the extraordinary *Isle of Dogs*, a tribute to Japanese culture, from the rest of his productions.

Dividing his time between Paris, New York, and the English countryside, Wes Anderson is one of the few totally free directors today, because he applies his freedom to all the constraints of the industrial art that is cinema. He has become one of those creators whose aesthetic universe is now familiar to spectators around the world. In the old days of cinephilia—which Wes claims to be a part of—an artist like him was called an "auteur." An author to the power of a thousand, then!

Thierry Frémaux,
Director, Cannes Film Festival

Wes Anderson in 1998, on the release of *Rushmore*.

INTRODUCTION

Wes Anderson in 1993. Photograph by Laura Wilson.

Wes Anderson unveiled his first short film, *Bottle Rocket*, at the Sundance Film Festival in January 1993, and in 2023 he celebrated thirty years in the business. In three decades, this contemporary of American filmmakers Paul Thomas Anderson, James Gray, and Darren Aronofsky became internationally known. More than this, he became a fashion and design icon. Because Wes Anderson, right down to his appearance, is a style, if not a school of thought. His cinema embodies an old-fashioned sophistication and elegance that coincides with the desire of the masses to view the world differently, by putting technology on pause and looking within for the answers that a comment on social networks will theoretically never provide. There is nothing reactionary or backward looking about what might appear to be a posture from another time. Wes Anderson is a matter of taste, increasingly shared by those who want to escape from a certain form of digital standardization of fashions and customs.

The Influencer

"Miniaturist," "Mannerist," "Surrealist." Wes Anderson's cinema is often reduced to its "pretty" forms, a shortcut to extracting its equally fascinating content. In the same way that he accumulates details in his images, the author-director nourishes his plots with multiple lines of interpretation—dramatic, comic, existential, historical, artistic. To immerse oneself in his filmography is to be dazzled and also to reflect on human nature, which Anderson believes to be profoundly good. After all, his characters always have the right to a second chance after making amends. Whether one likes or dislikes his approach (naïve, melancholy, and funny on the surface), audiences experience something different that transforms them a little. As a result, it is not incongruous to see an art of living and a way of apprehending reality "in Wes Anderson style" flourishing on Instagram or TikTok, and even in everyday life. After six months of intensive work on his case, the author of these lines himself came quite close to centering all his furniture, buying vinyl, and staring longingly at others without a word being uttered.

The Invisible Man

From his early days, Anderson cultivated a sense of secrecy and mystery that contributes to the fascination he still generates. Apart from promoting his films, he gives very few interviews, and when he does, he refrains from commenting on his private life. Very few personal details are circulated about him, starting with his childhood (in Texas), which he used as material for his first films. *Rushmore*

(1998) and *The Royal Tenenbaums* (2001), to name the most emblematic (although they were co-written with Owen Wilson, whom he met in college in Austin), refer to several key events in his youth: his parents' divorce (when he was eight), his place in a sibling family (he is the second of three boys), his artistic awakening at school (a teacher encouraged him to write and stage plays to channel his anger), and his experience of the control and frustration arising from his first creations.

On all this, and more (his relationship with the United States, France, fatherhood, the international situation, the world of yesterday and today, music, cinema, etc.), we would have loved to talk with Anderson. But, true to his legend, he was immersed in the preparation of his mysterious twelfth feature film, which began shooting in Germany in March 2024. Based on the principle that other people are the ones who speak best of you, we collected testimonials from a dozen of his closest associates (most of whom asked for the director's approval), foremost among them Robert Yeoman, his unfailing cinematographer since the feature *Bottle Rocket* (1996). With infinite patience and generosity, this respected professional gave us some valuable insights into Anderson's modus operandi and his evolution over the course of three fruitful decades spent establishing a unique universe of his own.

The Well-Loved Boss

In the course of writing this book and our various interviews, an unsuspected Anderson came to light. Less of a "control freak" and less aloof than one might imagine, attentive and solicitous of the well-being of his teams, gentleman Wes is clearly the artist Anderson. The child still seeking to find himself, the chronicler of dysfunctional tribes, the voluntary Parisian exile, has quietly built for himself a film family entirely devoted to his cause—without, however, falling into the trap of idolatry. It is because of this communion around his person and the extravagant projects he develops that Anderson is able to make the most of the potential of his collaborators, who eventually come to resemble him and adopt the same work ethic. All are aware of and happy to be living an unparalleled collective experience (to the point of sharing the same lodgings on the shoot) and to be writing the history of cinema in real time in the company of one of its most illustrious representatives today. Anderson is a master of images and a lover of words, an aesthete and a storyteller, an artist and a craftsman. He is also a go-between, who is part of the great movement of the arts and who perpetuates certain founding cinematic myths such as film, the square format (borrowed from the silent era), and handcrafted artifices. Filled with references to the films that cradled him, his cinema is as much oriented toward the past as it is anchored in the new millennium—and the significant antimodern current that goes with it. *Wes Anderson All the Films* is intended to be as accurate a reflection as possible of this atypical profile, of a persona that has succeeded in attracting a growing audience while remaining true to his values and aspirations.

Filming of *The French Dispatch*, immortalized by Roger Do Minh, still photographer.

Wes Anderson and his trusty cinematographer, Robert Yeoman, on *The French Dispatch*.

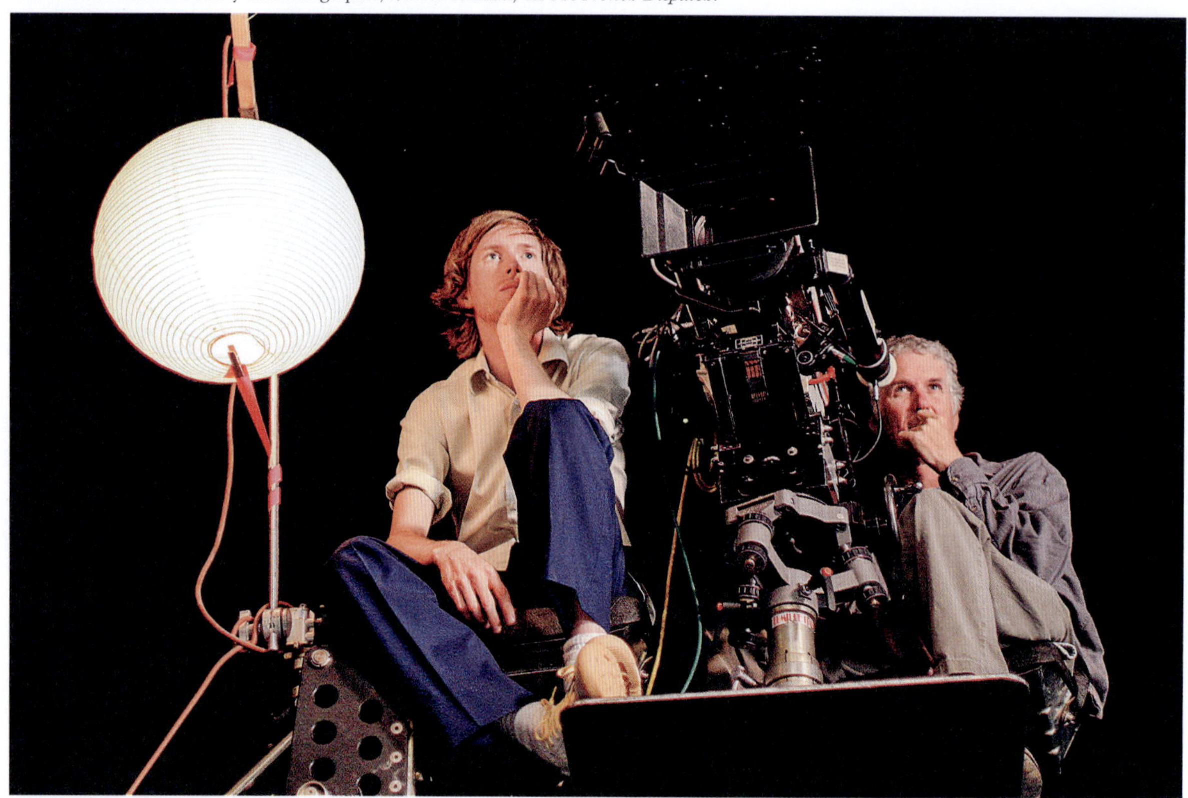

The influential art supervisor Adam Stockhausen on *The French Dispatch*.

WES ANDERSON
as seen by his colleagues

"Wes is a supremely creative human being and a master of the craft of filmmaking. In the years I have known him, he is always learning and growing and quick to apply what he has learned and to filter new experiences through his creative lens."

Jeremy Dawson, producer

"Wes is very loyal. He likes to work with the same team and have a small group on the set. It is a very intelligent way of doing things. Many thanks to him for taking us on all these wonderful adventures!"

Patricia Colin,
senior costume designer

"Wes is a being with a slender, graceful body, colorful clothes of childlike pop elegance, and a head of reddish-blond hair that touches the clouds."

Alexandre Desplat, composer

"Wes makes artistic choices that no other human being would. You can put ideas of your own in front of him, but he usually already has something in his mind that he's trying to get to. That's what an auteur does. He makes everything in his own vision. Wes is a great champion of artists, and I'm happy to be a part of the process."

Turlo Griffin,
conceptual artist and illustrator

"Wes brings a very strong vision to all aspects of his film. He is the master conductor and the cast and crew are his instruments. He challenges all of us to work outside of our comfort zone. When you work on his films, you are not just making a movie; you are embarking on a life adventure."

Robert Yeoman,
director of photography

"He is a true gentleman and a magician in the arts of film and storytelling."

Andy Gent,
senior puppet maker

Rupert Friend under the eye of Wes Anderson in *Asteroid City*.

ARRI
ARRIHEAD 2
WARNING
CHAPMAN

Tom Hanks (middle, standing) and Hope Davis (behind Hanks) on the set of *Asteroid City*.

BOTTLE ROCKET

United States • 13 min • Black and white • Mono • 1.33 : 1

Filming Dates: Spring–Autumn 1992
Screening in the United States: January 1993 (Sundance Film Festival)

Producer: Cynthia Hargrave
Associate Producers: Darren Kasmir, Lee Blumer
Executive Producers: L. M. Kit Carson, Michael Lang
Consigliere: Andrew Wilson

Screenplay: Wes Anderson, Owen Wilson
Directors of Photography: Bert Guthrie, Barry Braverman
Assistant Director: Christopher Michael Knudson
Film Editing: Tom Aberg, Laura Cargile, Denise Ferrari-Segell
Sound: Tom's Easy Way
Makeup: Solina Tabrizi
Stunts: Randy Fife

Starring: **OWEN WILSON** (Dignan), **LUKE WILSON** (Anthony), **ROBERT MUSGRAVE** (Bob Hanson), **ELISSA SOMMERFIELD** (Waitress at Diner), **ISIAH ELLIS** (Man on Street), **TEMPLE NASH** (Temple), **COL. BRIGGS BRANNING** (Man at Goff's)

"You don't intimidate people with guns; you shoot people with guns."

—

Temple

SYNOPSIS

Two friends, Dignan and Anthony, wander the streets discussing the virtues of the *Starsky and Hutch* series (William Blinn, 1975–1979). Equipped with bags, they nonchalantly scale a fence, then a gate, before entering a house with the obvious intention of robbing it. They leave without being disturbed, with a meager haul in their pockets. When the robbery is debriefed at a lunch counter, it becomes clear that they have robbed the house of Anthony's parents, and Anthony is furious because Dignan has taken his mother's earrings even though Anthony had expressly forbidden him to do so.

GENESIS

As is often the case with Wes Anderson, reality meets fiction, and vice versa. The idea for *Bottle Rocket* came from a personal experience he had while sharing a shabby Dallas apartment in the early 1990s with brothers Owen and Andrew Wilson and mutual friend Robert Musgrave. Faced with their landlord's categorical refusal to carry out any work to make the place more habitable (in winter, the cold seeped in through the broken windows), slackers Wes Anderson and Owen Wilson decided to stage a burglary of their own apartment[1] to demonstrate just how unsanitary and unsafe it was. Naturally, they were confounded by a private detective hired by the owner, who was a cheapskate but not stupid.

An Association of Wrongdoers

Arising from their disastrous association of wrongdoers, the two thieves, who had already written more or less successful four-hander screenplays, created *Bottle Rocket*, an absurd chronicle in which a duo of wannabe hoodlums dream of being kings of crime, without having the requisite determination or courage, let alone adventurous spirit. The characters are stubborn, more victims of everyday life than transforming it, to the point where, in the end, they challenge each other to a race because, in spite of everything, they have to keep going. Wes Anderson and Owen Wilson, gentle dreamers and facetious pessimists, have found each other.

CASTING

Wes Anderson did not have to look very far to find his actors: Owen Wilson; Owen's little brother, Luke; and Robert Musgrave and his friends had the advantage of proximity (the roles were written especially for them), availability, and being free of charge. After all, the initial budget was a meager $2,000. Most of the money came from Andrew Wilson, the only one of the gang who actually had a job, and an audiovisual one at that: he directed industrial films on which Wes Anderson occasionally collaborated to earn pocket money. Andrew, the eldest of the Wilson siblings, also provided black-and-white film and equipment, in the spirit of a Good Samaritan. For the supporting roles, the novice director and Owen Wilson, his co-writer, auditioned a number of acquaintances, including Robert Musgrave, who had to try twice for the role of Bob Hanson, an irresponsible cannabis farmer.

In 1992, Wes Anderson and Owen Wilson are about to take a giant leap forward.

From left to right, Luke Wilson, Wes Anderson, and Owen Wilson in the middle of editing.

FILMING AND PRODUCTION

In May 1992, Wes Anderson filmed for almost three days on the streets of Dallas, improvising as he went along, assisted by technicians on loan from Andrew Wilson. Eight minutes were in the can, but the money ran out. No matter. The group's idea was to proceed in stages, which was made possible by the ultra-sequenced script, with a succession of independent sketches—linked together in post-production by a catchy, jazzy soundtrack. In the end, Wes Anderson and Owen Wilson even hoped to have enough material for a feature-length film. Fate would dictate otherwise.

Mentor

Fate took the form of a certain L. M. Kit Carson, whom the Wilson brothers' father had met when he was running a public television station in Dallas. Trained as an actor (*David Holzman's Diary*, Jim McBride, 1967) and screenwriter (*Paris, Texas*, Wim Wenders, 1984), Carson was a fixture on the local independent scene, unrivaled in his ability to unearth rising talents. Impressed by the first draft shown to him by Wes Anderson and Owen Wilson, he became their mentor, advising them to lengthen the story to make a real short film. His wife, Cynthia Hargrave, also convinced of the duo's potential, became the producer for the project, whose financial setup was more a matter of resourcefulness than an ideal business plan. Expanded by five minutes (additional scenes were shot in autumn 1992), *Bottle Rocket* was finally ready for public release.

RECEPTION

The indispensable L. M. Kit Carson had his own means of access to the renowned Sundance Film Festival, run by actor, director, and producer Robert Redford, which showcases the best independent productions of the upcoming year. While *Bottle Rocket* did not yet show signs of a style that could be described as "Andersonian," it did demonstrate a vitality and spirit typical of the off-the-wall productions of the time. The offbeat, even outlandish dialogues between the quirky protagonists and the use of black-and-white are reminiscent of the films of Jim Jarmusch, one of the gurus of indie cinema since the early 1980s. This unexpected exposure at Sundance would also enable *Bottle Rocket* to be released in a full-length version.

They're not really criminals,
but everybody's got to have a dream.

BOTTLE ROCKET

COLUMBIA PICTURES PRESENTS
A GRACIE FILMS PRODUCTION "BOTTLE ROCKET" A BOYLE-TAYLOR PRODUCTION CO-PRODUCERS RAY ZIMMERMAN L.M. KIT CARSON MUSIC BY MARK MOTHERSBAUGH EDITOR DAVID MORITZ PRODUCTION DESIGNER DAVID WASCO
DIRECTOR OF PHOTOGRAPHY ROBERT YEOMAN EXECUTIVE PRODUCERS JAMES L. BROOKS RICHARD SAKAI BARBARA BOYLE MICHAEL TAYLOR WRITTEN BY OWEN C. WILSON & WES ANDERSON PRODUCED BY POLLY PLATT CYNTHIA HARGRAVE DIRECTED BY WES ANDERSON
SDDS
COLUMBIA PICTURES

BOTTLE ROCKET

1996

United States • 1 h 31 • Color • Dolby SR / SDDS • 1.85 : 1

Filming Dates: **October 17–December 18, 1994**
Release Date in the United States: **February 21, 1996**

Budget: **Approx. $7 million**
North America Box Office: **$560,069**

Production Company: **Columbia Pictures**
Producers: **Cynthia Hargrave, Polly Platt**
Co-Producers: **L. M. Kit Carson, Ray Zimmerman**
Executive Producers: **James L. Brooks, Barbara Boyle, Richard Sakai, Michael Taylor**
Associate Producers: **Michael Lang, Andrew Wilson**

Screenplay: **Wes Anderson, Owen Wilson**
Director of Photography: **Robert Yeoman**
First Assistant Director: **Jim Goldthwait**
Editing: **David Moritz**
Composer: **Mark Mothersbaugh**
Production Design: **David Wasco**
Set Decoration: **Sandy Reynolds-Wasco**
Sound: **Jeremy Gordon, Roxanne Jones**
Costumes: **Karen Patch**
Special Effects: **Margaret Johnson, Randy E. Moore**
Stunts: **Russell Towery**
Casting: **Liz Keigley**

Starring: **LUKE WILSON** (Anthony), **OWEN WILSON** (Dignan), **ROBERT MUSGRAVE** (Bob Mapplethorpe), **JAMES CAAN** (Mr. Henry), **LUMI CAVAZOS** (Inez), **ANDREW WILSON** (John Mapplethorpe, known as Future Man), **KUMAR PALLANA** (Kumar), **TAK KUBOTA** (Rowboat), **JENNI TOOLEY** (Stacey Sinclair)...

"You and I both respond to structure, and that's what's important."

Dignan to Anthony

SYNOPSIS

Anthony "escapes" (with his doctor's agreement) from the psychiatric hospital where he is a voluntary inmate to join his friend Dignan, who naïvely believes the absurd escapade he's planning will succeed. The eccentric Dignan wants to become a big-time thief. He brings along Anthony, who is less than enthusiastic. As a practice run, they break into Anthony's own house, then hold up a bookshop. Their goal: to convince Mr. Henry, a white-collar gangster, of their professionalism.

GENESIS

The long version of *Bottle Rocket* is the logical extension of the short film, which was originally conceived in a longer format. For reasons explained in the previous chapter, inseparable friends Wes Anderson and Owen Wilson presented the short film in 1993 at the Sundance Film Festival, their expanded script in hand, in the hope of getting noticed and raising funds to shoot additional sequences.

Sundance Kids

Once they were there the two videographers joined a writing workshop, albeit without much conviction. They were more interested in the directing workshop, which they ended up joining thanks to their mentor and benefactor, L. M. Kit Carson, whose influence was very real in the small world of American independent cinema. It was a big disappointment, as Anderson and Wilson had expected to film scenes and learn the craft, but they had to be content discussing their script and feature film project with kindly people who did not consider them their equals.

The Royal Road

The Sundance experience was not a fiasco, but it certainly felt like one. Anderson and Wilson never imagined they would have to start from scratch for this film. They made contacts and generated interest, but nothing concrete came of it: no one promised to finance new sequences. Their dream seemed to have come to nothing. But Carson was not one to be deterred, as he approached a number of Hollywood heavyweights. Among his acquaintances was producer Barbara Boyle, to whom he sent a video of the short film and the screenplay for the feature. Enthused, she forwarded the material to Polly Platt, a major player. Married between 1962 and 1971 to Peter Bogdanovich (champion of the New Hollywood movement born in the late 1960s, which saw the emergence of a generation of filmmakers freed from the tutelage of the studios), whose most emblematic films she produced, Polly Platt was also the first woman to become a member of the American film industry's main professional union, the Art Directors Guild. Her credits as a producer include films as diverse as *The Witches of Eastwick* (George Miller, 1987), *Big* (Penny Marshall, 1988) and *The War of the Roses* (Danny DeVito, 1989).

A New Mentor

At the time of these events, in early 1993, Polly Platt was still vice president of Gracie Films, a major film and TV production company founded by writer-director James Lawrence Brooks (also known as James L. Brooks or Jim), whose claim to fame was launching the animated series *The Simpsons* (1989–). It was Polly Platt who originally suggested that Brooks should meet Matt Groening, creator of that famous yellow-skinned family. In short, her opinion counted. The one she gave in the *Bottle Rocket* project's press kit was unequivocal: "The short was an exuberant, beautiful piece of work and what was extraordinary was the fascinating sense of humor that colored the piece. [. . .] I heard a new voice in the script. It was just exceptional writing, funny, different, with brilliant, completely original characters."[1]

Brooks, whom Platt had alerted, was in turn convinced, and met with the two thieves to ask them to rewrite the script. While Brooks liked their world, their tone, and even their (mostly nonprofessional) actors, he felt he needed to present something more straightforward to Columbia Pictures, Gracie Films' preferred distribution and exhibition partner. So Brooks set them up in a plush Los Angeles office, where Wes Anderson and Owen Wilson discovered a comfortable working environment that was a welcome change from their Texas bedroom.

Freeze Frame

The opening shot of *Bottle Rocket* is historic: the sound of a match striking precedes the appearance of the title, in black on a bright red background. It is historic because, for the first time, Wes Anderson uses the Futura typeface, which he uses in all his subsequent films, right up to *Moonrise Kingdom* (2012). Given the director's penchant for the written word, this is anything but insignificant. Letterer Jessica Hische went so far as to create a font especially for *Moonrise Kingdom*, which she marketed in 2014 under the name Tilda.

Wes Anderson and Owen Wilson in Utah, 1993, where they have just presented their short film *Bottle Rocket.*

"Jim's voice"

Eighteen months of hectic rewriting later, the script for the long version of *Bottle Rocket* was finally ready. Anderson would say that Brooks taught them how to articulate a screenplay. "Since then, I've heard Jim's voice when I write," he assures us.[2] The basis of the short film is there: most of the sequences (the initial robbery of Anthony's parents' house followed by a lunch counter scene, the pistol-shooting session, the meeting to prepare the bookshop robbery, and so on) are repeated with a different cut. On the other hand, the story opens with a close-up of Anthony's face, a way of making it clear that he is the film's protagonist, a regular young man with whom we can identify. In fact, it is more subtle than that; as the story unfolds, Dignan's character acquires an unexpected depth, to the point where, at the end, he appears as a different kind of hero, unpredictable and irritating, but endearing. After all, the last shot of the film is dedicated to him. While the short version of *Bottle Rocket* was a portrait of two irresponsible good guys for whom life was sliding away a little, the long version appears less frivolous and confronts these man-children with their (bad) choices and their adult responsibilities.

CASTING

For the long version, James L. Brooks did not question the original casting, which brought a vitality, authenticity, and freshness that were indispensable to the project. In his eyes, Luke Wilson (Anthony) had the presence of Robert Mitchum, and Owen Wilson (Dignan) was reminiscent of Montgomery Clift. This is what Wes Anderson and Owen Wilson reported.[3] (Were they joking?) The two Wilson brothers remained, as did their comrade Robert Musgrave in the role of Bob, the son of a good family, a cannabis grower in his spare time, and now a getaway driver. The happy band also had no trouble casting their Texan relatives and acquaintances. Andrew Wilson (the eldest Wilson brother) plays John Mapplethorpe, aka Future Man, Bob's brother and chief stalker. Kumar Pallana, a septuagenarian of Indian origin whose son runs a Dallas restaurant frequented by the gang, plays a bumbling safecracker. Temple Nash reprises his role as a gun seller in the

Robert Musgrave (Bob Mapplethorpe), in the background, was a friend of Owen and Luke Wilson (Dignan and Anthony), in the foreground.

Luke Wilson in *Bottle Rocket* in his first major role.

A star in Mexico, Lumi Cavazos (Inez) began a tentative American career with this film.

short film. Last but not least, Stephen Dignan (Rob, the bow tie–wearing bookstore clerk) and Brian Tenenbaum (Future Man's sidekick), two friends of Anderson and Wilson (who obviously liked their friends' stage names), also appear in the credits.

Making Room for the Professionals

Two roles, new in the long film, required professional actors because of their dramaturgical importance: Inez, the young maid in the motel where the gang ends up after the bookshop robbery, and Mr. Henry, a mafioso who hides his illegal activities behind a gardening business. Inez brings a romantic touch to the story (Anthony falls in love with her, damaging his relationship with Dignan and altering his relationship with the world), while Mr. Henry shifts the narrative into something more sarcastic, even postmodern, conveying the codes of film noir while at the same time caricaturing them—the film's vaguely Tarantinian side.

LUMI-nous

Relatively unknown in the United States, Mexican actress Lumi Cavazos first came to prominence as the lead in *Como agua para chocolate* (*Like Water for Chocolate*, Alfonso Arau, 1992), nominated for a Golden Globe for Best Foreign Film in 1993. In this historical drama, her character found in the art of cooking to be an outlet for her all-consuming but forbidden passion for her brother-in-law. It was a role with little dialogue, where emotions were conveyed through her glances and her art of preparing food. This is exactly what defines Inez, the Paraguayan cleaning lady surprised by Anthony's interest in her. The impossibility of their communication (she cannot understand English) is compounded by her natural modesty, which hinders the realization of this budding love. As Wes Anderson said, the character, who was not as present in the script, was enriched by Lumi Cavazos' personality.[4]

Mr. Caan

To play Mr. Henry, the gangster disguised as a respected citizen, Columbia wanted a big name to counterbalance the anonymity of the rest of the cast. Someone with a big impact was needed. Anderson initially considered Bill Murray, who remained unreachable (but it would only be a matter of time in his case). As it turned out, the director's agent was also that of James Caan, a Hollywood legend who had fallen from grace for acts of violence (for which he was not convicted), which led him to enter rehab and stay away from the cinema. In 1996, he made a comeback on the big screen, and the role of Mr. Henry was certainly an aspect of his renewed reputation. It has to be said that Wes Anderson and Owen Wilson had unwittingly written a tailor-made film. Who better than the man who played Santino "Sonny" Corleone in *The Godfather* (Francis Ford Coppola, 1972) or the martyred novelist in *Misery* (Rob Reiner, 1990)? Intense and explosive, James Caan imposed upon Anderson the presence of his Japanese karate teacher, Tak Kubota, with whom he plays the film's most zany scene, proof of the Texan filmmaker's ability to adapt. "These kids seem to have their heads in the right place," he confided about Anderson and his gang in the press kit. "They're talented, funny, nice to be with and are good souls, which is not a common trait to find in this business."[5]

Behind James Caan (Mr. Henry) and Owen Wilson hangs a portrait of Commander Cousteau, one of Wes Anderson's idols.

FILMING AND PRODUCTION

During preproduction, Anderson contacted Robert D. Yeoman, a cinematographer renowned for his work with William Friedkin (*Rampage*, 1987) and Gus Van Sant (*Drugstore Cowboy*, 1989), with whom he would like to work. To this end, he sent him a handwritten letter, dated March 1, 1994, accompanied by the synopsis and VHS of the *Bottle Rocket* short. This prompted the technician to meet this promising young director at the offices of Gracie Films. "My first impression was that he looked like a high school kid," recalls Yeoman. "We immediately hit it off and talked about movies we both liked, ones we didn't like, or which might inspire us for *Bottle Rocket*'s look, and so on. We seemed connected on so many levels! When I left, I knew I was in the presence of a very intelligent director who knew where he was going, with a clear vision for his film. I hoped I'd be hired, and was very excited when I got the confirmation call."[6]

Hesitant Beginnings of the "Wes Touch"

Filming began in and around Dallas in late 1994. Some of the locations used for the short film were reused, while others formed imposing new sets that hinted at Anderson's visions. The huge motel, with its deep red accents, is the setting for the romance between Inez and Anthony and has an early feel of the palace in *The Grand Budapest Hotel* (2014). As for the vast refrigerated warehouse, the scene of the ultimate heist, its endless corridors, airlocks, ladders, and open elevators (where Anderson places his camera to simulate vertical panning) are all precursory signature effects.

Visually, however, *Bottle Rocket* remains an object apart in Wes Anderson's filmography, where his

(L to R) Loyal cinematographer Robert Yeoman, producer Polly Platt, and Wes Anderson.

Dipak Pallana, center, ran an Indian restaurant in Dallas.

Luke Wilson on the set of *Bottle Rocket*.

Bottle Rocket would make Owen Wilson, the film's co-writer, one of Hollywood's hottest actors.

hands are not yet completely free. Columbia was keeping a close eye on things. "Originally, we wanted to shoot this feature with anamorphic lenses," says Yeoman. "The story featured three main characters, and we felt that the wide format would enable us to have more dynamic compositions. The studio was not convinced and asked us to shoot a test during the prep period. We shot a scene from the script with both anamorphic lenses [in a 2.40 format] and spherical lenses [in 1.85]. We purposely made the shots in anamorphic more interesting with stronger compositions and better lighting. For the spherical shots we made the compositions slightly awkward, and I lit the shots with less contrast. When the studio saw our tests they felt that there was no difference between the formats and told us we had to shoot spherical. [. . .] We were disappointed."[7]

Grand Angle

Anderson and Yeoman were nevertheless determined to make the film visually distinctive. To achieve this, they came up with the idea of using a rare short focal length: 27 mm. "Wes and I both loved *Rosemary's Baby* and heard that it was shot entirely on a 20 mm lens," says the cinematographer.[8] "There was a visual coherence and atmosphere that appealed to both of us. As the slightly wider spherical lenses came closest in terms of rendering, we opted for the Panavision 27 mm Primo. And so our adventure began . . . "

As usual, the two men would have had to change focal lengths from time to time, particularly for close-ups. Yeoman recalls with amusement the clever dodge he and Anderson had devised. "When our producer realized that we were only using one lens, he went to the set to ask us to vary it. So we put tape over the lens marking and continued to use it, but wc wrotc 50 mm, 75 mm, and 100 mm on the camera reports.

A few days later, the producer came back to the set, satisfied: 'I see you're using other lenses now.' 'Oh yeah!' I replied. Of course the entire movie was shot on the 27 mm except for a very few closeups of Lumi Cavazos which were shot on a 35 mm. I don't think the studio ever knew the difference."[9]

Changes in Tone

Another assertive directorial choice concerns the colors that define the evolution of the characters.

CABELL'S

Kumar Pallana (center), Dipak's father, became a mascot to Wes Anderson (far right).

In the first part (up to the bookshop robbery), Anthony, the hero, wears a firecracker-red sweater that contrasts with Dignan's neutral polo shirts and Bob's black suit. In the second part (from the motel stay to the clash between Anthony and Dignan), the world around them takes on an iridescent sheen that reflects a more positive state of mind. In this regard, Yeoman has an amusing anecdote about the phosphorescent blue of the motel pool. "We had to deal with the issue that the water was very green, which was not particularly attractive. It was too costly to drain the pool, clean it, then refill it, so we came up with the idea of putting blue gels on our underwater lights to change the color of the water. It was particularly effective in the night scenes."[10] Finally, in the last part of the film (where the gang re-forms), a form of chromatic neutrality takes over again, broken by the yellow jumpsuit worn by Dignan, who now takes center stage and will impose this extravagant outfit on his accomplices during the final robbery.

Jazzy

Some American observers may have thought at the time that the famous yellow jumpsuits worn by Dignan and his gang were a nod to the composer of the film's soundtrack, Mark Mothersbaugh. In his new wave band Devo, famous for the eccentric look of its members, he wore a similar outfit. This was a mere coincidence, since when the film was written and shot, Devo's lead singer was not yet attached to the project. Nevertheless, it was the sign of an obvious meeting of minds, which was confirmed during post-production of *Bottle Rocket*. Present at a test screening of the film, Mothersbaugh then contacted Wes Anderson to offer his services. The director did not hesitate for a second and was not sorry to do so: the musician's jazzy, slightly bossa nova–like score fits perfectly with the film's offbeat ambience and the actors' flippant performance. Happy with their collaboration, the two men went on to work together on *The Life Aquatic with Steve Zissou* (2004).

41184 **FOR WES ADDICTS** 41184

The most observant will have noticed that Owen Wilson ends up in a prison called Wasco. This is a nod to set designer David Wasco, with whom Wes Anderson began a long-term collaboration. The two men had become friends on the set of *Pulp Fiction* (Quentin Tarantino, 1994), where Wasco worked and where Anderson had gone when he was in talks with Miramax on the financing of *Bottle Rocket*.

RECEPTION

A disaster. A slap in the face. A humiliation. That is more or less how, years later, Wes Anderson would describe the test screenings organized to assess *Bottle Rocket*'s potential with an audience selected by the studio. One of these screenings in particular had the authors in despair: it took place in Santa Monica before an audience that grew increasingly sparse as the session progressed. Eighty-five people (out of 250) did not make it to the end! Too weird, too offbeat, not enough action . . . The comments were unequivocal. *Bottle Rocket*'s future had suddenly darkened.

Back to Work

Wes Anderson and Owen Wilson hung on to the last test screening, which they felt was more convincing than the others. Too late. For Columbia and James L. Brooks, the deal was over. "Jim knew what a good press screening was, we didn't," confesses the director.[11] Their mentor and producer knew how to judge the middle line between good and the bad. As an aside, he said he was satisfied with the film, but he knew how film studios work, their rigidity, and their expectations. As a result, the two writers were forced to rethink their plans, and Brooks had to take a little more money out of his own pocket than expected. "We wrote a new opening and we filled in all kinds of gaps and re-shot things," said Anderson.[12]

Serial Rejections

Bottle Rocket's facelift satisfied just about everyone, but another test awaited the team. Gracie Films and Columbia, convinced of the film's quality, submitted it to the Sundance Film Festival, which turned it down—despite the fact that the short had been favorably received three years earlier! There was consternation. Sundance was considered the ideal launching pad for this kind of vulnerable film. Without this label, *Bottle Rocket* was doomed to failure. James L.

Yellow (here, very bright!) became one of the emblematic colors of Wes Anderson's cinema.

Brooks wrote an angry letter to the selectors, claiming that they had failed to recognize the film's qualities and the talent of its makers. The Telluride (Colorado) and New York independent festivals—other major events—also rejected *Bottle Rocket*'s candidacy. For Columbia, this was the last straw. The studio, which had been targeting a massive audience of teenagers and young adults, completely altered its promotional campaign and distribution strategy, reserving Wes Anderson's first feature for a limited release in the United States. In other words, *Bottle Rocket* was sacrificed. Its box-office receipts, ten times lower than its budget, even put it in the category of Columbia's big flops.

From Cursed to Cult

There was a glimmer of light in the darkness, however: the film's critical reception was generally positive. Between immoderate enthusiasm, sincere encouragement, and polite reservations, Anderson had plenty of scope for licking his (gaping) wounds. As the director's reputation grew, *Bottle Rocket* quickly acquired cult status, made its way into DVD libraries, and was recommended to friends and acquaintances.

In retrospect, Wes Anderson's first feature appears to be an instructive trial run in which the director was still finding his feet, while at the same time putting in place elements that would infuse his cinema, such as certain themes (the gang, lies, childishness, betrayal) and visual gimmicks (binocular observation, notes and shots, races, slow-motion scenes, and the use of colors to convey emotions). *Bottle Rocket* was not totally out of place in the independent production scene of the time, which was dominated by Spike Lee, Jim Jarmusch, Steven Soderbergh, Gus Van Sant, Todd Haynes, and emerging filmmakers such as Richard Linklater, Kevin Smith, and even Quentin Tarantino, with whom Anderson shared a taste for offbeat dialogue and scenes, minus the violence. The clear break embodied by his next film, *Rushmore* (1998), makes *Bottle Rocket* a film apart, and therefore precious.

Roman Coppola on the set of *Asteroid City*, which he co-wrote with Wes Anderson.

Some Exclusive Scripts

Wes Anderson and His Writing Friends

Over the course of his career, Wes Anderson has called on a handful of recurring scriptwriters to work with him on some of the wildest and most inventive stories in contemporary cinema. All of them are close friends: Owen Wilson took a walk on the wild side with him in college; he and Noah Baumbach frequented the same New York intellectual circles; Jason Schwartzman, his protégé, whom he revealed in *Rushmore* (1998), introduced him to his cousin Roman Coppola. On the face of it, there is nothing to distinguish Wes Anderson's work from that of these prestigious co-writers. All the films in which they have actively collaborated are defined by their relationship with the group and the family, with feelings of exclusion and difference, with power relationships that flip into their opposites or balance out, with small lies that become big, with strategies of avoidance and confrontation. On closer inspection, however, nuances emerge.

Owen Wilson, Cool Brooding

Like Anderson, Owen Wilson has two brothers with whom he is close and parents he prefers not to discuss. Both men are also naturally more self-taught than schooled and have "different" brains that artistic endeavor has revealed. The three films they have written together are about vaguely rebellious but above all asocial minds, disconnected from reality, assuming the form of a disorganized gang (*Bottle Rocket*, 1993), a tyrannical leader (*Rushmore*), or a depressed sibling (*The Royal Tenenbaums*, 2001). Marked by absences or family tragedies, lacking emotional bearings, unable to communicate normally, hurtful, or manipulative, Wilson and Anderson's heroes drag along a tenacious brooding that they externalize in an excess of action (*Bottle Rocket*, *Rushmore*) or in a form of morbid vegetation (*The Royal Tenenbaums*). Redemption is certainly at the end of the road, but it comes through profound identity crises and renunciations that are initially perceived as insurmountable, all with an occasionally jubilant sense of derision.

Noah Baumbach, the Spirit of Adventure

Born four months after Anderson, on September 3, 1969, New Yorker Noah Baumbach, like his Texan friend, cultivates an intellectual dandyism and a taste for France. Both find in film an outlet for their existential angst, which stems from a painful parental divorce. In *The Life Aquatic with Steve Zissou* (2004) and *Fantastic Mr. Fox* (2009), their two collaborations, the main characters are driven by a certain arrogance but endowed with a charisma and a power of seduction that earn the admiration of followers ready to follow them to the ends of the earth—an end of the world that unfortunately seems to be a dead end. In their stubbornness, oceanographer Steve Zissou and the fox head of the family forget that they are responsible for the lives and well-being of those in their care. While this bad influence was present in an intimate way in *The Royal Tenenbaums* (through the father figure played by Gene Hackman), here it takes on an epic character: sometimes it leads to a hostage situation at sea, sometimes to the persecution of the entire fauna of a corner of the English countryside. With Baumbach, Anderson moves from the micro (the controllable family or friendship) to the macro (the outside world and its unpredictable dangers). Baumbach's presence at his side also coincides with Anderson's major foray into animation.

The Revolution

In choosing Jason Schwartzman to play Max Fischer, the brat of *Rushmore*, did Wes Anderson see the future that Truffaut imagined for Jean-Pierre Léaud in the saga of Antoine Doinel: he as a demiurge, and the actor as inspiration? In a way, that is exactly what happened, as Francis Ford Coppola's nephew went on to star—and grow—in other films, both short and long, by his mentor: *The Darjeeling Limited* (2007), *Hotel Chevalier* (2007), *Moonrise Kingdom* (2012), *Castello Cavalcanti* (2013), *The Grand Budapest Hotel* (2014), *The French Dispatch* (2021), and *Asteroid City* (2023). Schwartzman has even gone beyond his role as a simple performer at the service of Wes Anderson's vision by becoming one of his regular co-writers. After Schwartzman introduced Anderson to Roman Coppola, Anderson decided, for the first time, to write a six-hander screenplay: *The Darjeeling Limited.* Coppola, on the other hand, would be the sole co-writer of *Moonrise Kingdom* before Anderson called on the two cousins again to help him develop *Isle of Dogs* (2018) and *The French Dispatch*, for which they are credited as mere contributors to the initial idea; the same applies to *Asteroid City* for Coppola. What are the hallmarks of this collaborative effort? An emphasis on wandering (existential and initiatory), the end of innocence, the struggle against the established order, impossible loves, transgression. The result is a more mature cinema that coincides with an increasingly marked turn toward abstraction, of which Wes Anderson is now the sole repository.

Noah Baumbach, co-writer of *The Life Aquatic* and *Fantastic Mr. Fox*, is a dear friend of Wes Anderson.

JASON SCHWARTZMAN OLIVIA WILLIAMS BILL MURRAY
RUSHMORE
LOVE. EXPULSION. REVOLUTION.
TOUCHSTONE PICTURES PRESENTS
AN AMERICAN EMPIRICAL PICTURES PRODUCTION "RUSHMORE"
JASON SCHWARTZMAN OLIVIA WILLIAMS BILL MURRAY BRIAN COX
SEYMOUR CASSEL MASON GAMBLE RANDALL POSTER
MARK MOTHERSBAUGH KAREN PATCH DAVID MORITZ
DAVID WASCO BOB YEOMAN JOHN CAMERON
OWEN WILSON AND WES ANDERSON BARRY MENDEL AND PAUL SCHIFF
WES ANDERSON & OWEN WILSON WES ANDERSON
R RESTRICTED
Touchstone Pictures
www.Rushmore-themovie.com
Distributed by BUENA VISTA PICTURES DISTRIBUTION
© TOUCHSTONE PICTURES

RUSHMORE

United States • 1 h 33 • Color • DTS / Dolby Digital / SDDS • 2.39: 1

Filming Dates: **November 22, 1997–February 1, 1998**
Release Dates in the United States: **October 9, 1998 (New York Film Festival); December 11, 1998 (limited release); February 19, 1999**

Budget: **Approx. $9 million**
North America Box Office: **Approx. $17 million**

Production Companies: **Touchstone Pictures, American Empirical Pictures**
Producers: **Barry Mendel, Paul Schiff**
Co-Producer: **John Cameron**
Executive Producers: **Wes Anderson, Owen Wilson**

Screenplay: **Wes Anderson, Owen Wilson**
Director of Photography: **Robert D. Yeoman**
First Assistant Director: **Michael Cedar**
Film Editing: **David Moritz**
Musical Supervisor: **Randall Poster**
Composer: **Mark Mothersbaugh**
Production Design: **David Wasco**
Set Decoration: **Alexandra Reynolds-Wasco**
Sound: **Pawel Wdowczak**
Costumes: **Karen Patch**
Special Effects: **Ron Trost**
Stunts: **David Sanders**
Casting: **Mary Gail Artz, Barbara Cohen**

Starring: **JASON SCHWARTZMAN (Max Fischer), BILL MURRAY (Herman Blume), OLIVIA WILLIAMS (Rosemary Cross), SEYMOUR CASSEL (Bert Fischer), BRIAN COX (Dr. Nelson Guggenheim), MASON GAMBLE (Dirk Calloway), SARA TANAKA (Margaret Yang), STEPHEN MCCOLE (Magnus Buchan), CONNIE NIELSEN (Mrs. Calloway), LUKE WILSON (Dr. Peter Flynn), DIPAK PALLANA (Mr. Adams), ANDREW WILSON (Coach Beck)...**

"Take dead aim on the rich boys. Get them in the crosshairs and take them down. Just remember, they can buy anything but they can't buy backbone."

—

Herman Blume,
to the Rushmore students

SYNOPSIS

Max Fischer, a fifteen-year-old high school student at Rushmore Academy, a selective private school, does nothing like the others do. Enterprising and dynamic, he heads some fifteen clubs of varying degrees of eccentricity (backgammon, debating, calligraphy, theater...), which he runs with an iron fist, surrounded by a handful of disciples who follow him blindly. All these activities are detrimental to his academic performance, earning him regular reprimands from the principal, who is fed up with his hyperactivity. At the same time, Max strikes up a friendship with an eccentric, unhappily married industrialist, Herman Blume, and falls in love with a schoolteacher, Miss Cross. Several twists and turns lead him to leave Rushmore for a public high school and to organize reprisals against Blume, who betrayed him by courting Miss Cross behind his back.

Seventeen years old at the time of filming, Jason Schwartzman shines in the lead role as Max Fischer.

GENESIS

The box-office failure of their feature *Bottle Rocket* in early 1996 could have clipped their wings, but Wes Anderson and Owen Wilson had two trump cards up their sleeves: they had been noticed by the industry, and they still had plenty of stories to tell. At college, in addition to *Bottle Rocket*, they had already started work on *Rushmore* and sketched out what would become *The Life Aquatic with Steve Zissou*. In their minds, this "school film," largely inspired by their own school experience, would be their second feature. Several trips to Hollywood and their presence at the Sundance Film Festival enabled them to meet many people likely to support their projects. The disagreement with Columbia over *Bottle Rocket*, consummated by the film's complete failure, severed the economic link between the two men and their producer, James L. Brooks, whose friendship they nonetheless retained.

Unconventional

In Los Angeles, during the production of *Bottle Rocket*, Anderson and Wilson met Barry Mendel, an ambitious thirtysomething looking for his first film to produce. He was won over by these two boyish men, who seemed to have just emerged from adolescence and conveyed a universe and imagination of their own. Anderson's highly creative and unconventional personality and his approach to filmmaking in particular intrigued him. Under his impetus, the duo took over the writing of *Rushmore*, which exudes life experience: like Max, Wilson was expelled from high school and has always considered himself on the margins of the system; Anderson was also in love with an older woman and created and directed school plays. A master of stratagems, a dictator in a blazer, Max Fischer—an antihero—is also the perfect metaphor for the creator, narcissistic, obsessive, and arrogant. Self-portrait or caricature? A bit of both, certainly.

A Gang Apart

Although the character of Max Fisher is not exactly sympathetic on the face of it, Owen Wilson was keen to tone down any strong opinions. "I like people who get obsessed with something. For example, I'm not that interested in chess but I'm really interested in Bobby Fischer because he's just kind of obsessed with chess. There's something funny about those kinds of characters. These people don't have the self-awareness of how they're coming across to others and how kind of strange they are."[1] In his interactions with others, Max Fischer

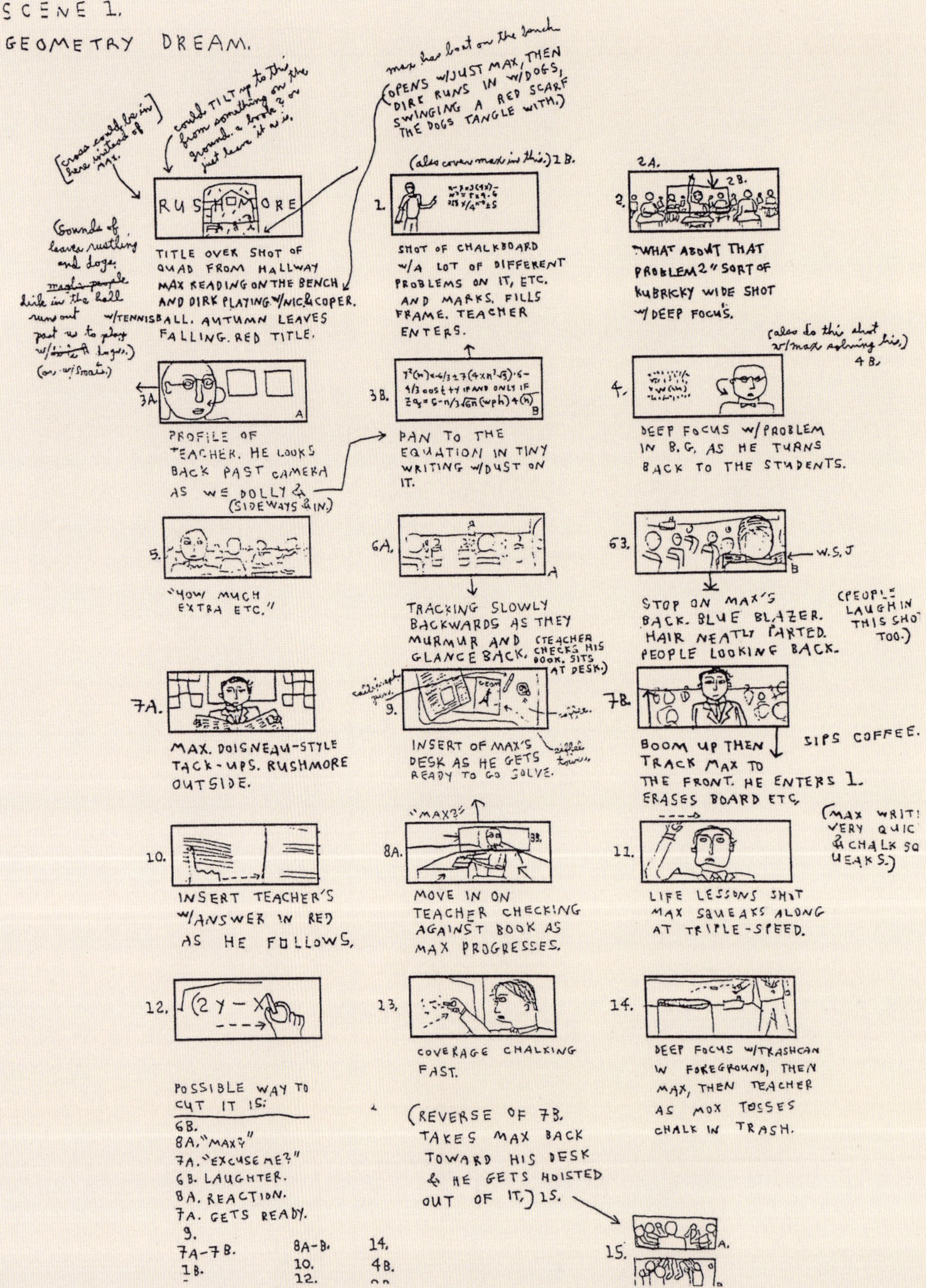

SCENE 1.
GEOMETRY DREAM.
RUSHMORE
TITLE OVER SHOT OF QUAD FROM HALLWAY MAX READING ON THE BENCH AND DIRK PLAYING W/NIC & COPER. W/TENNIS BALL. AUTUMN LEAVES FALLING. RED TITLE.
(OPENS W/JUST MAX, THEN DIRK RUNS IN W/DOGS, SWINGING A RED SCARF THE DOGS TANGLE WITH.)
(also cover max in this.) 1B.
1.
SHOT OF CHALKBOARD W/A LOT OF DIFFERENT PROBLEMS ON IT, ETC. AND MARKS. FILLS FRAME. TEACHER ENTERS.
2A.
2B.
2.
"WHAT ABOUT THAT PROBLEM 2" SORT OF KUBRICKY WIDE SHOT W/DEEP FOCUS.
3A.
A
PROFILE OF TEACHER. HE LOOKS BACK PAST CAMERA AS WE DOLLY & (SIDEWAYS & IN.)
3B.
B
PAN TO THE EQUATION IN TINY WRITING W/DUST ON IT.
(also do this shot w/max solving his.) 4B.
4.
DEEP FOCUS W/PROBLEM IN B.G. AS HE TURNS BACK TO THE STUDENTS.
5.
"HOW MUCH EXTRA ETC."
6A.
A
TRACKING SLOWLY BACKWARDS AS THEY MURMUR AND GLANCE BACK. (TEACHER CHECKS HIS BOOK. SITS AT DESK.)
6B.
B
W.S.J
STOP ON MAX'S BACK. BLUE BLAZER. HAIR NEATLY PARTED. PEOPLE LOOKING BACK.
(PEOPLE LAUGH IN THIS SHOT TOO.)
7A.
MAX. DOISNEAU-STYLE TACK-UPS. RUSHMORE OUTSIDE.
9.
INSERT OF MAX'S DESK AS HE GETS READY TO GO SOLVE.
7B.
BOOM UP THEN TRACK MAX TO THE FRONT. HE ENTERS 1. ERASES BOARD ETC.
SIPS COFFEE.
10.
INSERT TEACHER'S W/ANSWER IN RED AS HE FOLLOWS.
"MAX?"
8A.
8B.
MOVE IN ON TEACHER CHECKING AGAINST BOOK AS MAX PROGRESSES.
11.
LIFE LESSONS SHOT MAX SQUEAKS ALONG AT TRIPLE-SPEED.
(MAX WRITES VERY QUICK & CHALK SQUEAKS.)
12.
(2Y − X
13.
COVERAGE CHALKING FAST.
14.
DEEP FOCUS W/TRASHCAN IN FOREGROUND, THEN MAX, THEN TEACHER AS MAX TOSSES CHALK IN TRASH.
POSSIBLE WAY TO CUT IT IS:
6B.
8A. "MAX?"
7A. "EXCUSE ME?"
6B. LAUGHTER.
8A. REACTION.
7A. GETS READY.
9.
7A–7B.
1B.
8A–B.
10.
12.
14.
4B.
(REVERSE OF 7B. TAKES MAX BACK TOWARD HIS DESK & HE GETS HOISTED OUT OF IT.) 15.
15.
A.
B

Robert Yeoman and Wes Anderson on the set.

struggles to pretend and to establish communication with a minimum of etiquette.

This is what arouses both the interest of the moody Herman Blume and the mistrust of the delicate Miss Cross. In some respects, Max is the first "little genius" in Wes Anderson's filmography, a loner who is a victim of his excessive maturity and constantly out of step with his contemporaries (teenagers and adults alike)—in short, a totally asocial being.

Sold!

After a year or so of reflection and rewriting, the script for *Rushmore* was finally ready. Convinced he had a gem on his hands, Barry Mendel submitted it to New Line Cinema, a studio that specialized in horror films in its early days but gradually turned to independent cinema with some success. New Line was interested but overestimated the budget and finally threw in the towel after several months of tough negotiations between the various parties. Undeterred, the Mendel-Anderson-Wilson trio decided in mid-1997 to put the script rights up for auction. Four studios bid for the rights, and in the end Walt Disney Studios won the project, offering $10 million—a respectable sum for a film without stars and directed by someone whose first feature lost Columbia a lot of money. As it happens, Joe Roth, then president of Disney, loved *Bottle Rocket* and also believed in *Rushmore*, which would be produced by Touchstone Pictures, the studio's "adult" subsidiary.

CASTING

Already considered for *Bottle Rocket*, Bill Murray was the first actor contacted by Wes Anderson, who could think of no one better to play the dreamy, depressive Herman Blume, a wealthy industrialist whose outlook on life changes when he meets high school student Max Fischer, an incredibly subtle role requiring depth, eccentricity, and emotion. Murray had been hard to reach, but the star of *Ghostbusters* (Ivan Reitman, 1984) finally agreed to work with Anderson, who had almost given up. Murray's presence reassured the studio. Now it was time to find the rare pearl for the lead role, on whom the film's success would depend.

Casting a Wide Net

Even today, Anderson must be having nightmares: to find his young actor, the production exhausted

Max Fischer and his followers at the *Yankee Review*, of which he is editor.

fourteen casting directors who spent nine months crisscrossing the United States, Canada, and Great Britain, auditioning a total of eighteen hundred teenagers—a giant treasure hunt, concluded in October 1997, just a few weeks before shooting was due to start. Indeed, at the time of writing, Wes Anderson imagined Max as a skinny fifteen-year-old Mick Jagger, a description that initially colored the research and even prompted the production to send the script to cult actor Macaulay Culkin, who had stopped acting in 1994. This anecdote sums up the challenge facing Anderson and his teams. In the field, casting directors scoured drama classes, libraries, and high school cafeterias in search of the perfect Max. Without him, the film would not exist, as Anderson had made clear. His exacting standards and quest for perfection were not yet legendary, but they were already apparent during this crucial casting stage.

Chance Takes Care of Many Things

Only a twist of fate could save the film. This took shape at a party in San Francisco attended by Anderson collaborator Davia Nelson, invited by Sofia Coppola, the organizer of the event (the young filmmaker was about to release *The Virgin Suicides*, her first film). Nelson was there to relax, but she was also on the lookout—you never know. While there, she met Coppola's seventeen-year-old cousin, Jason Schwartzman. He was dark-haired, short, and stocky—in sum, he looked nothing like a young Mick Jagger. Nevertheless, the casting director sensed in him a way of being, a mood, a spirit that matched Max Fischer's profile. What if he was the one? Ostensibly, she turned the conversation to *Rushmore* and its difficulties in finding the rare bird, and this did not fall on deaf ears. Schwartzman recalls, "Davia said, 'We're looking for a teenage kid who's really horny and writes plays.' And I said, 'Whoa, that sounds like me.' So I gave her my address and phone number. When I got back to my house, there was a script waiting."[2]

Double Seduction

All that remained was to convince Anderson, whom Nelson had urgently contacted, to audition Schwartzman along with a dozen other candidates. On the big day, the apprentice actor arrived, wearing a blazer (like the other applicants) on which he had sewn his own Rushmore patch. The detail was not lost on the director, whose attention was instantly riveted on this uninhibited young man. The actor's dream quickly became reality. Anderson was won over by Schwartzman's personality—his funniness

Max Fischer, Russia's representative with the "Mini-United Nations."

and strangeness—his energy, and his ideas about the character. Schwartzman was the Max that Anderson had no longer expected to find.

Supporting Roles

The rest of the cast followed a clever mix of established and up-and-coming actors, chosen according to very precise criteria. For the character of Dirk Calloway, Max's submissive disciple who ultimately appears as Max's good conscience, Anderson took as his model Linus, Charlie Brown's best friend in *Peanuts*. Mason Gamble, a child who had been acting since he was seven, would play him. Englishwoman Olivia Williams, virtually unknown at the time (she had only filmed *The Postman*, Kevin Costner, 1997), assumed the role of Miss Cross, a teacher wounded by life (she lives in the memory of her deceased husband) who is destabilized by the interest of Max, then Herman Blume. Anderson, who originally wanted an American actress, changed his mind when he met her (it has to be said that Max dreamed of going to Oxford—a sign of destiny). Her compatriot, the solid Brian Cox, was cast as the intransigent, art-loving principal (his name is Guggenheim). Finally, Seymour Cassel, Anderson's favorite actor from his work with director John Cassavetes, was offered the role of

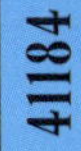

41184 **FOR WES ADDICTS** 41184

Wes Anderson first alluded to the famous French oceanographer Jacques Cousteau in *Bottle Rocket*, via a portrait hanging on a wall. He does it again here, in a scene in which Max reads *Un trésor englouti* (Flammarion, 1971) in French in his high school library, a book from the Odyssée collection that Cousteau published in collaboration with photographer Philippe Diolé. This is not the only nod to France: in another scene, Miss Cross puts Yves Montand's "Rue Saint-Vincent" (1960) into her cassette player.

II

FOR THE SAKE OF REALISM

In the scene where Herman Blume is attacked by bees in his hotel room, Anderson insisted that real insects be released into the room and that no one wear face protection, neither Bill Murray nor the technicians present that day (as a sign of solidarity with the actor). An ordeal according to Yeoman: "I remember bees landing all over me, including my face, as I was operating, and I was quite relieved when the shooting day was over!"[10]

Max's father, a hairdresser overwhelmed by the antics of his son. Max does not accept his humble origins and suffers from the absence of his mother, who died when he was a child.

FILMING AND PRODUCTION

Initially, Wes Anderson wanted to shoot in New England, where he was sure he would find a high school that could serve as the main setting for his film. In the end, however, he was unable to do so, so he decided to opt for Britain and its elegant buildings. Then, one day, his mother sent him photos of St. John's School, where he had studied, in Houston, Texas. It was a revelation. Why had he not thought of it sooner? By choosing a location that he knew well and that met all his requirements (old-style stone buildings on an enormous, clean-lined campus), he made his task considerably easier, especially when it came to designing the storyboard, which he was still drawing himself at the time. For Robert D. Yeoman, his cinematographer, it was also an obvious choice. "The architecture and landscaping of St. John's reminded me very much of the exclusive private schools of the Northeast in the US and was the perfect backdrop for our film."[3] The same logic of proximity applied to the choice of secondary setting for Grover Cleveland, the fictional public high school where Max fails after being expelled from Rushmore: its real-life counterpart, Lamar High School, is located across the street from St. John's. Anderson's father studied there briefly.

The Ideal Setting

"Wes and I visited every location with a viewfinder to map out our shots," explained Yeoman.[4] "We discussed lighting and camera moves and how best to achieve the shots on his storyboard. Often our production designer, David Wasco, would accompany us and we could discuss color and set decoration to create the environment. These discussions were key in setting the visual style of the film. [...] The fact that we shot in the fall aided us immensely; the turning colors of the leaves and often overcast or rainy skies added to the overall feeling." Anderson, who benefited from more favorable conditions than ever (a conciliatory production; an enthusiastic welcome from his former high school, where he employed students as extras; and a climate of trust established with a large part of the technical team since *Bottle Rocket*), did not allow himself to miss the opportunity to impose his style; in retrospect, *Rushmore* appears to be the first film in which his signature is asserted.

An Autumnal Atmosphere

The Texan filmmaker had an extremely precise idea of the colors he wanted for each sequence and each shot. Together with Yeoman and Wasco, he revisited vintage films (*Colonel Blimp*, Michael Powell

Max Fischer (Jason Schwartzman) stares at the schoolteacher (Olivia Williams) who is the object of his infatuation while Herman Blume (Bill Murray) dances in center.

and Emeric Pressburger, 1943; *The Age of Innocence*, Martin Scorsese, 1993; *Les Deux Anglaises et le Continent* [*Two English Girls*, François Truffaut, 1971] to immerse himself in their delicate aesthetics, which create an atmosphere both hushed and heavy. While green and brown tones—autumnal colors—dominate the exteriors, red and blue are occasionally used for the interiors and the characters' costumes, each time for a well-defined reason. As his cinematographer reminds us, Wes Anderson leaves no stone unturned. "At some point in the story Max changes from his blue Rushmore blazer to a green corduroy suit, in many ways signifying that he has moved on to another school. [...] When Max is kicked out of Rushmore and moves to a public school, we chose a location that did not have the vibrant colors of Rushmore. In the hallways and grounds there is trash. Even the corridors have little color and the remnants of ripped up posters on the walls. The light is mainly overhead fluorescents."[5]

Between "Magic" and DIY

Wes Anderson finally shot in wide format and with anamorphic lenses, both of which he had been denied on *Bottle Rocket* but had more or less granted himself. In agreement with Robert D. Yeoman, he again opted for a single focal length, the anamorphic 40 mm replacing the 27 mm used previously. "The lens has a slight distortion which he preferred. [...] Wes and I were both excited to shoot with it. These lenses have a different feeling in spatial depth and how the out of focus backgrounds are represented in the film. In some ways they are more 'magical,' for lack of a better word."[6] The only problem is that this type of lens requires a lot of light to maintain an ideal depth of field. Adapting to this constraint

Max Fischer's headwear is a tribute to France and also to the revolutionary Che Guevara, who frequently wore the beret.

Owen Wilson and Wes Anderson have fun on the set.

was not always easy for the cinematographer. "One of our most difficult locations for lighting was the factory that Mr. Blume owns. It was an immense space and was very dark. We used large tungsten lights on the foreground but to light the entire factory was beyond our means. I decided to use Lightning Strikes units, supplemented by the special effects team that showered sparks in various places in the background, suggesting welding and other construction. The effect was to throw some light in the deep backgrounds and show the great depth of Blume's factory."[7] This "magic" evoked by Yeoman is totally in keeping with the film's project, which Anderson likens to a "fable,"[8] to something "a little unreal," to a quest for theatricality, of which the opening of the curtains at the start of each new sequence is the most striking example. The result on *Rushmore* is exactly what the filmmaker had in mind on paper, and it sets the tone for his way of working, with total control, which he would never compromise on.

Rushmore was Bill Murray's first collaboration with Wes Anderson.

RECEPTION

During the first half of 1998, Wes Anderson set about postproduction on the film, the most important stage of which was undoubtedly the integration of songs from the British Invasion of the 1960s that he had selected with his musical director, Randall Poster. A folk song by the Kinks ("Nothin' in This World Can Stop Me Worryin' 'Bout That Girl," 1965) and a livelier one by the Who ("A Quick One While He's Away," 1966) capture the spirit of the film in their own way, divided between gentle melancholy (accentuated by certain slow-motion sequences) and hard-to-contain rage. In Randall Poster's view, the emotional charge conveyed by the music, brilliantly chosen by the director, would help popularize the filmmaker's singular vision.

The Artist and His Vision

Anderson was unsure of *Rushmore*'s glorious destiny. He was aware from the outset that the cinema he was championing was not destined to attract large audiences, and that he would have to ensure his artistic and financial autonomy in the not-too-distant future. A friend of his, cinematographer Michael Chapman, whom he had invited to a team screening ahead of the film's official presentation, was astonished that Disney had given him such a free hand. He took as an example the scene in which Max tampers with the brakes on Herman Blume's car to get him into an accident. "It's surreal. It's Godard!"[9] But Anderson did not care about verisimilitude or other people's tastes; what mattered to him was the coherence of events within the film. For him, the world of fiction is not the real world. He can do whatever he likes, including putting curtains on the screen. And he was willing to go all the way with artifice, even if it meant bewildering the viewer.

Early Recognition

By autumn 1998, *Rushmore* was ready for a tour of the North American and Canadian independent festivals. In Toronto, New York, and Telluride (Colorado), Wes Anderson's second feature met

Before being called *Rushmore*, the film's working title was *The Tycoon*.

with a generally mixed response. Critics praised its artistic qualities and the performances of the actors, especially Jason Schwartzman. The film's North American release on February 19, 1999, confirmed the trend, grossing $17 million in the US and Canada. Unfortunately, the film did not cross the Atlantic. In Europe, it went unnoticed despite equally favorable press. Here again, time would do it justice. Despite Anderson's youth (he only turned thirty in May 1999), *Rushmore* stood out as a film of maturity. The complex plot is part initiation story, part offbeat comedy, and part adult melodrama (after all, this is the meeting of three lonely people stricken by grief and depression). From a directorial point of view, the step forward taken after *Bottle Rocket* was staggering. Wes Anderson, with the help of Robert D. Yeoman and David Wasco, established a kind of aesthetic charter from which he would never deviate: symmetry and sophisticated composition of shots, chaptering of sequences (numerous annotations appear on screen for the first time), slow lateral and backward dolly shots, studied slow motion, and dramatic "roles" given to color and music. While not yet aiming for a form of abstraction (the cutting remains classic; the acting is not totally atonic), *Rushmore* established Wes Anderson as one of the most exciting filmmakers of his generation.

Bill Murray in *Caddyshack* (Harold Ramis, 1980), one of his first successes.

Bill Murray
The Indispensable

What would Wes Anderson's cinema be without Bill Murray, his great good luck charm who has starred in nine of his eleven feature films to date? The actor's gentle madness, capable of going from a cheesy smile to an aggressive gesture in a fraction of a second, and his ability to blend into the director's meticulous world and instinctively understand what is at stake are precious assets that Wes Anderson would not deprive himself of for anything in the world. From being purely professional at the outset, their relationship quickly became one of friendship and fusion, the two men having forged an almost filial bond over the years—Murray is eighteen years Anderson's senior—a putative father, in short. The unforgettable interpreter of Steve Zissou (*The Life Aquatic with Steve Zissou*, 2004) is also godfather to Wes Anderson's only daughter, Freya, whom he had with Lebanese artist Juman Malouf.

King of Comedy

To understand the origins of this prolific friendship, we need to recall what Bill Murray represents in the American imagination. Born in 1950, he first made a name for himself in the late 1970s as a comedian on the famous comedy show *Saturday Night Live*, where he was a mainstay alongside Dan Aykroyd and John Belushi, the future Blues Brothers. In 1979, increasingly in demand in Hollywood, he took on his first major role in *Meatballs*, a comedy directed by Ivan Reitman and co-written by Harold Ramis—

those who would make him a movie star over the next two decades.

The Phantoms of Glory

In 1980 and 1981, Murray appeared successively in Ramis's first film, *Caddyshack*, and Reitman's *Stripes*, both big hits in the US and packed with classic lines that made him one of the hottest comic actors of the moment. His nonchalance had become his signature. Three years later came the *Ghostbusters* whirlwind: as a placid ectoplasm hunter, Murray was the new global embodiment of cool. Instead of riding the wave of his burgeoning fame, the elusive troublemaker took the opportunity to complete the financing of *The Razor's Edge*, a drama in which he had written himself the lead role. The film was a resounding failure at the end of 1984. Wounded by this, Murray moved to France with his family for a few months to recharge his batteries. He did not return to the cinema until the late 1980s, when he agreed to star in the sequel to *Ghostbusters*, which was another box-office smash.

Quite a Character

The legend of Bill Murray—a personality whose unique talent is said to be compromised by his moods—would be incomplete without *Groundhog Day* (Harold Ramis, 1993), the admirable absurdist comedy in which he plays a weatherman forced to relive the same day over and over again in Punxsutawney, Pennsylvania. The film was at the origin of a trendy Murraymania that was bound to appeal to Wes Anderson, who had just directed his first short film, *Bottle Rocket*. Naturally, when it came time to think of an important name to appear in the long version of *Bottle Rocket*, the temptation to call on him was a big one. For practical reasons however, the role of the gangster Mr. Henry went to James Caan.

Blank Check

Anderson never missed out on recruiting Murray again. For his second feature film, *Rushmore* (1998), he cast him in the tailor-made role of depressive millionaire industrialist Herman Blume. Anderson was unable to reach him in person but knew that the actor's agents loved the script, and were pushing hard to get him to meet the writer-director. A few days later, they did, by telephone. The discussion was surreal: Murray talked about his passion for Akira Kurosawa for an hour before agreeing to star in *Rushmore*. Wes Anderson had won the first battle but was worried about what would happen next, given the actor's unfortunate reputation. "When I met him, I was immediately reassured because he was intelligent and involved in the film for the right reasons, ready to do whatever was asked of him,"[1] Bill Murray said. He agreed to work for scale and even advanced Anderson money for a helicopter scene that the production had refused. Anderson never cashed the check but preserved it religiously.

A Legendary Duo

An instant mutual esteem and an unspoken desire to leave a mark were probably at the root of one of the most fruitful collaborations in world cinema. For Anderson, Murray has played deceived husbands (*Rushmore*, *The Royal Tenenbaums* [2001], *Moonrise Kingdom* [2012]), an obtuse oceanographer (*The Life Aquatic*), a peremptory badger (*Fantastic Mr. Fox*, 2009), a filthy dog (*Isle of Dogs*, 2018), or a heartbroken newspaper boss (*The French Dispatch*, 2021), all without losing his composure and white clown melancholy. What would Wes Anderson's cinema be without Bill Murray?

As a clown in *Quick Change* (Howard Franklin, 1990).

Battered Characters

Small Mutilations

Physical injuries are used to develop characters and advance plots in Wes Anderson's films. *In Bottle Rocket* (1993), the protagonists display bruised physiques: Bob Mapplethorpe is adorned with a bandage behind his ear (a consequence of his brother's violence), and Dignan has a swollen face after a fight. Dressings, neck braces, and unsightly marks such as the wine stain on Agatha's face in *The Grand Budapest Hotel* (2014) are nothing compared to the amputations of other characters. Margot Tenenbaum is missing a finger in *The Royal Tenenbaums* (2001) and farmers shoot off a section of Mr. Fox's tail in *Fantastic Mr. Fox* (2009). In *The Island of Dogs* (2018), animals are experimentally mutated, advancing the idea of fulfilment and accomplishment through transcending life's injuries.

The countless furry mutant creatures in *Isle of Dogs*.

The battered ear and broken arm of Magnus Buchan, the high-school stalker from *Rushmore*.

Everyone at the bedside of Royal Tenenbaum, the boastful patriarch of *The Royal Tenenbaums*.

"Lazy Eye," the one-eyed scout from *Moonrise Kingdom*.

Francis Whitman (Owen Wilson, center), his face enveloped in bandages, from *The Darjeeling Limited*.

Danny GLOVER
Gene HACKMAN
Anjelica HUSTON
Bill MURRAY
Gwyneth PALTROW
Ben STILLER
Luke WILSON
Owen WILSON
The ROYAL TENENBAUMS
FAMILY ISN'T A WORD...IT'S A SENTENCE.
TOUCHSTONE PICTURES presents an AMERICAN EMPIRICAL PICTURE "THE ROYAL TENENBAUMS"
Danny GLOVER Gene HACKMAN Anjelica HUSTON Bill MURRAY Gwyneth PALTROW Ben STILLER Luke WILSON Owen WILSON
Music Supervisor Randall POSTER Music by Mark MOTHERSBAUGH Casting by Douglas AIBEL Costume Designer Karen PATCH
Editor Dylan TICHENOR A.C.E. Production Designer David WASCO Director of Photography Robert YEOMAN A.S.C.
Executive Producers Rudd SIMMONS Owen WILSON Produced by Wes ANDERSON Barry MENDEL Scott RUDIN
Written by Wes ANDERSON & Owen WILSON Directed by Wes ANDERSON
R
Touchstone Pictures
COMING SOON
royaltenenbaums.com

THE ROYAL TENENBAUMS

United States • 1 hr 50 • Color • DTS / Dolby Digital / SDDS • 2.39 : 1

Filming Dates: **March–May 2001**
Release Dates in the United States: **October 5, 2001 (New York Film Festival preview); December 14, 2001 (limited release); January 4, 2002**

Budget: **Approx. $21 million**
North America Box Office: **Approx. $52 million**
Worldwide Box Office: **Approx. $71 million**

Production Companies: **Touchstone Pictures, American Empirical Pictures**
Producers: **Barry Mendel, Wes Anderson, Scott Rudin**
Executive Producers: **Rudd Simmons, Owen Wilson**
Associate Producer: **Will Sweeney**

Screenplay: **Wes Anderson, Owen Wilson**
Director of Photography: **Robert D. Yeoman**
Film Editing: **Dylan Tichenor**
Music Supervisor: **David Moritz**
Composer: **Mark Mothersbaugh**
Production Design: **David Wasco**
Set Decoration: **Sandy Reynolds-Wasco**
Art Direction: **Carl Sprague**
Sound: **Pawel Wdowczak**
Costumes: **Karen Patch**
Casting: **Douglas Aibel**
First Assistant Director: **Sam Hoffman**
Makeup: **Naomi Donne**
Illustrations: **Eric Chase Anderson**
Stunt Arranger: **Michael Russo**

Starring: **GENE HACKMAN (Royal Tenenbaum), ANJELICA HUSTON (Etheline Tenenbaum), BEN STILLER (Chas Tenenbaum), GWYNETH PALTROW (Margot Tenenbaum), LUKE WILSON (Richie Tenenbaum), OWEN WILSON (Eli Cash), BILL MURRAY (Raleigh St. Clair), DANNY GLOVER (Henry Sherman), SEYMOUR CASSEL (Dusty), KUMAR PALLANA (Pagoda), ALEC BALDWIN (narrator)...**

"The Tenenbaums' house was central to the story and was like a character in the movie."

Robert D. Yeoman, director of photography[1]

SYNOPSIS

In the late 1970s, Etheline Tenenbaum, fed up with the antics of her husband, Royal, ejects him from the family home, where she raises her three highly gifted preteens alone. Chas is a financial genius, Margot writes critically acclaimed plays, and Richie is a tennis champion. Eli Cash, their neighbor and friend of roughly the same age, watches them all with envy. Twenty-two years later, all the siblings are depressed failures, while Eli has become a best-selling author. Will Royal Tenenbaum, the father who makes a thunderous come-back into the lives of the three siblings after years of absence, pull them out of this negative spiral?

GENESIS

Buoyed by the critical success of *Rushmore* (1998) and their renewed partnership with Touchstone Pictures, Wes Anderson and Owen Wilson were already thinking about their next project in 1999. It could have been *Black Irish*, the working title of a parodic Western they had begun writing but which, for reasons unknown, never saw the light of day—perhaps the failure of *Wild Wild West* (Barry Sonnenfeld, 1999) had dissuaded them? In the end, the two friends settled on a subject that they had only tentatively addressed up to that point, but which obsessed them intimately: family. Coming from them, the treatment could only be unusual. From the outset, they planned to describe a clan whose children would be geniuses, each in their own field. Soon, in their minds, there would be three of them (two boys and a girl), experts in finance, sports, and writing, respectively. At this stage, Anderson and Wilson had no script, but they were driven by the desire to bring to life these characters, whom they imagined to be as whimsically fantastical as they were isolated. They are also convinced that, as they became adults, their imperceptible malaise, in combination with their gifted condition and a toxic family environment, would become an unbearable burden.

OUR FATHER, THIS NONENTITY

The writing process took about a year. Initially, the story revolved around Richie, the youngest son, a former tennis champion who suffers burnout in the middle of a tournament and returns to the family home after a long sea voyage. He finds his older (adopted) brother and sister in the same depressed state as himself. And with good reason: their glorious past is also buried. How do you rebuild your life when you have been at the top and have now fallen so far? The answer: back home, where it all began. Anderson and Wilson hold the threads of their lives together, and it remains to be seen who will pull them. The father, a character who was not central at the outset, will play this role and become increasingly important. As the film progresses, the viewer realizes that he is the one primarily responsible for his children's suffering, which he tries—unsuccessfully—to repair by imposing himself on their lives after years of estrangement. This narrative device is not far removed from the one the two screenwriters employed in *Rushmore*, when the antihero, Max Fischer, decides to make amends with those he has hurt, despite their reluctance.

TRUE OR FALSE?

For those who might have wondered, Wes Anderson has always declared that the members of *The Royal Tenenbaums* were not romanticized versions of his own parents and two brothers. "Certainly the

Irina Gorovaia (top) and Amedeo Turturro (bottom) play Margot and Richie Tenenbaum as children.

Gene Hackman's performance in *The French Connection* (William Friedkin, 1971) left a lasting impression on Wes Anderson.

The character of Royal Tenenbaum was written especially for Gene Hackman, despite his initial reluctance to accept the role.

Wes Anderson was so keen to work with Gwyneth Paltrow (shown here with Luke Wilson) that he arranged the filming schedule around her availability.

inspiration for the characters comes from real people that Owen and I have known [Tenenbaum is the name of a friend of theirs], people who have influenced us in life, not only family members but also good friends. [...] My father is nothing like the character of Royal. But the way Etheline, the mother in the family, encourages everyone comes from my life, and also the way each of the characters connects to someone else."[2] Does the director tend to downplay the autobiographical aspect of his film? During preproduction, Anjelica Huston, chosen to play Etheline, was astonished by her resemblance to Wes's mother, Ann Anderson, also an archaeologist. And when Wes handed her his mother's old glasses to put on, the actress laughed and asked whether or not she was playing his mother. "I think he was astonished by the idea," recalls Anjelica Huston.[3] In psychoanalysis, one would be discussing repression.

Poetic License

Not only was the film motivated by the desire to evoke filial ties, but it was also motivated by the ambition to recreate an imaginary New York, the city with international influence into which sensitive Texans Wes Anderson and Owen Wilson quickly blended. Why imaginary? Because, for them, *The Royal Tenenbaums* is a romantic, idealized vision of the Big Apple, nourished by Anderson's assiduous reading of the *New Yorker*. The legendary writer J. D. Salinger, whose work appeared in the magazine, is the tutelary figure hovering over the director's early work. "The entire film is steeped in some kind of New York literary history," said Anderson,[4] justifying his poetic license. The film's similarity to an illustrated novel (the viewer watches the characters in a book come to life, with the narrative appropriately chaptered and largely narrated by a voice-over) follows the same intellectual path.

CASTING

From the outset of the project, even before writing the script itself, Wes Anderson, with the approval of Owen Wilson, imagined that the main characters, with their overinflated egos, would be played by first-rate actors, if not stars. The credit that *Rushmore* brought him enabled the director, now considered one of the most promising of his generation, to dream big, knowing that the planned

Compare the sets of *The Royal Tenenbaums* on the top and *The Magnificent Ambersons* (Orson Welles, 1942) on the bottom.

budget of around $20 million (double that of the previous film) would nevertheless impose financial sacrifices on the chosen stars. The two authors had no qualms about casting Gene Hackman as Royal Tenenbaum, the colorful patriarch who is the film's key figure. A New Hollywood legend, Hackman, the embodiment of detective Jimmy "Popeye" Doyle (*French Connection*, William Friedkin, 1971), was a hard-to-get actor with a full schedule and a reputation for his strong character. Convincing him would be no easy task.

Landing the Big Fish

Aware of the obstacles but determined to succeed as he had done with Bill Murray for *Rushmore*, Anderson sent his agent early on in 1999 to arrange a meeting with Gene Hackman. Hackman was cordial, even willing to read the script in due course. However, he asked the director not to write specifically for him. They did not know each other, so why should Anderson know what suited him? This was an unassailable argument, and one that would be taken into account in future negotiations. A few months later, with the script finalized, Anderson tried his luck again with the actor, who this time proved distant. Too much work, a feeling of not having been listened to, the reasons why Hackman initially turned down the role were all valid but left the director in doubt. Luckily for him, the actor's agent, who was very supportive of the project, was able to use his influence with his protégé. He passed on the many letters (and pleas) sent by Anderson to tip the balance in his favor. Ready for anything, the director even commissioned his illustrator brother Eric—who created the character sketches and paintings for the film—to draw a picture of Royal Tenenbaum in the midst of his family, to demonstrate the importance of the role. Whether Hackman was moved by the idea or just worn down, we shall never know, but he finally agreed, much to everyone's relief.

A Golden (Acting) Family

The hard part was over. Enthused by their first collaboration, Bill Murray had long since agreed to play the secondary role of Raleigh St. Clair, a brooding neurologist married to the unfaithful Margot Tenenbaum. The latter is played by Gwyneth Paltrow, a true star at the peak of her career, having just won an Oscar for her role in *Shakespeare in Love* (John Madden, 1998). The actress did not hesitate for a second, excited at the prospect of working with Wes Anderson, who found in her the ideal profile of the capricious woman-child to embody the character of the Tenenbaum daughter. The only constraint: the production had to organize the shooting schedule around her limited availability. The other star in the credits is an old ally. A *Bottle Rocket* fan who became a friend of Owen Wilson's after starring with him in *Meet the Parents* (Jay Roach, 2000), Ben Stiller was biding his time. The role of Chas Tenenbaum, a temperamental widower obsessed with controlling his two sons, suited him like a glove. The veteran cast was

More firecracker yellow for the tent Richie's depressive character sets up in the family home.

rounded out with Anjelica Huston as well as Danny Glover, Mel Gibson's unforgettable sidekick in the *Lethal Weapon* saga (Richard Donner, 1987). Anderson, who has always admired Glover, thought he had the stature and presence to stand up to Gene Hackman as Henry Sherman, Etheline Tenenbaum's suitor. For the voice of the narrator, the director called on the solid Alec Baldwin, whose warm, ironic timbre was just right for the fable that the director wanted to stage, following *Rushmore*. Finally, the Wilson brothers, inseparable from Wes Anderson since his early days, finally landed two key roles: Luke dons the tennis outfit of Richie Tenenbaum, the younger brother secretly in love with his adopted sister, Margot; Owen dons the cowboy hat of Eli Cash, the family's drug-addicted parasitic neighbor.

FILMING AND PRODUCTION

The script had not yet been finalized when Wes Anderson's collaborators, under his guidance, began scouring New York for the house that would serve as the film's main set. Initially tempted to shoot the film in a studio (which would have made things easier, given the whimsical nature of the story), the filmmaker eventually preferred to set the action in a real location, to tie it in with the vision of New York he had in mind. For the same reason, the immediate exteriors also had to be real. The guiding principle: the megalopolis must be identified but remain somewhat abstract. This meant aiming for little-known sites and habitats that fell outside the New York stereotype. The challenge was such that it took over a year to find a location that met Anderson's requirements.

A Sad Prescience

In one striking sequence, Richie Tenenbaum slits his wrists in his bathroom to the tune of "Needle in the Hay" by Elliott Smith (1995), the singer Wes Anderson had unsuccessfully approached to sing the cover of the Beatles' famous "Hey Jude" that opens the film. This scene was sadly prophetic: on October 21, 2003, barely two years after the release of *The Royal Tenenbaums*, Elliott Smith died tragically at the age of thirty-four after a violent argument with his girlfriend. According to the investigation report, the young woman had taken refuge in the bathroom, only to open the door and find the singer in agony, a knife plunged into his chest. Although the theory of suicide was advanced, the investigation into this suspicious death has not yet been closed.

Owen Wilson (Eli Cash) and Luke Wilson (Richie Tenenbaum) in front of a painting by Wes Anderson's friend Hugo Guinness.

Anjelica Huston (Etheline Tenenbaum) makes her first notable foray into Wes Anderson's cinema.

The Magnificent Anderson

The imposing mansion in *The Magnificent Ambersons* (Orson Welles, 1942) was the director's aesthetic reference. On the advice of a friend, he scoured the Hamilton Heights neighborhood of Harlem, in the northwest of Manhattan, where he discovered the house of his dreams: an old Victorian mansion in red brick, four stories high and with a roof, on which Richie's aviary and the Tenenbaum flag, flown on the existing turret, could be installed. While some of the interiors were unsuitable for the desired shots (the production team found others in neighboring buildings for Etheline's office or the kitchen, for example), the assets of the location outweighed its constraints, according to cinematographer Robert D. Yeoman. "It had recently been sold, and our producers made a deal with the new owners that we could paint the interior and make minor changes as long as we did not alter the bones of the house. [...] The rooms were often small and the staircase difficult to work in, but it was essential to create the sense of a family home and connect the rooms to each other. [...] We were able to paint and dress the house exactly how Wes wanted. [...] The neighborhood was perfect for the taxi pickups, coming and going from the house, etc."[5]

Aesthetic Erasure

The Royal Tenenbaums is distinguished by its strong ochre tones, which were to become the norm in Wes Anderson's cinema. From the sets to the costumes and props, everything was designed to achieve this stylized ambiance, according to Robert D. Yeoman. "The color palette of the film was carefully con-

Gene Hackman dazzles as Royal Tenenbaum. Among his numerous awards for his performance is a Golden Globe for Best Actor in a Musical or Comedy.

trolled, and we shot many tests in prep. Pink, red, blue, gray, and brown were all emphasized."[6] The result reinforces the timelessness of the story, which seems to take place in a parallel universe despite its obvious proximity to the New York we know. The famous yellow cabs are humorously replaced by dented, weathered cars nicknamed "Gypsy Cab Co." All other visual aspects of New York are rearranged, even erased. "The plan was to use the architecture of New York City without showing the typical landmarks that you usually see in movies. When we shot a single of Pagoda by the river we placed him so that he blocked the Statue of Liberty in the background. We chose other locations that were not immediately recognizable."[7] This is the case, for example, of the hospital where Richie Tenenbaum is taken after his suicide attempt, an abandoned facility located in Newark, New Jersey, was refurbished for the film.

Pampered Actors

Filming began in March 2001 in the Hamilton Heights neighborhood. As producer Barry Mendel points out, the timing was tight. "It's a film with 240 scenes in it and we have 60 days to shoot it, so mathematically that means we are shooting four scenes a day. It was a breathless pace."[8] To ease the pressure, the actors were provided with the best possible facilities. In the house, a special room was reserved for them to rest and exchange ideas between scenes, thus fostering a collegial atmosphere. Improvisation was also kept to a minimum, as the work plan, sets, and staging had been locked down beforehand. On set, Anderson regularly played the music he would be using in the film (ranging from Ravel to Bob Dylan to Nico) to give the actors an idea of the emotional color of the scenes they would be playing—a welcome initiative.

Gene Hackman Ironizes

Following in the footsteps of *Rushmore*, Anderson and Yeoman, the director of photography, opted for a wide-format, 40 mm anamorphic lens with the occasional addition of an anamorphic zoom. In addition to its skillfully composed, increasingly detailed shots, *The Royal Tenenbaums* is distinguished by its sweeping camera movements, which were not always easy to set up, according to Yeoman. "When Royal and Etheline are walking through the park the entire scene is shot with a long dolly track. Because of the strict rules of the park, we were not allowed to move any rocks or bushes, so the track had to be laid around or above [...] anything that was natural. It was quite a long track, and Gene Hackman said to me, 'You know they have this thing called a Steadicam.' Wes did not feel that the feel of the Steadicam moves [was] right for the film, so all moving shots were either off of a dolly or hand held with a Panavision Panaflex Platinum."[9]

The all-star cast includes (first row, center) Ben Stiller; (second row, l to r) Bill Murray, Gene Hackman, Luke Wilson; and (third row, behind Hackman) Danny Glover and Anjelica Huston (Etheline Tenenbaum).

FOR WES ADDICTS

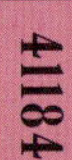

The hands stamping the library card at the beginning of the film are those of Wes Anderson. The director also lends his voice to one of the two commentators of the tennis match lost by Richie Tenenbaum—the other voice is that of Andrew Wilson. Finally, the Braverman Grant, the theatrical award that Margot Tenenbaum receives, is a direct reference to Barry Braverman, a filmmaker who made corporate films for Owen Wilson's father, helped Wes shoot the short version of *Bottle Rocket* (1993), and continued to work with him on *The Darjeeling Limited* (2007) and *Moonrise Kingdom* (2012) as part of the lighting team.

RECEPTION

At the beginning of 1999, *Rushmore* had created a great deal of anticipation around Anderson's next film, which was amplified by the announcement of the big names in the credits. Logically, it was with some excitement that observers flocked to the preview of *The Royal Tenenbaums* at the New York Film Festival on October 5, 2001. The filmmaker explained that he had been planning the film's appearance for a long time: "I love the New York Film Festival, and so it was something I had in mind before we even started shooting the movie. [...] It's a New York movie and [...] to me it's the best place to start."[10]

A Divisive Style

The good word from New York was certainly shared at the time of the limited release at the end of December 2001 (and again at the time of the national release on January 4, 2002), but reservations were expressed above all about the increasingly disembodied approach advocated by the director. Although not quite Robert Bresson, the apostle of stylistic sim-

Wes Anderson, perfectly in the center of the picture. Photograph by Laura Wilson.

plicity whom Wes Anderson admires, not least for the French filmmaker's distanced, understated acting, there is a perfectly unusual tone to *The Royal Tenenbaums* that dismayed some critics. (Surely one of the characteristics of innovative artists is to initially provoke a form of incomprehension?) In France, the press was also divided between enthusiastic and measured opinions. All the world's press, however, agreed on one thing: Gene Hackman was an absolute knockout! The actor had delivered his best performance since *Unforgiven* (Clint Eastwood, 1992), which won him the Oscar for Best Supporting Actor in 1993.

Double Triumph

There was a lot of talk about Gene Hackman at the annual awards ceremonies. The actor won four of them, including the prestigious 2002 Golden Globe for Best Actor (in a comedy or musical film), but he was not nominated for an Oscar. However, Wes Anderson and Owen Wilson were nominated for an Oscar for their original screenplay. The famous statuette eluded them, but their reputation as auteurs was firmly established—although no one suspected that *The Royal Tenenbaums* signaled the end of their screenwriting collaboration. As for Wes Anderson's star, it shone ever brighter and without borders. With $71 million in worldwide takings (including $52 million in the US and Canada), *The Royal Tenenbaums* set a kind of record that would stand for twelve years, until the breakthrough with *The Grand Budapest Hotel* (2014). But that is another story…

In *The Life Aquatic*, will Ned Plimpton (Owen Wilson, right) kill his father (Bill Murray)?

(Not) Great Families

Love and War

As its title suggests, *The Royal Tenenbaums* (2001) established, almost from the outset, Wes Anderson's perception of blood ties: disaffected, distorted, and amplified by his own experience as a child traumatized by his parents' divorce. *Bottle Rocket* (1996) had already given a glimpse of this. In his first feature, the main characters never mention their parents, whose existence remains ghostly, sometimes suggested by the presence of a little sister whom Anthony Adams visits at school, sometimes by the vast family home occupied by heir Bob Mapplethorpe and his older brother. The surname of Dignan, the third character, is not specified, as if to deny his ancestry. (Owen Wilson, the actor who plays him and is the co-writer of the film, also has a notoriously complicated family history.) Revisiting *Bottle Rocket* from this angle gives the film a troubling scope. The famous Andersonian melancholy stems from this discordant family music.

Original Sin

Following on from *Rushmore* (1998), with its tormented, motherless hero who seeks an empirically incestuous affair with an older schoolteacher, *The Royal Tenenbaums* normalized what might have been a simple twist in the plot in the first two films. Inspired by the writings of J. D. Salinger,

Woodrow Steenbeck (Jack Ryan) and his sisters, orphaned by their mother, in the desert heat of *Asteroid City*.

the members of this fictional tribe are all victims of their immediate environment, starting with their father. Royal, a fickle, inconsistent, and narcissistic man, wears out his wife's patience and dries up her love. Driven out of the family home, then rejected by his children, the unworthy progenitor disappears from the radar, plunging his descendants into confusion and depression, since he is indeed both the cause of the unhappiness and its solution. (One might even say that title of the film reduces the family entity to the name of the patriarch.) Wes Anderson is a pessimist by nature, not a nihilist or even a skeptic. He believes in human nature and its capacity for resilience, but salvation comes through difficult trials that the characters' emotional handicaps seem to render insurmountable. It is no longer a question of killing the father but of bringing him back to life in their lives. This is one of the main challenges of Andersonian cinema.

Peter Pan Syndrome

The thoughtless Royal is a "child" who has not grown up, like most of the male adults in Wes Anderson's filmography. His greatest pleasure is running wild with the two offspring of Chas, his eldest son, who is obsessed with control and security—a neurosis that also links him to early childhood. Assuming responsibility, recognizing and correcting mistakes, educating, protecting, and providing for his children are the prerogatives of a normally constituted father. Not so with Anderson. "I hate fathers, and I never wanted to be one," says Steve Zissou to his presumed son, Ned, in *The Life Aquatic with Steve Zissou* (2004). It was a sentence as frank and direct as an uppercut that Ned took in stride, aware of the time it would take the oceanographer-star to come to terms with their filiation. We find traces of this childish behavior in Peter Whitman, who, in *The Darjeeling Limited* (2007), takes a trip with his brothers to India while his partner is about to give birth. Or war photographer Augie Steenbeck in *Asteroid City* (2023), unable to tell his four children that their mother has died. Another irresponsible oaf is the head of the family in *Fantastic Mr. Fox* (2009), who endangers his family by stealing from humans, despite his wife's warnings. The thrill of petty theft and its execution (planned with the precision of a treasure hunt) outweighs the consequences for his household. The only woman in Wes Anderson's filmography of comparable immaturity is Midge Campbell in *Asteroid City*. "I love my daughter, but I'm a bad mother because, unfortunately for her, she's not my priority," she confesses bluntly to Augie Steenbeck. She adds coldly that she feels no guilt, no doubt "because of my history with violent men" (her father, but also her brother and uncles). The paternal loop has been sordidly brought full circle.

"Mama, kiss it better..."

Largely inspired by the filmmaker's own mother (also an archaeologist), Etheline Tenenbaum seems to have crystallized the prototype of the benevolent, protective mother, the opposite of their father. Perhaps too much so. It is she who, in an irresistible impulse, brings her depressed children back home, enclosing them in their cozy cocoon, breaking their flight. The tame falcon that Richie, the

Bewildered members of the dysfunctional *The Royal Tenenbaums* family.

youngest son, watches circling in the sky with satisfaction, if not envy, illustrates this generalized alienation. Mrs. Fox shows the same excessive vigilance with her only son, Ash, as does Laura Bishop who, in *Moonrise Kingdom* (2012), is nonetheless reproached for her marital liberties by her rebellious daughter. There are exceptions to the rule, but they benefit from extenuating circumstances. Patricia Whitman, in *The Darjeeling Limited*, has "abandoned" her three (adult) sons to retire to a monastery in India. The call is imperious; it goes beyond motherhood. Then there is the prison guard in *The French Dispatch* (2021), who finds the child mysteriously taken from her at birth. Finally, there are the dead mothers, whose absence weighs heavily on the shoulders of Max (the antihero of *Rushmore*), Ned (*The Life Aquatic*), and the Steenbeck girls (*Asteroid City*), the latter of whom seek to revive, through rituals and spells, the missing woman whose ashes are contained in a Tupperware container.

Sibling Enmity

Chas, Margot, and Richie Tenenbaum have a complicated relationship. The first has always been jealous of his youngest, Royal's darling; the second, who was adopted, has never found her place; the third suffers in silence from the forbidden feelings he has for his sister in spirit. Siblings are the space where filial wounds are openly expressed (sometimes culminating in fights), without fear of parental judgment or a possible breakup. "I wonder if the three of us could have been friends in real life," Jack Whitman innocently asks his two brothers in *The Darjeeling Limited*. The same question arises in *Bottle Rocket*, for driver Bob Mapplethorpe, a victim of his elder brother's beatings and harassment. For Wes Anderson, the second of three boys, the feeling of belonging to the same lineage implies duties and obligations, regardless of the attachment one may feel for the other. One does not exclude oneself just like that, on pain of incurring the wrath of one's siblings. "You're a traitor to our family," one of his little brothers says to the teenage runaway in *Moonrise Kingdom*. This sanctity of fraternal ties can also be the envy of many. Eli Cash, a neighbor and friend of the young Tenenbaums, has always dreamed of being one of them, to the point of sleeping with Margot, whom he does not love (and vice versa), in order to be legally "inducted" into the family (which does not happen).

One Person Missing

Eli Cash also (theoretically) has parents, although we never see them on screen. As a child, he was very much a part of the Tenenbaum household, even secretly sending Etheline his report cards to get her attention. In spirit, he is a would-be orphan in search of affection and recognition. A major figure in novels (by Dickens, Hugo, Malot, Twain, Dahl, Rowling, etc.), the orphan is central to the work of Wes Anderson, who knows his classics: Sam (*Moonrise Kingdom*), Zero (*The Grand Budapest Hotel*, 2014), and Atari (*Isle of Dogs*, 2018) tragically lost their parents when they were young; Max (*Rushmore*), Ned (*The Life Aquatic*), the Whitman brothers (*The Darjeeling Limited*), Woodrow Steenbeck (*Asteroid City*), and Gigi (*The French Dispatch*) are all motherless or fatherless. This condition, which they have not chosen, is more of a driving force than a hindrance. The sense of injustice they feel ontologically makes them impervious to the dramas and obstacles they encounter along the way. Relatively autonomous, they move forward in life with a goal (to become an adult, a hotel concierge, a sailor, or a policeman; to save dogs; to save the planet), armed with certainties that have thrived on the fertile ground of their original or occasional distress. Most of them have above-average IQs and show intelligence honed by adversity.

The Ideal Family

Ultimately, Anderson's portrait of the ideal family is the one we choose for ourselves, against all odds. It may, of course, be a traditional family (*The Royal Tenenbaums*, *Fantastic Mr. Fox*) or a single-parent family (*Rushmore*, *The Life Aquatic*, *The Darjeeling Limited*, *Asteroid City*), but nothing beats the home whose foundations you lay yourself. There is no happier, more accomplished character in the filmmaker's melancholic world than Klaus Daimler, second-in-command to oceanographer Steve Zissou, when he receives Zissou's affection in *The Life Aquatic*: "Don't you know me and Esteban always thought of you as our baby brother?" he says tenderly. The same goes for Sam (*Moonrise Kingdom*), a Khaki Scout who is finally adopted by the policeman looking for him, saving him from reform school in the process; for bellboy Zero (*The Grand Budapest Hotel*), the moral and legal heir to M. Gustave, concierge turned millionaire; and for ward of the state Atari (*Isle of Dogs*), elected master of Chief with the blessing of his first pet, Spots, who in turn looks after the puppies he has just had with his loved one.

Suzy Bishop (Kara Hayward) will soon "betray" her brothers by fleeing the family home.

Bill MURRAY
in a new comedy by
Wes ANDERSON
THE
LIFE AQUATIC
with
STEVE ZISSOU
Owen WILSON Cate BLANCHETT Anjelica HUSTON Willem DAFOE Jeff GOLDBLUM Michael GAMBON Bud CORT
TOUCHSTONE PICTURES presents an AMERICAN EMPIRICAL PICTURE
"THE LIFE AQUATIC WITH STEVE ZISSOU" Bill MURRAY Owen WILSON Cate BLANCHETT
Anjelica HUSTON Willem DAFOE Jeff GOLDBLUM Michael GAMBON Bud CORT
Casting by Douglas AIBEL Music Supervisor Randall POSTER Music by Mark MOTHERSBAUGH Costume Designer Milena CANONERO
Edited by David MORITZ Production Designer Mark FRIEDBERG Director of Photography Robert YEOMAN, ASC Executive Producer Rudd SIMMONS
Produced by Wes ANDERSON Barry MENDEL Scott RUDIN Written by Wes ANDERSON Noah BAUMBACH
R
SOME LANGUAGE AND NUDITY
COMING SOON
Directed by Wes ANDERSON
Touchstone Pictures

THE LIFE AQUATIC
WITH STEVE ZISSOU

2004

United States, Italy • 1 h 59 • Color • DTS / Dolby Digital / SDDS • 2.35 : 1

Filming Dates: **September 16–December 2003**
Release Dates in the United States: **November 20, 2004 (Los Angeles preview), December 25, 2004**

Budget: **Approx. $50 million**
North America Box Office: **$24 million**
Worldwide Box Office: **$35 million**

Production Companies: **Touchstone Pictures, American Empirical Pictures, Scott Rudin Productions, Life Aquatic Productions Inc.**
Producers: **Wes Anderson, Barry Mendel, Scott Rudin**
Co-Producer: **Enzo Sisti**
Executive Producer: **Rudd Simmons**
Associate Producer: **Daniel Beers**

Screenplay: **Wes Anderson, Noah Baumbach**
Director of Photography: **Robert Yeoman**
First Assistant Director: **Sam Hoffman**
Second Unit Director: **Roman Coppola**
Editing: **David Moritz**
Production Design: **Mark Friedberg**
Set Decoration: **Gretchen Rau**
Art Direction: **Stefano Maria Ortolani**
Music: **Mark Mothersbaugh**
Sound: **Scott A. Jennings, Pawel Wdowczak**
Costumes: **Milena Canonero**
Makeup: **Gino Tomagnini**
Visual Effects Supervisor: **Jeremy Dawson**
Casting: **Douglas Aibel**
Animation: **Henry Selick**

Starring: **BILL MURRAY (Steve Zissou), OWEN WILSON (Ned Plimpton), CATE BLANCHETT (Jane Winslett-Richardson), ANJELICA HUSTON (Eleanor Zissou), WILLEM DAFOE (Klaus Daimler), JEFF GOLDBLUM (Alistair Hennessey), MICHAEL GAMBON (Oseary Drakoulias), NOAH TAYLOR (Vladimir Wolodarsky) BUD CORT (Bill Ubell), SEU JORGE (Pelé dos Santos), SEYMOUR CASSEL (Esteban du Plantier)...**

“A week before she killed herself, my mother told me that you’d known about me since the day I was born.”

—

Ned Plimpton to Steve Zissou

SYNOPSIS

Underwater exploration star Steve Zissou presents his latest documentary at an Italian festival. He announces his intention to kill the mythical jaguar shark that has devoured his best friend in front of a skeptical audience—no one believes him anymore, neither the public or his sponsors, who are tired of his eccentricities. The oceanographer is nevertheless determined to turn his next expedition into a revenge and the subject of a new documentary. Despite the headwinds, he boards the *Belafonte*, his aging ship, with his crew, who follow him blindly, and a certain Ned Plimpton, a pilot who presents himself as his son. A pregnant journalist, and Zissou's spurned wife also join the odyssey.

Steve Zissou (Bill Murray) and his team in the middle of a fake underwater forest.

GENESIS

The figure of Steve Zissou (a surname borrowed from the nickname of photographer Jacques-Henri Lartigue's brother Maurice) is one of a series of projects that Wes Anderson developed in college in the early 1990s as part of his screenwriting courses. He imagined this character based on Jacques Cousteau, his youthful idol, captain of a boat—named the *Belafonte*—whose expeditions were meticulously prepared by his wife, the real brains of the couple. This storyline continued to evolve over the years, assuming a scope that required solid directing experience. After *Rushmore* (1998) and *The Royal Tenenbaums* (2001), Anderson finally considered himself ready for the adventure.

A Change of Partner

Anderson draws on two visions. In his fertile mind, it was not only a question of parodying the maritime epics of Cousteau (of whom Steve Zissou would be, on the face of it, an unsympathetic version) but also of filming cutaway shots of a boat. When he was a child, the future creator often enjoyed drawing behind the scenes in this way. Anderson dreamed of transposing this approach to the screen. Having laid the foundations of his script, all that remained was to consolidate the framework and to paper the walls. One man was going to help him do just that. Noah Baumbach, a native New Yorker, befriended Anderson in 1997, at a time when these two hopefuls of American cinema were in opposite camps: Anderson was an up-and-coming filmmaker, and Baumbach was stagnating (he did not make his breakthrough until 2005 with his fourth film, *The Squid and the Whale*, produced by his friend). Since the late 1990s, they had enjoyed a close friendship, comparable to that between Anderson and Owen Wilson, his erstwhile alter ego. So when Wilson, absorbed in acting, was less available to write, Anderson turned to Baumbach, with whom he spent days in New York restaurants polishing the story.

Alone Against the World

Steve Zissou was fleshed out and brought to life. His irascible and authoritarian character, at the same time seductive and elusive, shapes the action and the profile of the other protagonists. It soon becomes clear that his hold over men does not work with women, who oppose him. His wife despises him; the journalist hired to cover the expedition finds him mediocre; the documentary script girl, disgusted by his dictatorial behavior on board, stirs up a mutiny. When he is abandoned by his producer, Zissou's ego takes a beating from all sides. Soon it is no longer a simple adventure film, punctuated by action scenes and centered around the central character. Zissou somehow escaped his creators. "As we wrote the script with Noah Baumbach, [...] the subject gradually shifted to a more general questioning of the figure of the filmmaker. We talked a lot about *La Nuit américaine* (François Truffaut, 1973) and *8½* (Federico Fellini, 1963). In the end, *The Life Aquatic* tells the story of a man in desperate need of rallying people around his film project. But Cousteau's world remained very present."[1] Anderson might add that Zissou's frantic quest for funding, as a cursed and misunderstood demiurge, is akin to the exuberance of visionary director Orson Welles.

An Enchanted World

The writing took on another decisive turn when it came to describing the underwater world that the crew of the *Belafonte* are led to explore in certain scenes. For Anderson and Baumbach, the perfection of the images produced by the abundant documentaries—including breathtaking footage by Canadian director James Cameron—on the silent world was a stumbling block. As they lacked the resources to compete, they decided to adopt the opposite approach, opting for an imaginary, poetic, and totally artificial underwater world. Fish, crustaceans, mollusks, and coral reefs would be handmade and animated frame by frame, using a technique known as stop motion. The result was a unique underwater world, like the reinvented

Freeze Frame

Cousteau-style red hats, flashy jumpsuits, turtleneck jumpers, Zissou branded running shoes, Anjelica Huston's mermaid outfit. The wardrobe of *The Life Aquatic* partly defines its old-fashioned charm. This was the work of Italian costume designer Milena Canonero, a veritable star in her field, winner of four Oscars (two when she worked on *The Life Aquatic*), who began a long-term collaboration with Wes Anderson. Accustomed to the precision and demands of the great directors (Stanley Kubrick, Francis Ford Coppola, Barbet Schroeder, Steven Soderbergh), this was the first time that she slipped into a comic universe with its own codes. For team Zissou's strange blue suits, she had to use her imagination to achieve the effect of sardines glistening underwater—even coating them in iridescent blue paint—and enabling them to withstand torrential downpours, explosions, and the multiple immersions of the characters in the sea. This essential work made Milena Canonero indispensable to Wes Anderson.

New York of *The Royal Tenenbaums*. This specific dimension of the film would be taken on by Henry Selick (see "Filming and Production"). The acclaimed director of *The Nightmare Before Christmas* (1993) was the worthy heir of Ray Harryhausen, the famous special effects designer revered by Anderson, who popularized stop motion in the 1950s and '60s by incorporating animated sequences into films such as *The 7th Voyage of Sinbad* (Nathan Juran, 1958) and *Jason and the Argonauts* (Don Chaffey, 1963).

CASTING

After two memorable supporting roles in *Rushmore* and *The Royal Tenenbaums*, Bill Murray was finally offered the lead role—his only one to date—in a film by Wes Anderson, who was really keen to showcase his immense talent as an actor, which had been reduced a little too much to comedy. By the time preparations for the film began, Murray had already shattered that image by playing the unforgettable broken character in *Lost in Translation* (2003) for Sofia Coppola, a role that won him a Golden Globe and an Oscar nomination in 2004. So the timing was ideal. The actor, to whom Anderson had briefly mentioned the project during the filming of *Rushmore*, was eager to slip into the skin of Steve Zissou, whose stubbornness touches him. "He makes a fool of himself all the time, but he doesn't stop and react to it. The beauty of Steve Zissou is that he doesn't ever lose his momentum. For me, it was a very different kind of performance [...] because you're not stopping and selling every moment as you would in an ordinary comedy."[2]

Counterpoint

In 2003, when *The Life Aquatic* was being developed, Wes Anderson had no intention of doing without Owen Wilson, who had been making hit comedies and big studio films at a breakneck pace. The two men probably discussed this project during their college years in Texas. Although not involved in the writing, Wilson would be unlikely to shy away from the role, especially as the character of Ned Plimpton, presented as Steve Zissou's unknown son, could enable him to explore new territory. For once, Wilson was not destined to play a high-spirited outlaw, a cool guy, a dreamy good friend, or an insufferable dandy. Ned is a simple, generous man who expects nothing from Zissou, whose exploits he enjoyed before he realized their relationship. He is a good, self-effacing man who must be played without affectation, in minor mode, so as not to overshadow the

Steve Zissou is a tribute to Jacques Cousteau.

main character. Wilson took on the task seriously and professionally. To prepare, he joined Anderson in Rome a few months before shooting began and rehearsed his scenes with him. During these work sessions, the two developed Ned's Southern accent, which they imagined to be old-fashioned and very nineteenth century, in order to anchor the character in the kind of alternative reality they had in mind. The restraint and delicacy of Wilson's performance was much appreciated by the critics.

Strong Women

When Anderson contacted Cate Blanchett to offer her the role of Jane Winslett-Richardson, the nosy, pregnant journalist constantly trying to provoke Steve Zissou, the Australian American actress was enthusiastic. Who would not dream of working with Wes Anderson? She particularly appreciated his art of the offbeat, which he managed to combine with action and a certain gravitas. As luck would have it, between her positive response and the start of filming, she actually became pregnant. The production company feared that she would withdraw, but this would be a misreading of Cate Blanchett, who considered her-

Owen Wilson (Ned Plimpton, left) and Bill Murray (Steve Zissou) in *The Life Aquatic.*

self even better suited to the role in this new context. Informed viewers would be able to watch her scenes, some of which are very physical, with an even more admiring eye. When it came to casting Eleanor Zissou, the mistress-wife who no longer accepts her husband's improprieties, Anderson did not hesitate: Anjelica Huston had been approached from the script stage, not only for her special presence and charisma but also for her exemplary demeanor on the set. She did not disappoint.

Other Excellent Protagonists

There are three other notable actors in this film: Willem Dafoe (who plays Klaus Daimler, the zealous second-in-command of the *Belafonte*), Jeff Goldblum (who plays Alistair Hennessey, Zissou's rival), and Bud Cort (who plays Bill Ubell, the management controller sent by the production company of the documentary directed by the oceanographer). Dafoe benefited from a combination of circumstances: Wes Anderson wanted a German actor before being convinced by his meeting with the Italian American actor, organized by the latter's agent. A relative stranger to comedy, the actor from *The Last Temptation of Christ* (Martin Scorsese, 1988) gave a surprising performance as Klaus Daimler, the diligent assistant who considers Steve Zissou to be an older brother and takes a dim view of Ned Plimpton's arrival among his mentor's entourage. Goldblum was chosen by Anderson for his elegance and magnetism. It takes a lot to stand up to Steve Zissou, and Goldblum's character, Alistair Hennessey, is his nemesis, another star oceanographer with much greater resources. Well known to film fans, Bud Cort had his moment of glory in the 1970s, playing one of the title roles in *Harold and Maude* (Hal Ashby, 1971), a film that Anderson idolized. Highly committed to his role as a stooge scorned by everyone in *The Life Aquatic*, he learned Tagalog, the language of the Philippines, for his scenes with the Asian actors who played the pirates kidnapping his character. In a different genre, the Brazilian singer Seu Jorge, a star in his own country and an actor in *City of God* (Fernando Meirelles, 2002), plays the role of Pelé dos Santos, a seafaring troubadour who reinterprets David Bowie songs on his guitar in bossa nova style.

Cate Blanchett (top and bottom right) portrays a journalist in The Life Aquatic.

Seu Jorge (left) is a music star in Brazil. In *The Life Aquatic*, he performs David Bowie classics in Portuguese.

FILMING AND PRODUCTION

Most of the filming took place in Rome's famous Cinecittà studios, while the scenes aboard the *Belafonte*, which give the film its spectacular dimension, were filmed off the coast of the Italian capital. Three other locations were also chosen: the Teatro di San Carlo in Naples, an opera house, was the setting for the first sequence; the seaside town of Nettuno and its coastal tower, south of Rome, were the secluded place where Zissou lived; and Ponza Island, in the Tyrrhenian Sea, was the setting for the Port-au-Patois stopover.

Archive Research

In the period leading up to filming, which began on September 16, 2003, the production team spent a great deal of time trying to find the two boats needed—one for the sequences at sea and another, which would be dismantled, for the interiors. They finally found them in South Africa, after a quest complicated by Anderson's requirements: the functional ship had to date from World War II, be a minesweeper, measure around fifty meters in length, and be reminiscent of Cousteau's *Calypso*. The parts and materials salvaged from the dismantled ship were loaded onto the functional ship, which the artistic teams would embellish with two towers and an observation deck, and repaint to give it the look of a tired but credible old tub. The ship headed for Rome to anchor in the surrounding area and unload its precious contents, which were taken to the Cinecittà backlot—the area around the studios dedicated to the creation of exterior sets. On site, dozens of hands were busy making Anderson's dream come true: to portray the interior of the ship in a cross-sectional shot. An open, sectioned half

Preparatory drawings for the *Belafonte*, the boat that Wes Anderson films in cross-section.

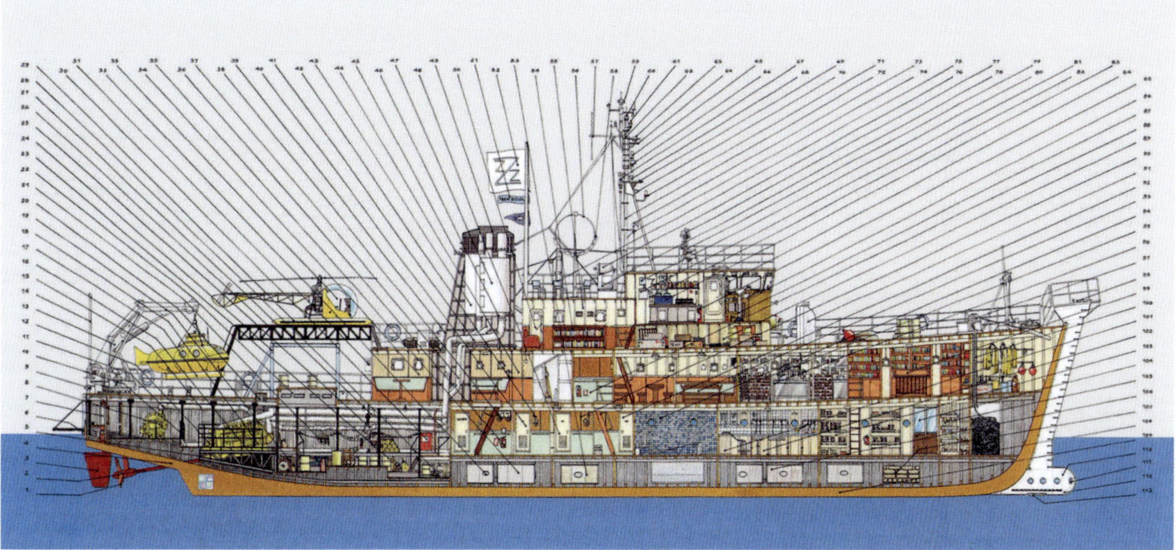

ship, with all its customized parts, three stories high, was built lengthways on a huge platform. This enabled Anderson, as he wished, to move a crane-mounted camera around to explore the bowels of the *Belafonte* in a single movement. The structure was so breathtaking in its own right that it attracted tourists to Cinecittà in droves. Finally, to represent Alistair Hennessey's imposing ship, which Anderson wanted to be distinct from the *Belafonte*, NATO provided the production team with a ship in perfect condition.

Panic on Board!

For the cast and crew, the sequences out at sea were by far the most inconvenient to shoot. On their first outing, to familiarize themselves with the boat, they all got seasick due to the rough water. To prevent this from happening again, anti-seasickness patches were applied behind the ears of the cast and crew, a method far from satisfying for cinematographer Robert Yeoman. "When I got back to my flat in the evening, I was very dizzy, as if I'd been drugged. After several weeks, the nurse took me aside and said: 'It's only one patch a week! [Not 1 per day…] I suppose that explains everything, although I wish she'd told me sooner."[3]

Aside from the physical complications, filming at sea is a real headache for Wes Anderson's trusted operator. "Zissou and his crew were generally in the middle of the ocean, with no land in sight. As the boat's engines were very noisy, we had to turn them off while we were filming in order to get a better sound recording. Unfortunately, without these engines, we would immediately drift away, carried away by the current, and would often turn one hundred and eighty degrees to find ourselves

The boat used for the sea scenes. Another boat was dismantled and decorated as a set for the interiors and lateral section.

BELAFONTE

Wes Anderson gives direction through a megaphone.

facing land in the background."[4] This drifting also led to a problem with the light. A carefully prepared shot could easily find itself in full backlight while everything was being set up. A solution was quickly found by Yeoman and his colleagues: "Our maritime team used *gommones* [Zodiacs], small fast inflatable boats placed at the bow and stern of the ship. They guided us as best they could in the desired direction."[5]

Another World

Robert Yeoman had a more amusing job. This consisted of recreating archive images for Steve Zissou's documentaries, excerpts of which are occasionally shown to the viewer. Shot on old Kodak Ektachrome film, they have a retro feel that sets them apart from the rest of the film. The same can be said of the stop-motion sequences created by Henry Selick and his team, which included a special cinematographer, Patrick Sweeney. The director-animator began by submitting around fifty sketches of imaginary or reinvented underwater creatures that had to be made, and Anderson selected a number of them. To create them, Selick and his puppeteers used a new type of silicone, adapted to the translucent appearance of fish skin to make them more realistic. The story's famous jaguar shark, spotted and glistening, benefited not only from this technique but also from the incredible efforts made by the puppeteers: it measured ten feet long and weighed more than 150 pounds, making it without doubt the biggest "puppet" ever conceived! Given its dimensions, it was impossible to animate it entirely by hand frame by frame like the other creatures in the film. Its swimming movements were therefore computer assisted, while its mouth and fins were managed in the normal way by the animators. Its encounter with the crew of the *Belafonte*, who were squeezed into a tiny submersible (a mock-up, made of steel and fiberglass, designed by some Italians), is one of the most poetic moments in Wes Anderson's cinema.

RECEPTION

Had Touchstone Pictures taken an ill-considered risk in betting $50 million on a purely art house film? This is the debate that was occupying observers as 2004 drew to a close. Although fairly well received by the press in the United States (*Rushmore* and *The Royal Tenenbaums* were more convincing), *The Life Aquatic* frustrated a not inconsiderable number of influential American critics who felt it was not spectacular enough or that it was too long. The punishment was terrible: with less than $25 million in box

The *Belafonte*'s two research dolphins are, in fact, remote-controlled animatronic robots.

office receipts in North America, it was a bitter failure, and the box office in the rest of the world would not make it up. The partnership with Touchstone Pictures, which began with *Rushmore*, ended on a negative note, even though, over time, the film acquired a reputation befitting its qualities. It is precisely because it escapes from all the boxes into which people wanted to put it that *The Life Aquatic* has become a cult film.

When Audacity Is Not to Everyone's Taste

Fourteen years after its release, the film was back in the news. Speaking to American journalist Alex Blumberg on his podcast *Without Fail* (hosted by Gimlet Media), Nina Jacobson, former head of Disney (parent company of Touchstone Pictures), explained that at the time she did everything she could to give as much money as possible to Wes Anderson, whose project she was enthusiastic about. "I will always remember, at our first big screening of the movie, afterwards people would come up and congratulate me on what a *brave* movie it was, at which point I knew that I was fucked, because 'brave' is code for 'stupid' in Hollywood."[6] Was her dismissal from Disney in 2006 linked to the failure of *The Life Aquatic*? In her opinion, it was more the result of internal conflicts and petty settling of scores.

FOR WES ADDICTS

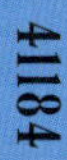

The producer of Steve Zissou's documentaries, played by Irish British actor Michael Gambon, has a curious name: Oseary Drakoulias, in homage to two great names in music. Guy Oseary was none other than Madonna's right-hand man, having run the Maverick label in the 1990s before becoming the pop star's official manager. George Drakoulias was a producer for the American Recordings label, and helped to launch the rock band the Black Crowes.

The baroque imagination of Federico Fellini (image from *Amarcord*, 1973) is a source of inspiration for Wes Anderson.

The Wes Connection

A Man Subject to Influences

Before traveling in the literal sense of the word (he eventually became an enlightened, stateless man, dividing his life between the United States and France), Wes Anderson found escape through cinema and many other forms of artistic expression. Painting, photography, comics, literature, music...no creative field escaped his sagacity and his profound desire to embrace culture in order to enrich his work.

Cinema in All Its Forms

An ardent film buff since his high school days, Anderson developed this passion at the University of Texas and since then never ceased to be interested in the seventh art, whatever its origins. This universalist, encyclopedic approach is reminiscent of that of Martin Scorsese, who once invited him to discover the restored version of Jean Renoir's Le Fleuve (1951), which subsequently became one of Anderson's favorite films. It was after this memorable screening that he decided to set the action of *The Darjeeling Limited* (2007) in India. Two other Frenchmen play an important role in his imagination, François Truffaut and Louis Malle—the former for his relationship with a wounded childhood and the autobiographical aspect, and the latter for his documentaries on India and the delicacy of his portraits.

American cinema was obviously not to be neglected, either. Alfred Hitchcock—an Englishman who made his career in Hollywood—and Orson Welles are two tutelary figures who Anderson quotes over and over again. Hitchcock's *Rear Window* (1954) was largely inspired by his principle of frames within frames (the windows of the apartments in the building opposite) observed by the hero through binoculars, all stylistic figures that can be found in Anderson's "voyeuristic" films. In the case of Welles, the influence is more diffuse but nonetheless pervasive, to the point of arousing the enthusiasm of the Texan director, his fervent admirer. "He likes the big effect, the very dramatic camera move, the very theatrical device. I love that!"[1] Two American classics made a lasting impression on him: *The Graduate* (Mike Nichols, 1967) and *Harold and Maude* (Hal Ashby, 1971), works bathed in pop melancholy about impossible love affairs, a theme found at the heart of *Rushmore* (1998), *The Royal Tenenbaums* (2001), *Moonrise Kingdom* (2012), and *Asteroid City* (2023). In a different genre, his taste for stop-motion animation was born out of the vision of the creatures of special effects genius Ray Harryhausen (*Jason and the Argonauts*, Don Chaffey, 1963) and those of the Rankin/Bass studio (*Rudolph the Red-Nosed Reindeer*, Larry Roemer, 1964, a TV Christmas special).

Inspired by a number of international directors (such as the Italian Federico Fellini and his surrealist visions, and the Indian Satyajit Ray and his caste struggle), Anderson has also shown a marked interest in Japanese cinema, in particular the films of Akira Kurosawa and Yasujirō Ozu—although they are far removed from each other—the moving war frescoes of the former contrasting with the static minimalist dramas of the latter. Perhaps it is a way of blurring the lines and freeing himself from his supposed masters.

Lines of Genius

Drawing was second nature to Anderson, who practiced it from an early age. He even storyboarded his first two feature films, *Bottle Rocket* (1996) and *Rushmore*, and often translated his visions for his collaborators in sketches. Painting, comics, photography, and the graphic arts are an obvious nourishment for this image enthusiast. The production company he had been working with since 2006 is called Indian Paintbrush. As early as *Bottle Rocket*, he took on this dimension in his work by invoking the English painter and photographer David Hockney, famous for his flat compositions, his work on color, his play with perspective, and his obsession with swimming pools. These are recurring motifs for Anderson (*Bottle Rocket*, *Rushmore*, *The Royal Tenenbaums*, *Fantastic Mr. Fox*).

From Hockney to Henri Rousseau, it is a single step that the filmmaker cheerfully takes in *The Wonderful Story of Henry Sugar* (2023), a succession of *tableaux vivants* in which a colorful jungle recalls the exotic works of the French painter. The false simplicity of Rousseau, classed as "naïve," links him to illustration and comic strips,[2] of which Wes Anderson is particularly fond. For *Moonrise Kingdom*, he revealed the major influence of portrait painter Norman Rockwell, one of the fathers of American illustration. Another acknowledged reference is to Charles Schulz, the creator of the famous comic strip *Peanuts*, whose main character, Charlie Brown, always displays the depressive air that characterizes the Andersonian hero.

Adept at initiating great departures, Wes Anderson is capable of offering his collaborators models from Renaissance painters such as the Florentine Agnolo Bronzino for *Rushmore*, or Japanese masters of prints such as Hiroshige and Hokusai for *Isle of Dogs* (2018). "I've always...been sensitive to a certain imagery that comes from Japan," he says. "These works convey the beauty of the country's landscapes and architecture in an extremely simple and pure way."[3] More secret (this is a matter for connoisseurs) is the correspondence between Wes Anderson and Joseph Cornell, an American sculptor of the last century who was famous for his wooden boxes with glass fronts in which the artist arranged various objects salvaged from here and there, somewhere between

Another eccentric Fellini vision, from *Amarcord*.

Charles M. Schulz, father of the *Peanuts* characters and their funny, sometimes melancholy world.

The complex, ambiguous worlds of Roald Dahl fascinate Wes Anderson.

abstraction and surrealism. These little "poetic theaters," in Cornell's own words, bear a striking resemblance to the sense of the absurd sketch and director's composition.

A Repertoire of Books

While the vast majority of Wes Anderson's scripts are original, they sometimes implicitly quote preexisting writings. The most striking example is *The Grand Budapest Hotel* (2014), "loosely based" on the memoirs of the Viennese author Stefan Zweig, according to the director[4] on the film's release. Anderson recaptures the Mitteleuropa atmosphere of the novelist's books and his gallery of characters, who are confronted with the disturbing march of the world from the 1910s to the 1940s.

In the same way, the name of J. D. Salinger has often been associated with that of Anderson, who has never denied his admiration. Quite the contrary, in fact. The neurasthenic portrait of adolescence painted in *The Catcher in the Rye* (1951) and the wanderings of the iconoclastic Glass family (recounted in many of the writer's short stories) undoubtedly infuse Anderson's darkly acidic work.

Mark Twain is the second great American author of significance to the director of *Moonrise Kingdom*—a proclaimed tribute to the truant escapades of Tom Sawyer and Huckleberry Finn. Twain's satirical, moralistic tone and complex approach to childhood were bound to appeal to Wes Anderson. But it is another storyteller, with his unbridled and cruel imagination, for whom Anderson has an even greater admiration: the Welshman Roald Dahl, the only one whose works he has adapted (notably *Fantastic Mr. Fox*) and whose importance in his life he explained at the time of the broadcast of *The Wonderful Story of Henry Sugar*, one of the four short films commissioned by Netflix, which owns the rights to the Dahl catalogue. "I think I came to Dahl right at the moment when he reached the peak of his popularity. [...] We loved our school book fair, which was filled with new books and old books, and Dahl was always a big presence. We loved these books, and we knew his picture from the back, we knew the guy telling us the story, and his voice was so strong that you sort of felt like you knew him. And there is something about that—about feeling that you have a personal relationship to the author telling the story."[5]

Music at the Heart of Everything

Wes Anderson's films are to pop what Martin Scorsese's are to rock: benchmarks for film soundtracks. In fact, the two filmmakers shared the services of the same musical director (whose role is to suggest titles and negotiate the rights and licenses for each song borrowed): Randall Poster, an expert in the field who has worked hand in hand with Anderson since *Bottle Rocket*. Their understanding was such that Poster would go to the ends of the earth to satisfy his friend's whims, which is exactly what he did to obtain some of the tracks featured on the soundtrack to *The Darjeeling Limited*. "Wes knew that he wanted to use music from the films of [Indian filmmaker] Satyajit Ray. And that forced me to travel to Calcutta to try and find these recordings, because it wasn't like you could go to Tower Records—there still was a Tower Records at that point—and buy all the great Indian film scores."[6]

Wes Anderson's eclectic musical tastes reflect his immense curiosity: blues, rock, pop, world music, jazz, classical. (One of the first sequences he had in mind for *The Royal Tenenbaums* was when Richie Tenenbaum, played by Luke Wilson, one of the two gifted sons, collapses on a tennis court to Maurice Ravel's String Quartet played by the Britten Quartet.) He draws from the songs an energy and intentions that he transmits as much as possible to the actors and technicians on the set. For *Rushmore*, for example, he choreographed certain scenes using music he had selected in advance of the shoot with Randall Poster—mainly the British Invasion of the 1960s. It makes one wonder why he has yet to make a musical.

The bittersweet tone of *The Graduate*, bathed in pop-rock tunes, appeals to a music-loving director.

On the Move!

Perpetuum Mobile

Wes Anderson's characters always have a goal to reach, a quest to accomplish (killing a legendary shark, robbing the rich, recovering their exiled dog). They are never content to stand still, and they use every possible means of locomotion to achieve their ends. Motorized vehicles (cars, motorbikes, airplanes, boats), sports equipment (bicycles, skis), and public transport (trains, funicular railways, lifts, cable cars) are omnipresent and entirely congruent with the filmmaker's aesthetic. The vertical and lateral dollies that Anderson is so fond of are the result of using a cargo lift, crossing a landscape on a train, or a crazy ski descent. Many of the settings are revealed to the viewer by means of these multiple movements, the most common of which is walking.

The small town of *Asteroid City* and its main road, ideal for getting around.

The three Whitman brothers ride motorcycles, helmetless, across India in *The Darjeeling Limited*.

The sinister Jopling criss-crosses the Central European capital of *The Grand Budapest Hotel* on his (customized) BMW R 11, a German model from the 1930s.

Royal Tenenbaum rides a bumper car with his grandsons in *The Royal Tenenbaums*.

Mr. Gustave and Zero board a sleigh in *The Grand Budapest Hotel* to catch up with Jopling, who has put on skis.

HOTEL CHEVALIER

United States, France • 13 min • Color • Dolby Digital • 2.35 : 1

Filming Dates: **September 2005**
World Premiere: **September 3, 2007 (Venice International Film Festival)**
Release Dates in the United States: **September 25, 2007 (four Apple stores); September 26, 2007 (free to view on iTunes for a month, before projection as a prologue to *The Darjeeling Limited*, from October 26, 2007)**

Production Companies: **American Empirical Pictures, Première Heure, Searchlight Pictures, 20th Century Fox**
Producers: **Wes Anderson, Patrice Haddad (in association with)**
Co-Producer: **Alice Bamford**

Executive Producers: **Jérôme Rucki, Nicolas Saada**
Associate Producer: **Pierre Cléaud**
Screenplay: **Wes Anderson**
Director of Photography: **Robert Yeoman**
First Assistant Director: **Émilie Cherpitel**
Editing: **Vincent Marchand**
Art Direction: **Kris Moran**
Music Supervisor: **Randall Poster**
Sound: **Stuart Wilson**
Costumes: **Milena Canonero**
Makeup: **Frances Hannon**

Starring: **JASON SCHWARTZMAN (Jack Whitman), NATALIE PORTMAN (Jack's girlfriend), MICHEL CASTEJON (waiter)...**

Jack: Whatever happens in the end, I don't want to lose you as my friend.

Woman: I promise I will never be your friend. No matter what. Ever.

—

SYNOPSIS

A man lies in his luxurious Parisian palace hotel room. A phone call interrupts his reverie. At the other end of the line, there is a woman. He is distant, she announces that she is coming over, and he is unable to dissuade her. He gets ready and waits for her. She arrives with a bouquet of flowers in her hand and a toothpick in her mouth. The man's embarrassment is perceptible. They had clearly loved each other, but something had broken their relationship. Will the evening they spend together, and the contusions he discovers on her body, be enough to lift the mystery in the eyes of the viewers, who are awaiting explanations?

GENESIS

At the beginning of 2005, Wes Anderson was in Paris for the end of the promotional tour for *The Life Aquatic*, due to be released in France on March 9. His friend Jason Schwartzman (who had made his name with *Rushmore* six years earlier) was also there, shooting *Marie Antoinette* (Sofia Coppola, 2006). Schwartzman offered his mentor a place to stay while he was there, and the cohabitation lasted for two months. Not only did it strengthen the bond between the two men, but it also prompted Anderson to approach the actor—who had become very popular—with a project for a short film, or even a feature-length film: a love story set in the French capital, where he would soon be renting his own apartment.

Work in Progress

While in Paris, the two men spent a lot of time with Roman Coppola, also passing through Paris. The cousin of Jason Schwartzman, Sofia Coppola's elder brother gradually became part of Anderson's inner circle, working as a second-unit director on *The Life Aquatic*. The trio took advantage of their geographical proximity to come up with a story, based on an idea by Anderson, about three angry brothers who travel to India to reconcile. During his discussions with his two friends, Wes realized that Jason's character, the youngest of the brothers—a dark, distrustful, and seductive writer—had a lot in common with the one he had in mind for his behind-closed-doors story. By agreement with his two companions, he made Jack Whitman the hero of a short film that would be the prologue to the film they were developing, which would become *The Darjeeling Limited* (2007). The three authors would then have fun alluding in their script to this particular episode in Jack's life, written entirely by Anderson and set chronologically two weeks before the start of the voyage to India.

CASTING

As the writing progressed, the director began to think more and more about Natalie Portman for the female role. She was an actress he admired and whose career he had followed closely since *Closer* (Mike Nichols, 2004); her participation in the project would be a godsend.

No Smoking

Through producer Scott Rudin, who worked on *The Darjeeling Limited* and put together *Closer*, Wes

Natalie Portman accepted the role of Jack's girlfriend without a second thought.

Anderson obtained Portman's contact details. When he approached her, he feared that she would be put off by the nude scenes scattered throughout the story, as she had always refused to shoot them. Much to his surprise, the young woman agreed, albeit on one condition: "She didn't want to smoke."[1] For this reason, for example, in the final scene, instead of offering her a cigarette on the balcony, Jack hands her a toothpick. The rehearsals confirmed the merits of Anderson's choices. The chemistry between Schwartzman and Portman was palpable and guaranteed to make an impact on screen.

FILMING AND PRODUCTION

Anderson wanted to shoot *Hotel Chevalier* quickly, before being caught up in the preparation of *The Darjeeling Limited*. To avoid tedious discussions with Searchlight Pictures (the 20th Century-Fox subsidiary behind the film), he decided to self-produce without informing the studio. The rest was a matter of resourcefulness and coping. "It was like making a student film."[2]

In Commando Mode

Anderson was not just another "student": his reputation opened many doors for him. The Hotel Raphaël (in the 16th arrondissement of Paris), where he had stayed a few years earlier in a yellow-tinted room that made an ideal Andersonian setting, authorized him to shoot for two days in its establishment toward the end of September 2005. Anderson also asked Marc Jacobs, the artistic director for Louis Vuitton, to design Jack Whitman's suitcase, which he reused in *The Darjeeling Limited*—he even commissioned others for the film. His brother, Eric Anderson, designed the motifs (animals and palm trees). Finally, by virtue of his long-standing and positive relationship with the manufacturer Panavision, the director obtained the free loan of two cameras and lenses necessary for the work of the director of photography, Robert Yeoman, who appreciated this novel configuration. "Wes wanted to keep it small-scale: a skeleton crew and a minimum of equipment. We only used the lighting we could plug into the sockets in the room."[3] For the famous nude scenes, which are "always a bit tense and awkward"[4] to set up, the

Natalie Portman makes a brief appearance in *The Darjeeling Limited* wearing the same yellow robe.

operator, working alone with Wes Anderson, had no problems whatsoever. And with good reason: Natalie Portman is filmed with great modesty. It is worth noting that, for the soundtrack, the director used "Where Do You Go To (My Lovely)" (1969), which blends English and French with a gentle nostalgia. British songwriter Peter Sarstedt was born in India—which cannot be a coincidence.

RECEPTION

Once the short film had been finalized, Anderson set off on the adventure of *The Darjeeling Limited.* It would be time to consider screening *Hotel Chevalier* when both projects were completed. An agreement was finally reached between the director and Searchlight—who belatedly discovered the existence of this prologue—enabling *Hotel Chevalier* to benefit from good visibility. The critics were more complimentary than they were for the feature film, praising the boldness and piquancy of this thirteen-minute film, which remains a unique item in Anderson's oeuvre.

FOR WES ADDICTS

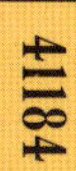

If Searchlight Pictures discovered the existence of *Hotel Chevalier* only when *The Darjeeling Limited* had been completed, the American distributor still consented to place the short film as a prologue to the feature film for theatrical release. The enthusiastic welcome given to *Hotel Chevalier* then prompted Searchlight to promote it to be selected for the short film Oscar (it was not accepted). It was then offered as a bonus in video editions of *The Darjeeling Limited.*

OWEN WILSON ADRIEN BRODY JASON SCHWARTZMAN
OPENING NIGHT FILM 45TH NEW YORK FILM FESTIVAL 2007
IN AN AMERICAN EMPIRICAL PICTURE BY
WES ANDERSON
OFFICIAL SELECTION VENICE FILM FESTIVAL 2007
venezia 64.
Competition
·THE·
DARJEELING
·LIMITED·
FOX SEARCHLIGHT PICTURES AND COLLAGE PRESENT
"THE DARJEELING LIMITED" OWEN WILSON ADRIEN BRODY
JASON SCHWARTZMAN AND ANJELICA HUSTON COSTUME DESIGNER MILENA CANONERO MUSIC SUPERVISOR RANDALL POSTER
FEATURING MUSIC FROM THE FILMS OF SATYAJIT RAY AND MERCHANT IVORY CO-PRODUCERS JEREMY DAWSON ALICE BAMFORD ANADIL HOSSAIN
EDITED BY ANDREW WEISBLUM PRODUCTION DESIGNER MARK FRIEDBERG DIRECTOR OF PHOTOGRAPHY ROBERT YEOMAN, ASC EXECUTIVE PRODUCER STEVEN RALES
PRODUCED BY WES ANDERSON SCOTT RUDIN ROMAN COPPOLA LYDIA DEAN PILCHER
WRITTEN BY WES ANDERSON & ROMAN COPPOLA & JASON SCHWARTZMAN DIRECTED BY WES ANDERSON
IN SELECT THEATRES THIS FALL
WWW.FOXSEARCHLIGHT.COM
FOX SEARCHLIGHT
श्रीमाली जाति सम्पत्ति व्यवस्था ट्रस्ट
महालक्ष्मी मन्दिर उदयपुर

THE DARJEELING LIMITED

2007

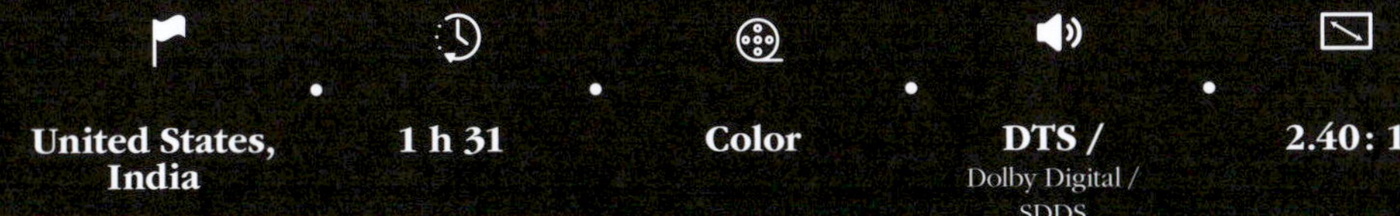

United States, India • 1 h 31 • Color • DTS / Dolby Digital / SDDS • 2.40 : 1

Filming Dates: **January 15, 2007–May 2007**
Release Dates in the United States: **September 28, 2007 (New York Film Festival preview); September 29, 2007 (limited release); October 26, 2007**

Budget: **Approx. $16 million**
North America Box Office: **Approx. $12 million**
Worldwide Box Office: **Approx. $35 million**

Production Companies: **Searchlight Pictures, Collage, American Empirical Pictures, Dune Entertainment, Cine Mosaic, Indian Paintbrush, Scott Rudin Productions**
Producers: **Wes Anderson, Scott Rudin, Roman Coppola, Lydia Dean Pilcher**
Co-Producers: **Alice Bamford, Jeremy Dawson, Anadil Hossain**
Executive Producer: **Steven Rales**
Associate Producer: **Molly Cooper**

Screenplay: **Wes Anderson, Jason Schwartzman, Roman Coppola**
Director of Photography: **Robert Yeoman**
First Assistant Director: **Émilie Cherpitel**
Second Unit Director: **Roman Coppola**
Editing: **Andrew Weisblum**
Production Design: **Mark Friedberg**
Set Decoration: **Aradhana Seth**
Art Direction: **Adam Stockhausen**
Music Supervisor: **Randall Poster**
Sound: **Pawel Wdowczak**
Costumes: **Milena Canonero**
Makeup: **Frances Hannon**

Starring: **OWEN WILSON (Francis Whitman), ADRIEN BRODY (Peter Whitman), JASON SCHWARTZMAN (Jack Whitman), AMARA KARAN (Rita), WALLACE WOLODARSKY (Brendan), WARIS AHLUWALIA (chief steward), ANJELICA HUSTON (Patricia Whitman), IRRFAN KHAN (father of the dead boy), BARBET SCHROEDER (mechanic), CAMILLA RUTHERFORD (Alice), BILL MURRAY (businessman), NATALIE PORTMAN (Jack's ex-girlfriend)...**

"Do you trust me?"

Francis Whitman to his brothers

SYNOPSIS

Peter Whitman only just manages to catch the train where he is to meet his two brothers, Francis and Jack, for a journey of initiation that will enable them to renew their strained family ties, which their reunion at their father's funeral a year earlier was not sufficient to consolidate. Francis, the eldest, physically scarred by a motorbike accident, has a secret plan: to take his brothers to meet their mother, who has been living in a monastery for many years and of whom they have had no news. This quest assumes increasingly mystical and spiritual overtones as the train travels deeper into India.

A newcomer to Wes Anderson, Adrien Brody (center) blends seamlessly into the director's idiosyncratic world in *The Darjeeling Limited*.

GENESIS

Wes Anderson's fascination with India did not emerge spontaneously. It was a long process that began when he was a child and was refined as an adult. Around the age of eight, he befriended a boy of Indian origin, a neighbor in Houston, Texas, who told him about his homeland. Intrigued by what he did not fully understand, Anderson became more interested in India, first through books and then, at high school and in college, through the films of Satyajit Ray (*The Apu Trilogy*, 1955–1959) and the documentaries of Louis Malle (*Calcutta*, 1969; *Phantom India*, 1969). Much later, in the early 2000s, Martin Scorsese's vision of a restored version of *Le Fleuve* (Jean Renoir, 1951) completed this already rich body of work and triggered an irrepressible desire to go and shoot on location.

Three Brothers, Three Writers

Anderson first had a kind of vision, or at least a desire, to tell the story of three brothers on a train. After the maritime and family peregrinations of *The Life Aquatic* (2004), the railway misadventures could not be more logical. But the story remained at the draft stage until the famous screening of *Le Fleuve* in 2004. It was decided that the protagonists would go to India. But for what reasons and to do what? Anderson did not have the answer, as he was absorbed in *Fantastic Mr. Fox* (2009), on which he was working with Noah Baumbach, the co-writer of *The Life Aquatic*. In 2006, the director realized that his animated film had been postponed indefinitely; it was time for him to take up the Indian story that had been in the back of his mind. It became clear once again that there were three characters, so three writers were needed. As one of three siblings, Anderson wanted to feed this fiction with his own experience and that of his writing partners, who were inevitably close to him. Two names came to mind: Jason Schwartzman, his protégé whom he discovered in *Rushmore* (1998), and his cousin Roman Coppola, who was second unit director on *The Life Aquatic*.

Consolidation

Before beginning work on the script, Anderson had to ensure that the project was viable. After being let down by Touchstone Pictures following the failure of *The Life Aquatic*, he nevertheless saw producer Scott Rudin renew his confidence in him.

Introduced as an actor by Wes Anderson, Indian-American Waris Ahluwalia is a trained jeweler and owns his own jewelry brand.

Rudin had connections at 20th Century-Fox, notably at Searchlight Pictures, the studio's art house subsidiary, for which he had just directed *Notes on a Scandal* (Richard Eyre, 2006). A deal was struck. At the same time, a man whose importance would grow in the Anderson system emerged from the shadows: Steven Rales, a millionaire American industrialist with a passion for art house cinema, who had been promoted by Searchlight to executive producer—the legal and financial supervisor of a film, in other words its agent. *The Darjeeling Limited* was the first film to involve Searchlight's brand-new California-based production company, Indian Paintbrush. This marks the beginning of a long-term collaboration with Anderson.

Heading for India

Anderson, Schwartzman, and Coppola began working in Paris, where the three friends found themselves at the same time, due to a fortunate combination of circumstances (see *Hotel Chevalier*). After a while, feeling that their imaginations were limited by the promiscuity in the Parisian cafés where they wrote, the director invited his two friends to go to India. In his eyes, it was the only way to finalize a screenplay that he wanted to be less tightly scripted than his previous works—leaving more room for landscapes, to the detriment of action—and which the Indian experience would be a considerable influence. In March 2006, they embarked on a journey that would open both their eyes and their hearts. Anderson's intuition was right: "India is not a country like any other. It is a place where many aspects of daily life are radically different from our own, and that really influenced the script. Even though 90 percent of the story is about Francis, Peter, and Jack negotiating, arguing, and trying to understand each other, we felt it was very important that these conversations took place on board a train travelling through this ancient country in real conditions."[1] The means of transport in question (see below) and India (its people, its crowded places, its ancestral rituals) were to be "characters" in the film in their own right.

CASTING

The writing, which took the authors about a year to complete, gives pride of place to the three main protagonists, whose first names were not chosen at random. They refer to the American directors Francis Ford Coppola (Roman's father), Peter Bogdanovich, and Jack Nicholson, three of the figures of New Hollywood who give the film an adventurous and contemplative spirit that Anderson had never seen before. Francis, the eldest, is the leader who likes to control his world and events. Peter, the middle child, is the rebel who refuses to accept his responsibilities—he has left his partner behind, who is in the advanced stages of pregnancy. Jack, the youngest, is a romantic who writes short stories inspired—too much so—by his surroundings. The three brothers carry their grief for their father, with all its attendant suffering, on their shoulders: Francis's face is disfigured by a huge bandage, Peter wears his father's sunglasses all the time, and Jack plays at Casanova to take his mind off things. To play these siblings, one needs actors who do not necessarily resemble each other, but who complement one another, capable of respecting the dialogue to the letter and the Andersonian daze, while interacting spontaneously in an unfamiliar environment.

Owen Wilson, Naturally

For Francis, the essential cog in the plot, the originator of the family expedition and its inherent tensions, Wes Anderson could think of no one better than Owen Wilson. He would be perfect to play this moody, fragile individual whose car accident seems more like a suicide attempt—like Eli Cash's when he drives his car into the Tenenbaums' house on Etheline's wedding day. The idea of giving Francis a battered physique came to the director while he was near St. Peter's Basilica in Rome, observing a man in a motorcycle jacket whose face was covered in bandages. "He had foam pads on the side of his head, his eyes were all black—and he was walking around the place in this sort of startled daze, with tears just sort of standing in his eyes."[2] Now a star that everyone wants to be, Owen Wilson willingly agreed to be involved once again with the man he considered a brother.

A Long-Awaited Comeback

At the time of writing, there was no doubt that Jason Schwartzman would inherit the role of Jack, the carefree sibling, preoccupied above all by his libido, which masks a wounding love affair. His desire to play for his mentor again, nine years after *Rushmore*, was strong. Wes Anderson had obviously followed his acting career closely, the most spectacular achievement of which was the role of Louis XVI that he has just played in *Marie Antoinette* (Sofia Coppola, 2006).

Francis Whitman (Owen Wilson) is the victim of a car accident. Photograph by Laura Wilson.

A Newcomer

For the third brother, Anderson first thought of Luke Wilson before changing his mind, as he had been obsessed with another actor for some time. Adrien Brody, who won an Oscar in 2003 for *The Pianist* (Roman Polanski, 2002), would be ideally suited to Peter, this "middle-of-the-road" brother—like Wes—with a lost look and a nervous disposition. It was a proposal that delighted the interested party, an early fan attracted by the director's unique universe and the delicacy with which these three

Wes Anderson (left, in white) and cinematographer Robert Yeoman capture the action on a dolly gondola pushed by Indian grip Sanjay Sami. Photograph by Laura Wilson.

The Mysterious Mr. Rales

A millionaire who made his fortune with his brother in hardware in the 1980s and '90s, Steven Rales founded his production company, Indian Paintbrush, in 2006. A fan of art house cinema, he immediately took Wes Anderson under his wing and, over time, became a sort of unofficial patron, supporting all his films from *The Darjeeling Limited* onward. How did the two men meet? It's a mystery. Neither Rales, who has not spoken to the press since 1985, nor Anderson have ever mentioned the pact that binds them and gives the director a comfortable production environment, full autonomy, and total control over his work.

men go through painful ordeals by approaching them in a comic and wonderfully strange way. To facilitate the desired osmosis, Italian designer Milena Canonero created slightly different gray suits for the brothers. Under their jackets they each wear a beige, white, and black shirt, of which they have several, according to Anderson's wishes, so that they stay in character and never stray. These sets of clothes also enable the actors to arrive on the set in the morning already dressed and coiffed.

The Regulars and One Unknown

The inimitable Bill Murray, Anderson's favorite actor, agreed to make a friendly appearance. He opens the film as a harried businessman chasing his departing train. For five minutes, everything suggests that he is the hero of the story, before Peter (Adrien Brody) catches up with him, overtakes him, and rushes aboard the train, which the businessman misses, much to his dismay. Another of the filmmaker's loyal followers, Anjelica Huston, plays the beautiful role of Patricia Whitman, the mother deemed unworthy by her three sons because she left to look after orphans in a convent on a supposedly mystical whim. The daughter of director John Huston had always dreamed of playing such a character, who reminded her of the British actress Deborah Kerr, directed by her father in *Heaven Knows, Mr. Allison* (1957). Wallace Wolodarsky, one of the original screenwriters of *The Simpsons* (Matt Groening, 1989–), who was also close to Wes Anderson and occasionally an actor (he played a referee in *Rushmore*), took on the character of Brendan, Francis's personal assistant and whipping boy. Amara Karan, a young Englishwoman of Sri Lankan origin, was chosen to play the appealingly pleasant train hostess who bewitches Jack. She was an amateur actress, and after this film she gave up her career in finance to devote herself exclusively to cinema.

Bill Murray (top) in a supporting role and Amara Karan (bottom) as Rita, a railway hostess.

FILMING AND PRODUCTION

As mentioned in the genesis of the film, Anderson established from the outset that the story would take place mainly in the reduced space of a real train traveling through India, in the region of Rajasthan. This idea, which was attractive on paper, would require a great deal of effort and ingenuity on the part of the entire film team. When producer Lydia Dean Pilcher, a regular partner of Indian director Mira Nair, was approached to join the project just before shooting began, she quickly realized the scale of the task, particularly the bureaucracy, and at times even thought she would not be able to complete it. "We were going to a region under the aegis of the North West Railways, who had never before been asked to hire ten wagons and a locomotive for three months in order to dismantle them, build interiors, and run them on a working track!"[3]

Melting Pot

To establish the visual universe, Wes Anderson and artistic supervisor Mark Friedberg boarded an ordinary tourist train. They wanted to immerse themselves in the landscapes they traveled through, the crowded conditions encountered by the passengers, the length of the journeys, and the local history. They concluded that their rail journey must be the result of several influences. After all, the Indian railway was developed under British rule in the nineteenth century. Their Darjeeling Limited (a name that evokes both tea and the Bengali region where it originated) would therefore have a typically Eastern style in a Western guise. Traditional fabrics and prints are used and recycled to blend perfectly with the Art Deco

One of the film's many Indian extras. Photograph by Laura Wilson.

The elephants are also extras. Photograph by Laura Wilson.

The three Whitman brothers on a train, customized with the help of local craftsmen

influences of the interiors, in shades of green and blue. Friedberg also drew on the incomparable skills of local craftsmen. For example, they repainted the exterior of the train, featuring a multitude of animal motifs. Locals were also hired for the sequence in the Indian village where the brothers went with the body of a child they had been unable to save from drowning. In addition to their contribution as extras, some of the locals built a large traditional hut at the request of the production, which they colored as they saw fit without the prior approval of Friedberg and Anderson—a happy "accident" in the end.

Cramped

In terms of staging, shooting on the train encountered a number of constraints that the director of photography, Robert Yeoman, tried to anticipate. "A model of the train cabin was built in a warehouse. We rehearsed many scenes there with the camera to see how best to block it and move it around in this tiny space."[4] Faced with reality, the technician was a little disappointed. Although the electricity in the compartments had been rewired and the windows changed, he still had to deal with a few unforeseen problems, particularly with the lighting. "Because of the cramped conditions, we rushed to fit all the lights into the train, generally opting for overhead fluorescent lamps. The windows were fitted with special slots in which we could place pre-cut ND gels [neutral density filters] to reduce exposure to the outside. Finally, the corridors were so narrow that we placed the dolly rail in the ceiling and suspended the camera so that it was out of the way of the three actors. [...] There was only room for the three actors, myself, a camera operator, a dolly operator, a boom operator,

88772
प्रवेश
ENTRY

The film's train ran a regular daily route in the Rajasthan region.

Freeze Frame

The characters' arms in *The Darjeeling Limited* are constantly cluttered with suitcases, trunks, and bags in the most beautiful orange-brown, embellished with animal motifs designed by Eric Chase Anderson. The luggage was created especially for the film by legendary American designer Marc Jacobs, Louis Vuitton's artistic director between 1997 and 2013. It was dragged through the desert and exposed to water, proving to be particularly hard-wearing—fortunately so, as the production only had one set.

and Wes. I think Wes appreciated the small size of the group. There were no distractions; we could all concentrate on what we had to do."[5]

Nonstop

For the purposes of filming, the Darjeeling Limited traveled on tracks from the city of Jodhpur to Jaisalmer (in the Thar Desert, near the Pakistani border). Yeoman has not forgotten these daily outings: "We would leave the station at first light. We would cross the desert for five hours, then go back the same way. As we were shooting in winter, the days were short and those ten hours were our only window of opportunity. [...] It was very sunny most of the time, which allowed us to get consistent lighting for all the scenes [...] The sunlight also gave more saturation to the colors."[6] Filming on a moving train is obviously no picnic. Because of the frequent stops (to make way for trains on scheduled service crossing the tracks of the Darjeeling Limited) or the unpredictable running delays, the production had to use its imagination. For Wes Anderson, stopping the filming was out of the question, both literally and figuratively. In the event of a prolonged break in the middle of nowhere, the director sometimes asked his crew to dismantle an entire carriage with its cabins and transport them by truck to the desert, where filming was to continue. It was much more relaxing to film the final scenes in the orphanage-monastery, where the character played by Anjelica Huston had retreated. Reconstructed in Udaipur in a derelict royal hunting lodge, this magical and spacious location, imbued with spirituality, ultimately provided satisfactory working conditions.

RECEPTION

It is impossible to describe the film's release without mentioning the tragic event that marked it: in the month preceding it, Owen Wilson attempted to take his own life. Years later, the actor spoke at length about the depressive state from which he had suffered since the age of eleven, a period during which he had developed an anxiety about death that he had never divulged to anyone. This retrospective insight into his inner demons makes the characters he has played and co-written for Wes Anderson all the more disturbing: the asocial Dignan (*Bottle Rocket*, 1993), the neurasthenic Herman Blume (played by Bill Murray in *Rushmore*), the drug addict Eli Cash (*The Royal Tenenbaums*, 2001), the hapless Ned Plimpton (*The Life Aquatic*), and, of course, the presumed suicidal Francis Whitman (*The Darjeeling Limited*).

Loyalty

Star actor Owen Wilson logically did not take part in the promotion of *The Darjeeling Limited*, which received a lukewarm reception from the moment it opened at the New York Film Festival on September 28, 2007. Observers were baffled by the film's length and its shorter-than-usual script—it was criticized for having too many contemplative scenes and outdoor shots. And yet previously there had been a tendency to criticize Anderson's lack of innovation. This

On Wes Anderson's urging, Anjelica Huston, who hates flying, agreed to travel to India, where she was dazzled.

was only the director's fifth feature-length film, but the growing expectations aroused by his films went hand in hand with disproportionate reactions. It is partly because of these contradictions that the director attaches less and less importance to the criticisms leveled at his work. He moves forward, indifferent to fashions, unwittingly dictating a trend. His trend. He was also beginning to win the loyalty of a regular audience who did not care about the critics. Unjustly underestimated, *The Darjeeling Limited* was the second of his films to attract the biggest audiences in France, ahead of *Moonrise Kingdom* and behind *The Grand Budapest Hotel*. It was also a great success in Germany and Spain. In Europe, it received a warmer welcome than in the United States, where Wes Anderson suffered his second failure. No man is a prophet in his own country.

41184 **FOR WES ADDICTS** 41184

Those with a keen ear will recognize the tune played briefly by the tiny music box operated by Anjelica Huston toward the end of the film: this is "Waterloo Road" (1968) by the British group Jason Crest. The version chosen for the end credits is the cover version, titled "Les Champs-Élysées" (1969) and sung by French singer Joe Dassin.

Léa Seydoux (center) with Rodolphe Pauly (left) and Peter Gadiot (right) for one of the three Prada Candy spots.

Marketing Culture

The Impact of Advertising

Between two feature-length films (sometimes in the same year), Wes Anderson regularly made ads that created a stir every time. On February 26, 2012, his two fantastic little films (one a domestic comedy, the other an action comedy) for Japanese car manufacturer Hyundai had the honor of being shown, exclusively worldwide, during the breaks of the eighty-fourth Academy Awards ceremony. It was a form of consecration for the American director, who never altered his approach when he received commissions of this kind. The dozen or so commercials he designed all bear his imprint.

A Question of Genes

The fees received are undoubtedly a source of motivation for the director, but not the only one. His father, Melver Leonard Anderson, worked in advertising and public relations, so there must be some traces of that in his DNA. In Wes Anderson's fictional films, which are highly visual and offbeat, there is a certain marketing effectiveness, in the noble sense of the term: the viewer's attention is captured and maintained due to a display of inventiveness and ingenuity, as illustrated by his two ads for IKEA in 2002—the very first that the Texan directed. In one, a family settles scores in the living room; in the other, a couple squabbles in the kitchen. Suddenly, a salesman from the brand appears and asks them what they think about the product, as the shot pulls back and reveals they are all in a room mock-up in the store. Funny, unexpected, and effective. The same surprise effect is at work in "The Apartomatic" (2010), the ad that Wes Anderson co-wrote with Roman Coppola for Stella Artois. A young woman, momentarily left alone in a room in her handsome companion's home, cannot resist touching a console full of switches. Her manipulations trigger a series of more or less catastrophic events (from the automatic opening and closing of curtains to the sudden eruption of flames) that culminate in the young woman being swallowed up by a sofa, with only a glass of beer left on top.

Experiments on a Real-Life Scale

Advertising occasionally appears to be a field of experimentation for Wes Anderson—a laboratory of ideas, in short. In the series of short commercials (thirty seconds each) he made in 2007 for AT&T, he devised a staging device that enabled a TV news reporter to change scenery without moving, in a sophisticated rotating movement. He used and improved on this principle in *The Wonderful Story of Henry Sugar*, sixteen years later. In 2012, he immersed himself in a futuristic world for Sony's Xperia smartphones, filming, frame by frame, little robots that could be considered prototypes of the canine androids in *Isle of Dogs* (2018) or the alien creature in *Asteroid City* (2023). As for the three spots for Prada's Candy eau de parfum, these were made at the end of 2012 with the collaboration of Roman Coppola—again. Léa Seydoux's performance as a muse would undoubtedly have strengthened Coppola's decision to give the French actress a supporting role in *The Grand Budapest Hotel* (2014). The film was shot at the same time.

Acknowledged Influences

In 2005, his two ads—the least successful—for Dasani (Coca-Cola's purified water brand) showed two actors dressed respectively as a hamster and a bear in giant cages. (Was this a manifestation of his taste for animal fur, which we see again in his two animated films?) Joking aside, Anderson found advertising to be a humorous way of expressing himself or paying tribute to the filmmakers who had forged his artistic personality. The ads for American Express (2006) and SoftBank (2008) are pastiches of *La Nuit américaine* (François Truffaut, 1973) and Jacques Tati (with Brad Pitt as Monsieur Hulot), respectively. The three Prada Candy segments (broadcast in April 2013), in which Léa Seydoux is torn between two men, are tributes to *Jules et Jim* (François Truffaut, 1962), whose reference was passed on to French cinematographer Darius Khondji for inspiration. The idea was to create a Parisian atmosphere in Budapest. "For financial reasons, we shot on location in a café, a cinema, and a large flat. We had more or less the same team as for Castello Cavalcanti (2013), shot just before."[1] His lighting, which highlights the Prada pink, heralds the candy tones of *The Grand Budapest Hotel*.

An advertisement for H&M.

True to Himself

In "Come Together," made in 2016 for H&M and released for the festive season, Wes Anderson took a straightforward look at *The Darjeeling Limited*. Adrien Brody plays a meticulous train conductor reminiscent of the one his character had to put up with in the 2007 film. The clever lateral tracking and pastel colors are typically Andersonian, almost making you forget that this is an ad and that the characters are all wearing H&M. Wes Anderson's talent lies in his ability to remain himself, whatever the medium.

Lit by French photographer Darius Khondji, the three Prada spots feature a re-created Paris . . . in Budapest.

MESSIEURS
•
DAMES

GEORGE CLOONEY MERYL STREEP JASON SCHWARTZMAN BILL MURRAY OWEN WILSON

A FILM BY WES ANDERSON

FANTASTIC MR. FOX

"IT'S THE BEST ANIMATED FILM OF THE YEAR, AND MAYBE THE BEST FILM, PERIOD."

– *The Philadelphia Inquirer*, Steven Rea

FANTASTIC MR. FOX

2009

United States • 1 h 27 • Color • DTS / SDDS / DOLBY • 1.85: 1

Filming Dates: **Early 2008–June 2009**
Release Dates in the United States: **October 30, 2009 (AFI Fest); November 13, 2009 (limited); November 25, 2009**

Budget: **$40 million**
North America Box Office: **$21 million**
Worldwide Box Office: **$58 million**

Production Company: **20th Century Fox**
Producers: **Allison Abbate, Scott Rudin, Wes Anderson, Jeremy Dawson**
Co-Producers: **Molly Cooper**
Executive Producers: **Steven Rales, Arnon Milchan**

Screenplay: **Wes Anderson, Noah Baumbach**
Director of Photography: **Tristan Oliver**
First Assistant Director: **Kev Harwood**
Editing: **Andrew Weisblum**
Director of Animation: **Mark Gustafson**
Production Design: **Nelson Lowry**
Art Direction: **Francesca Maxwell**
Music: **Alexandre Desplat**
Puppet Fabrication Supervisor: **Andy Gent**
Visual Effects Supervisor: **Tim Ledbury**

Starring: **GEORGE CLOONEY (Mr. Fox), MERYL STREEP (Mrs. Fox), JASON SCHWARTZMAN (Ash), BILL MURRAY (Clive), WALLY WOLODARSKY (Kylie), ERIC ANDERSON (Kristofferson), MICHAEL GAMBON (Bean), WILLEM DAFOE (Rat), OWEN WILSON (Coach Skip), JARVIS COCKER (Petey), WES ANDERSON (Weasel), ROMAN COPPOLA (Squirrel Contractor), JUMAN MALOUF (Agnes), ADRIEN BRODY (Rickity), ROBIN HURLSTONE (Walter Boggis), HUGO GUINNESS (Nathan Bunce)...**

“It is strange to make a film about the countryside without blue or green, but these colors were banned from the start!”

—

Turlo Griffin, designer/illustrator[1]

SYNOPSIS

A couple of foxes, Mr. and Mrs. Fox, masters in the art of stealing chickens, have to interrupt this adventurous life because Felicity is expecting a child. Two years go by and Mr. Fox, a well-known journalist, seems to have settled down, but when he sees a property advertisement, he visits a house built into a gigantic tree and ends up buying it. His lawyer, Clive Blaireau, warns him, however, that the owners of the three farms bordering the house are not very friendly. What better thing for Mr. Fox to do? To rob his new neighbors, without his wife knowing, with the help of his inseparable companion, Kylie the possum. The terrifying Bean, Bounce, and Boggis then decide to get rid of Mr. Fox. For the cunning fox, this is a time of reckoning, not only for Felicity, who is worried and suspicious, but also for his only son, Ash, who resents his father's lack of interest in him.

The beech tree where the Fox family lives was inspired by the tree that stood next to author Roald Dahl's property.

GENESIS

Obsessed with *Fantastic Mr. Fox* (by Welsh children's author Roald Dahl), the first book he ever read and owned, Wes Anderson had always dreamed of adapting this story of a fox hunted down by vengeful farmers whom he has robbed. In particular, he was deeply affected by all the scenes that took place underground, because when they were children he and his brothers loved digging holes and tunnels. In 1996, shortly after the release of *Bottle Rocket*, the filmmaker contacted Michael Siegel, the literary agent who, in agreement with Felicity Dahl, the widow of Roald (who died in 1990), managed requests for adaptations of the work of the author of *Charlie and the Chocolate Factory* (1964). The dialogue was initiated and would never be broken off, even though Anderson was moving ahead with other projects. When *The Royal Tenenbaums* went into production in early 2001, the director returned to Michael Siegel and Felicity Dahl. The critical success of *Rushmore* (1998) and the anticipation generated by his next film made him even more credible in the eyes of the Dahl clan, who were determined not to allow just anybody to exploit the writer's work. Liccy, as the sixty-year-old woman was nicknamed, agreed to meet Anderson because she liked his work. During this informal meeting, she gently but firmly hammered home her credo: no deal without a script. At the same time, she granted him the rights to the book for a short period so that he could start writing. First, however, Anderson had to shoot *The Royal Tenenbaums*, which went on to become a huge hit in 2002.

Country Life

On August 18, 2002, Wes Anderson published an article in the Sunday supplement of the *New Yorker* about his second meeting with Liccy, which had taken place in the spring of the same year. She received him at the famous Gypsy House, the family home in the English countryside northeast of London. The visit left an indelible impression on the director, who confided how moved he was to discover the shed in the garden where Roald Dahl had written most of his children's books. He also

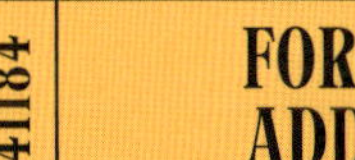

41184

FOR WES ADDICTS

41184

The tree house acquired by the Fox family at the beginning of the film is a direct allusion to Wes Anderson's childhood passion for tree houses, which was triggered by his reading of Johann David Wyss's *The Swiss Family Robinson [Der Schweizerische Robinson]*, an 1812 novel in which a shipwrecked family builds this kind of structure on an island. This obsession also appears in *The Royal Tenenbaums* (Margot writes a play called *The Levinsons in the Trees)* and in *Moonrise Kingdom* (the hut built by the scouts at an extravagant height).

The exterior and an interior shot of Roald Dahl's famous "Gipsy House" in England.

recognized in the gigantic beech tree next to the property the model of the tree inhabited by the *Fantastic Mr. Fox* family. He was not done with his—agreeable—surprises. At the end of the day, Liccy delivered the original manuscript and the notebook full of sketches of the foxes and farmers drawn by Roald Dahl himself. Following this inspiring meeting, Anderson made an agreement with Liccy to return to write the screenplay in the company of Noah Baumbach, his new co-writer—and friend—with whom he had been working in parallel on the project that would become *The Life Aquatic* (2004). An important detail: the filmmaker was still vacillating over the form to be given to *Fantastic Mr. Fox*. Would it be a purely animated film, or would it include live action (for the human characters)?

Dissensions

To create *Fantastic Mr. Fox*, Wes Anderson needed the green light from Touchstone Pictures, which had supported him since *Rushmore*. The subsidiary of the Disney giant, however, preferred him to tackle *The Life Aquatic*, which seemed more mature, more concrete. With Noah Baumbach, the director therefore gave priority to developing his maritime adventure film and put the Roald Dahl adaptation on hold. Two and a half years later, just before the official American release of *The Life Aquatic* (December 25, 2004), the media announced that Wes Anderson was to direct *Fantastic Mr. Fox* in animation for Revolution Studios, the young company launched by Joe Roth in 2000. The latter was none other than the former chairman of Disney and one of the first mentors of the director, whom he launched into orbit by promoting the production of *Rushmore*. The confirmed news was a major blow to Touchstone Pictures, which was not even able to console itself with what proved to be the catastrophic box-office performance of *The Life Aquatic*.

A Vast Project

In the wake of this earth-shattering announcement, Wes Anderson and Noah Baumbach, as planned with Liccy Dahl, set up shop at Gypsy House for three weeks of intense study, as the project promised to be a colossal one. Roald Dahl's book does not have much to say about it: it boils down to the siege of the burrow and Mr. Fox's underground actions to gain access to the villains' larders. The characters are few and sketchy (the six members of the Fox family, the farmers, a badger, and a rat), and apart from the humans, no one has a name. In the course of their conversations and walks through the county of Buckinghamshire, Anderson and Baumbach imagined a more complex world with a teeming fauna, from which emerge a few complementary characters (such as Kylie the possum, the hero's disciple), and significant dramatic stakes. They incorporated the idea of a slightly dysfunctional fox family in which Mrs. Fox (christened Felicity, in homage to their hostess) vainly imposes her law upon her husband, and the only son (as compared to four other fox cubs in the book), Ash, has the greatest difficulty in attracting his father's attention. The arrival in this troubled household of Kristofferson, the Foxes' nephew, a potential orphan (his father is very ill, and his mother is not mentioned), does not help matters. Gifted in everything, to the point of dazzling Mr. Fox, he unwittingly clashes with his cousin, who

Mr. Fox is voiced by George Clooney, who makes his animated film debut with *Fantastic Mr. Fox.*

Bill Murray gazes at the lawyer Clive Blaireau, to whom he is about to lend his voice.

Boggis, Bunce, and Bean, the three villains of the story, dig up the war shovel.

achieves very little. At the end of their stay, the two authors presented a first version of the script to Liccy, who was enthusiastic. Not only had the spirit of Roald Dahl not been betrayed, but he would surely have liked the acerbic wit expressed in this adaptation.

A False Start

On *The Life Aquatic*, Wes Anderson hit it off with Henry Selick; the director of *The Nightmare Before Christmas* (1993) brought the film's creatures and underwater fauna to life, animated frame by frame. This conclusive experiment encouraged the Texan filmmaker to turn to the stop-motion technique—which he had always loved—for *Fantastic Mr. Fox*. In accordance with his wishes, Henry Selick was brought on board as director of animation, a prospect that also delighted producer Joe Roth. Anderson was so enthusiastic that he approached Cate Blanchett, whom he had just directed in *The Life Aquatic*, with the idea of voicing Felicity Fox. The project, which had the invaluable support of Sony for the cast, was now launched. Anderson and Baumbach went back to the script, but fate seemed to have other plans. At the beginning of 2006, Henry Selick suddenly threw in the towel to devote himself to *Coraline* (2009), a feature film he was to direct for the brand-new American animation studio Laika. His departure put production of *Fantastic Mr. Fox* on hold. Was this one bad twist too many?

Back on Track at Last

Disappointed but never short of ideas, Anderson returned to work on *The Darjeeling Limited*, which he had begun developing with the help of Jason Schwartzman and Roman Coppola. At the same time, things became complicated with Joe Roth, who also abandoned *Fantastic Mr. Fox*. The rights to adapt this work came onto the market, and 20th Century-Fox—with its seemingly predestined name—seized the opportunity in October 2006. It just so happened that this same studio, via its subsidiary Searchlight Pictures, was producing and distributing *The Darjeeling Limited*, which Wes Anderson was about to start shooting. The project was then miraculously reactivated with the same producer, Scott Rudin, at the helm, who had supported the director since *The Royal Tenenbaums*.

Mrs. Fox benefits from the talent of Meryl Streep, who also makes one of her rare forays into voice acting.

It was decided between them that the director would enter preproduction on *Fantastic Mr. Fox* at the same time as his current shoot in India. To this end, a new American animation director, Mark Gustafson, and an English art supervisor, Nelson Lowry, were chosen. The nationality of the latter was important, as Wes Anderson wanted his animated film to be made in England, which has a long tradition of stop-motion animation.

CASTING

Immediately after completing *The Darjeeling Limited*, Wes Anderson immersed himself in *Fantastic Mr. Fox*, recording the voices before the actual filming, as is usually the custom in animation. The actors he had in mind had all agreed to be part of it: George Clooney (Mr. Fox), Jason Schwartzman (Ash Fox), Bill Murray (Clive Blaireau), and Meryl Streep (Felicity Fox). The latter was a welcome replacement for Cate Blanchett, who had been approached three years earlier but was ultimately unavailable in autumn 2007, the period chosen by Wes Anderson for his recording.

Country Life, Part Two

For his first animated film, the director was brimming with out-of-the-ordinary ideas. One of them was to have the actors act not in the studio but in real conditions, in the middle of the countryside, to obtain more realistic performances from them. To this end, production rented a large mansion in Connecticut, where a large part of the cast gathered in October 2007. Videos posted on the internet show George Clooney running and rolling in the grass—or perched on a sidecar alongside Wally Wolodarsky (the voice of Kylie the possum)—as he spouts his lines! The star of *Ocean's Eleven* (Steven Soderbergh, 2001), chosen for his debonair and heroic side, spared no effort during this recording session, which used every conceivable setting: the house, the surrounding fields, the barn, the cellar, and even a lake. A form of improvisation was encouraged. For example, the unexpected roar of a boat passing in the distance, picked up by the sound engineers, was retained and remixed to create the sound of an airplane. Eric Anderson, who was in charge of some of the sound effects, was also spontaneously hired to voice Kristofferson's cousin, as he had had the opportunity to play him during the tests.

Emergency Plan

Unable to travel to Connecticut due to her hectic schedule, Meryl Streep recorded her dialogue a little later in a Paris studio opposite Wes Anderson, who provided her cues. To put herself in the shoes of Felicity Fox, she said she was inspired by her encounter with a fox in the middle of London. From the bathroom window of the apartment she occupied during the filming of *Mamma Mia!* (Phyllida Lloyd, 2008), she met the gaze of the stray animal, which stared at her for several minutes. Jason Schwartzman was also unable to take time off for the countryside session because of the European promotion of *The Darjeeling Limited*, for which he was responsible in his dual capacity as actor and co-writer. So it was in London, where he was with Anderson for a film festival, that he recorded the voice of Ash Fox in twenty minutes. A logistical problem delayed the delivery of a special microphone, and the two men had to wait a long time for it in the studio booked for the occasion. When the precious accessory arrived, they had only a short time in which to work before attending the presentation of *The Darjeeling Limited* (like nothing had happened…).

In terms of aesthetics and frame-by-frame animation, Wes Anderson wanted the handmade, manufactured aspect to be visible.

Wes Anderson in a rare appearance on the set. He controlled the filming remotely, from his home.

FILMING AND PRODUCTION

With the voices in the can, Wes Anderson could move on to the animation phase, which would last almost two years. In the meantime, Nelson Lowry, briefed in advance by the director, called on all the art departments to develop the film's visual environment. Here again, Anderson's methodology was unprecedented: he agreed with Lowry, Mark Gustafson, and director of photography Tristan Oliver that he would control practically everything remotely, from his computer in Paris. This choice led to a number of minor tensions, which disconcerted the British team, who were used to being closer and warmer.

Down to Work!

Among the first collaborators to enter the fray were the illustrators, responsible for graphically conceptualizing the sets and characters imagined by the director and the artistic supervisor. Turlo Griffin was one of these artists whose work is essential to any purely imaginary creation. In 2007, he had only been practicing his craft for four years. This was a promising talent that Nelson Lowry spotted when he was in charge at Moving Picture Company, a special effects company based in London. Griffin was offered the chance to work on the film's environments (landscapes, buildings, interiors—in short, everything that makes up its visual world), with the director's blessing. "I think Wes liked the way I drew. [...] Chris Appelhans [another artist] had done some incredible concept paintings in the beginning, establishing the autumnal brown/ochre landscapes in the film. [...] But there were still a lot of environments to create and I worked on most of them. The first thing I drew was the beech tree in which the foxes live, both inside and out."[2]

In total, Griffin spent eighteen months on the film, from September 2007 to spring 2009, producing hundreds of illustrations in the traditional way. "In general, I drew with colored pencil on colored paper, scanned the result, then changed the contrast in Photoshop, enhanced it, lit it again and added other elements (like the Foxes' living room furniture, for example) until my composition was approved."[3] A painter at heart, Griffin also asked to do the paintings of Felicity Fox, the budding artist in the story. "These little canvases, intended to accompany the miniature sets, were a real pleasure to paint. I painted a number of these."[4]

Rat, voiced by Willem Dafoe, adopts the postures of a spaghetti western villain.

Fox Dreams

Another essential link in the chain is the "character designer," the person who creates the features and look of a character before it is produced in hard copy, like Félicie Haymoz from Switzerland. Having worked with Mackinnon & Saunders, the Manchester design studio chosen by Anderson and Lowry to make the film's puppets, she came highly recommended to the two men, whose main visual reference was *Le Roman de Renard* (Ladislas and Irène Starewitch, 1937), the first French animated film, which was characterized by its anthropomorphism tinged with bestiary elements. Haymoz says, "The beginning of the project was laborious and very stressful for me. I drew all day, and at night I dreamt of foxes! [...] When I spend time with a character, I put myself in their shoes and imagine what they wear and what accessories they use on a daily basis. If a character's trousers or scarf seem right, they bring out the rest, they impose a direction. [...] I think that's what Wes Anderson liked about my drawings. I was able to spend weeks obsessing over costume details because he pays so much attention to these elements."[5]

Avoid "Clean" Above All

The head of the puppet fabrication department on *Fantastic Mr. Fox*, Andy Gent, also from Mackinnon & Saunders, had the onerous task of turning the preparatory work done by the designer-illustrators into reality. His watchword: forget everything he had previously learned. "Wes wasn't at all interested in clean, crisp animation similar to that generated by a computer, a trend that everyone was following at the time. He wanted his work to have the look of old-fashioned films like *Le Roman de Renard* or the stop-motion scenes of Ray Harryhausen from the 1950s–1970s. He surprised and even shocked us! And of course he made the right decision for *Fantastic Mr. Fox*, with the right technique, the right rendering."[6] The viewer had to clearly understand that the puppets were handmade (Anderson liked to feel that there was some trickery involved, which he believed helped to infuse the film with magic), and they also

Young Ash Fox and his cousin Kristofferson are voiced by Jason Schwartzman and Eric Anderson (Wes's younger brother).

had to inspire a sense of fear in younger viewers and enable them to identify with the protagonists. Here again, the director convinced Gent. "The characters are very bestial, of course, but not frightening. Seeing them move and speak so delicately most of the time is a very clever way of making them exist in a world where children are likely to love them. Roald Dahl himself didn't shy away from telling difficult stories and I remember him saying, 'You shouldn't hide these things from children.'"[7]

So British

More than five hundred puppets were produced in the end, including 102 for Mr. Fox alone, in several guises, each requiring six different sizes. Around 150 sets and four thousand accessories were also produced in the various artistic departments. Particular attention was paid to the interiors. Given that the film cost almost nothing in digital effects or action scenes (which are rare because they take up time and therefore money), Anderson required his collaborators to source the best materials, fabrics, and other aspects to achieve the cozy effect he was looking for. He even asked his New York tailor to provide him with items for Mr. Fox's wardrobe.

A Small Revolution

From a directorial point of view, Wes Anderson was obliged to revise his cinematographic syntax. The long panoramic shots that are characteristic of his style are few and far between in *Fantastic Mr. Fox*, for one simple reason: the miniature sets are limited in space and do not correspond to each other; it is therefore difficult, unless one cheats with digital technology, to imagine complex movements for the characters. He therefore favored still shots and more extensive cutting than usual. It was for this reason that, for the first time in preproduction, he systematized the use of animatics—an animated storyboard designed to preview the many scenes planned. The choice was crucial for the rest of his career, since from then on he would prepare all his feature films in this way. Anderson asked the animators to film at a rate of twelve frames per second (as opposed to twenty-four in a live-action film) to give the image a jerky aspect that enhanced the impression of being handmade. The director of photography, Tristan Oliver, had to design his lighting to highlight the ochre tones favored by the director, who purged the image of greens and blues. Only one character, cousin Kristofferson, wears blue to indicate that he is not just some other local character.

RECEPTION

A few weeks before the film's release, Tristan Oliver gave an interview to the *Los Angeles Times*, which caused a certain amount of controversy. The latter complained about Wes Anderson's lack of presence during the making of the film in unflattering terms. "He can spend a whole day locked in an empty room with a computer. He's a bit like the Wizard of Oz. Behind the curtain."[8] Oliver later claimed that his words had been distorted. Not one to hold a grudge, Wes Anderson called on his services again for *Isle of Dogs*.

Background

These minor disagreements in no way affected the film's enthusiastic reception in the press. According to Rotten Tomatoes, an online film and TV review site, *Fantastic Mr. Fox* is by far the most popular Wes Anderson film in English-speaking countries, with 93 percent favorable opinions. In France, where it received an average of 4.3 stars out of 5 on the reference site AlloCiné, the response was similar. According to the modest director, there was a simple explanation for this plebiscite: "I received better reviews because the stakes were not high."[9] Unfortunately, the box-office results did not live up to the expectations raised by this excellent reception. North American takings ($21 million) were half the budget. The question of a sequel, which could have been envisaged in the event of a huge box-office success, did not even arise. The main source of satisfaction for Anderson was that he has not disappointed Liccy Dahl, with whom he would have to negotiate again in the not-too-distant future. As well as *Fantastic Mr. Fox*, he was an early fan of *The Wonderful Story of Henry Sugar*.

White Cap

From time to time in the film, young Ash reads a comic book called *White Cap*, about a superhero fox who wears a white cape. We can see only the cover, but Christian De Vita, the illustrator, had drawn other posters and even a few scripted pages (by him and Wes Anderson). There was talk of *White Cap* being made into a comic book, but unfortunately this project never came to fruition.

Fantastic Mr. Fox marks Wes Anderson's first animated film and the start of his collaboration with composer Alexandre Desplat.

Wes Anderson and a mini version of Mr Fox.

A Highly Animated World

Wes and His Puppets

In the early 2000s, when news of the *Fantastic Mr. Fox* (2009) project surfaced, only the uninitiated were surprised by Wes Anderson's interest in the works of Roald Dahl and animation: he had been passionately fond of both from a very early age. Furthermore, the filmmaker communicated a great deal through drawings: for example, he designed the entire storyboard for *Bottle Rocket* (1996), his first feature film. The finely stylized compositions of his films and the spleen emanating from the characters make his world highly compatible with the adult animation toward which he was moving. Even though it was originally a children's story, *Fantastic Mr. Fox* aims to please all audiences, with an aesthetic halfway between naïve painting and conceptual art, and to offer a dual reading: on the one hand, the story of an amusing battle between clever animals and narrow-minded farmers, and on the other, a reflection on parenthood.

The English School

After the short underwater sequences in *The Life Aquatic* (2004), for which Wes Anderson opted for volume animation, commonly known as stop motion, the director continued to use this technique in *Fantastic Mr. Fox*, setting handmade puppets in motion frame by frame. The best-known example is the work of Aardman Animations, a British company famous for its short films (including the first adventures of Wallace and Gromit, *A Grand Day Out* [Nick Park, 1989], and *The Wrong Trousers* [Nick Park, 1993]), commercials, and music videos ("Sledgehammer," Peter Gabriel, 1986, and "My Baby Just Cares For Me," Nina Simone, 1987). The success of *Chicken Run* (Nick Park, 2000) and *Corpse Bride* (Tim Burton, 2005) also demonstrated that there was an alternative to the CGI animation favored by Pixar, which was taking over the family film market.

A Strange Meeting

Wes Anderson and British artistic supervisor Nelson Lowry recruited many of the technicians used to working for Aardman or Mackinnon & Saunders, an English workshop specializing in volume animation—it supplied the puppets for *The Corpse Bride*. Among them was Andy Gent, head of the puppet fabrication department on *Max & Co* (Samuel and Frédéric Guillaume, 2007), a Swiss children's film. This experienced artist, who grew up with a father who was a nonconformist cabinetmaker working in both wood and metal, is an expert in his field. He had feared the end of stop motion because of the growing prominence of computer-generated images, but he was delighted to see Anderson's interest in this traditional technique. He first had to pass a test that left him with an amusing memory. "My first meeting with Wes was in Paris, in a flat, where I was accompanied by Nelson Lowry [...] I had brought some sculptures from the studio. Our meeting was very short because Wes was very busy. He looked at the puppets and touched the models carefully, then asked me: 'How do you reproduce eye blinks?' I replied that we could make them with Vacuum forming plastic [sous vide molding] or modelling clay. He was very polite, nodded, and said 'very interesting,' then left the room and I didn't see him again for several months!"[1]

A New Approach

While Gent waited patiently for news, Anderson notified his teams that he would be physically absent from the shoot, which would take place at 3 Mills Studios in northeast London. Thanks to a sophisticated network of cameras, he was be able to view and comment on the tedious work of each animator from a distance—it would take more than a year and a half to complete. For the rest, he would communicate directly by email with the main station managers to correct, amend, and validate all the artistic choices being made. Gent was not surprised by this unusual way of working, nor by Anderson's

Manufacturing and maintenance of the film's puppets.

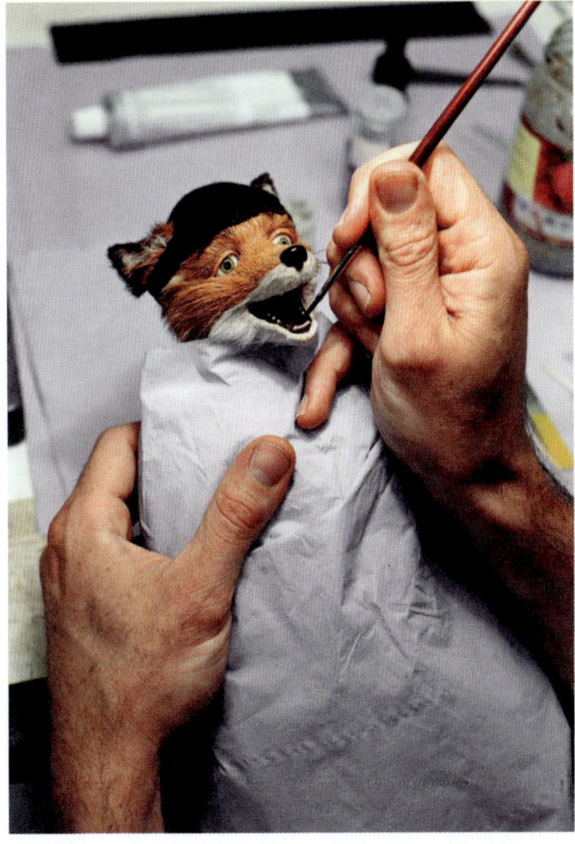

unpredictable character, as he was prepared by his Paris interview for this. He was not surprised to learn that his puppets would not blink, and he had to create particularly expressive irises. In the end, although a few blinks were created, they were rarer and more fleeting than in a traditional animated film, and they were replaced by numerous frowns and exaggerated widening of the eyes, adding an extra touch of fantasy. Gent was delighted. "You can feel the craftsmanship, and at the same time, it is very realistic. [...] Wes's style is not cold; it is warm, tactile, textured. He plays a lot with scale, using tiny puppets in large sets to create the illusion of vast panoramas, which is a very clever and charming way of going about things."[2]

Respecting the Vision

Gent started work about a year before filming began. He worked closely with the character designers, the illustrators who imagine and draw up the silhouettes of the characters and their outfits, such as Félicie Haymoz from Switzerland. He said, "I think mainly about the puppet, [...] indicating everything that might be useful in making it: the textures of the clothes, the accessories, the hair, and

Animation director Jason Stalman during the making of *Isle of Dogs*.

so on. I also try to express the character's personality, by presenting them in a neutral posture that allows the whole of their body to be seen, because I am thinking of the sculptor who is going to reinterpret my drawing."[3] This preparatory work was crucial and necessary, but the hardest part remained for Gent and his team. "A drawing often allows you to go very far, but it is the sculpture that answers all the three-dimensional problems. It is an unpredictable process and you have to let it evolve. [...] We test and develop it throughout the film."[4] The director's demands obviously do not make the task any easier. "We have to make sure that our work respects Wes's requests, his mentions and references. [...] For *Isle of Dogs*, I think he gave me forty-two films to watch before I even started to do anything, in order to capture the atmosphere, the period, the way people spoke, the way they looked and felt."[5]

Controlled and Empowered at the Same Time

Once all this information has been assimilated, the puppet department has to get down to business. Gent says, "We start by showing Wes a plasticine figure [an intermediate stage in the production process], he tells us what he thinks of it, we take it back, and so on. Once he's got what he wants for the character, we move on to the molding, then the technical process of transforming it into puppets. In the meantime, we examine (under his supervision) fabrics and numerous samples of materials, colors. [...] Then the animators confirm that it works or suggest adaptations."[6] A considerable number of emails were exchanged, feeding into each other's thinking. Sometimes Gent received some unusual ones, as he explains: "To the question, 'What kind of color does this character need?,' he could send me an overall photograph of a Gucci

Some of Andy Gent's creations. The puppet master (bottom) shows off the large bird that gambols over the Asteroid City credits.

boutique and reply, 'Somewhere in there,' as was the case for the Nutmeg character in *Isle of Dogs*!"[7]

Under the Sun

Andy Gent's work is not confined to animated films for Wes Anderson; he also occasionally worked on the director's live-action feature films. This was the case, for example, on *Asteroid City* (2023), where the puppeteer developed the famous large roadrunner, the strange bird (perhaps best known from the Looney Tunes and Merrie Melodies cartoons featuring Road Runner and Wile E. Coyote [Chuck Jones, 1949–]) that hops around in stop motion during the opening and closing credits—it even dances at the end. It was an experience appreciated by the English artist. "Unusually, I was able to work on set with Wes. Being in Spain filming, mainly, under the sweltering midday sun, was very different from what I experience in the studio! It was very dynamic. The day was incredibly fast-paced. We were obviously shooting much faster, so there was no comparison [with studio animation]."[8]

Second Life

For Gent, Anderson's view of volume animation has not changed too much. His own, on the other hand, has been enriched by contact with this meticulous filmmaker, whose requests and wishes he learned to anticipate. "Working on a film with Wes is both stimulating and fun. Often you don't really know where he's going to take you. [...] It's always a challenge, but understanding his language and trusting him makes it easier."[9] This collaboration was all the more valuable for Gent, as it extended beyond the shoot. After being repaired and cleaned, his puppets, like the dubbing actors, go on promotional tours for the films. These authentic "stars" are a source of wonder for children and adults alike. Some of them would be featured in museums, showrooms, and other exhibition spaces dedicated to the very special world of Wes Anderson.

The Obsession with Symmetry

A Perfect Calculation

Introduced in *Rushmore* (1998), his second feature film, the symmetrical composition of Wes Anderson's shots has assumed increasingly spectacular proportions over the years. There are several reasons for this aesthetic bias, which goes against the pictorial rule of thirds, in which an image is divided into nine equal parts with certain constants and changing lines of force. Symmetry is the ideal backdrop for the characters' psychorigidity, but it also helps to organize the chaos that occurs on either side of the center of the image, where the viewer's attention is focused, and therefore helps them understand it. It is also a simple, highly visual way of instantly creating a sense of discrepancy (and therefore also facetiousness and burlesque) that echoes the filmmaker's deadpan humor.

The hushed world of *Isle of Dogs* before the organized chaos begins.

The bellboy Zero (center) is well supported by two superiors in *The Grand Budapest Hotel*.

Chas Tenenbaum (Ben Stiller) with Uzi and Ari, appropriately distributed. Like father, like sons.

Ned Plimpton (Owen Wilson) and Klaus Daimler (Willem Dafoe) challenge each other in the middle of the ship's gangways in *The Life Aquatic*.

A fantastic sense of perspective in *Fantastic Mr. Fox*.

OPENING FILM
FESTIVAL DE CANNES 2012

Ascot Elite Entertainment Group, Focus Features and Indian Paintbrush Present an American Empirical Picture "Moonrise Kingdom" Casting by Douglas Aibel Co-Producers Molly Cooper Lila Yacoub Costume Designer Kasia Walicka Maimone Original Music by Alexandre Desplat Music Supervisor Randall Poster Editor Andrew Weisblum, A.C.E. Production Designer Adam Stockhausen Director of Photography Robert Yeoman, A.S.C. Executive Producers Sam Hoffman Mark Roybal Produced by Wes Anderson Scott Rudin Steven Rales Jeremy Dawson Written by Wes Anderson & Roman Coppola Directed by Wes Anderson

Moonrise Kingdom

A Film by Wes Anderson Director of The Royal Tenenbaums and The Life Aquatic

Bruce Willis
Edward Norton
Bill Murray
Frances McDormand
Tilda Swinton
Jason Schwartzman
Bob Balaban

MOONRISE
KINGDOM
NEW PENZANCE ISLAND
SUMMER
1965

ASCOT ELITE Entertainment Group

FOCUS FEATURES

MOONRISE KINGDOM

United States • 1 h 34 • Color • Datasat / Dolby Digital • 1.85 : 1

Production Dates: **May–June 2011**
World Premiere: **May 16, 2012 (Cannes Film Festival)**
Release Dates in the United States: **May 25, 2012 (limited release); June 29, 2012**

Budget: **Approx. $16 million**
North America Box Office: **Approx. $45.5 million**
Worldwide Box Office: **Approx. $68 million**

Production Companies: **Indian Paintbrush, American Empirical Pictures, Scott Rudin Productions, Moonrise Productions**
Producers: **Wes Anderson, Jeremy Dawson, Steven Rales, Scott Rudin**
Co-Producers: **Eli Bush, Molly Cooper, Lila Yacoub**
Executive Producers: **Sam Hoffman, Mark Roybal**
Associate Producers: **Octavia Peissel**

Screenplay: **Wes Anderson, Roman Coppola**
Director of Photography: **Robert Yeoman**
First Assistant Director: **Nate Grubb**
Film Editing: **Andrew Weisblum**
Production Design: **Adam Stockhausen**
Set Decoration: **Kris Moran**
Art Direction: **Gerald Sullivan**
Music: **Alexandre Desplat**
Sound: **Pawel Wdowczak**
Costumes: **Kasia Walicka Maimone**
Makeup: **Nuria Sitja**
Visual Effects Supervisor: **Danny S. Kim**
Casting: **Douglas Aibel, Henry Russell Bergstein, Deborah Maxwell Dion**

Starring: **JARED GILMAN (Sam), KARA HAYWARD (Suzy), BRUCE WILLIS (Capitaine Sharp), EDWARD NORTON (Scout Master Ward), BILL MURRAY (Walt Bishop), FRANCES MCDORMAND (Laura Bishop), HARVEY KEITEL (Commander Pierce), BOB BALABAN (The Narrator), TILDA SWINTON (Social Services), JASON SCHWARTZMAN (Cousin Ben)...**

“Who’s got Snoopy?”

Scout Master Ward, concerning the troop dog

SYNOPSIS

Summer 1965. Suzy Bishop is bored at home, between her overbearing mother, moody father, and teasing little brothers. Scout Master Ward is worried about the disappearance of one of his Khaki Patrol scouts, Sam Shakusky. Shakusky has arranged to meet Suzy in a secluded spot on the imaginary island of New Penzance, New England, where they live. The two twelve-year-olds have been secretly in love for a year and are planning to flee their hostile environment (Sam, an orphan, is bounced from foster home to foster home). Alerted to their disappearance, the authorities launch a search. They are led by Captain Sharp, head of the local police and, incidentally, the lover of Laura Bishop, Suzy’s mother. Gradually, the masks come off: Ward is not as organized as he seems; Suzy’s father cannot control his nerves; Sharp is more sensitive than expected. Could Sam and Suzy be more mature than the adults around them?

Kara Hayward and Jared Gilman both debut in *Moonrise Kingdom*. They were paired again in *Paterson* (Jim Jarmusch, 2016).

GENESIS

No sooner had *Fantastic Mr. Fox* (2009) been finished when Wes Anderson was thinking about his next film. The idea of a love story between two preadolescents had been on his mind for several years. It was fueled by a vivid memory: in fifth grade, the young Texan had fallen in love with a classmate but had never dared approach her. What might have happened if he had declared himself? In a way, the film is an extension and embodiment of his childhood fantasy. He also imagined that the beautiful heroine was an avid reader of mawkish fantasy novels. The adventure that the two lovebirds embark on could be an illustration of this, in a kind of *mise en abyme* that the director is fond of. As the script was not very clear in his mind, he spent a whole year working on it, despairing of developing it as he wished, inhibited, perhaps, by the overwhelming shadow of two masterpieces on the subject of childhood that obsessed him: *L'Argent de poche* (François Truffaut, 1976) and *Black Jack* (Ken Loach, 1979).

The Rescue Mission

In the throes of a creative impasse, Anderson approached Roman Coppola about his project, with whom he was about to direct an advert for Stella Artois. The contribution of the co-writer of *The Darjeeling Limited* (2007) proved decisive. The two of them came up with the script in a month and finalized it six weeks later. The romance between two twelve-year-olds that Anderson had imagined involved few adults. With the help of Roman Coppola, the presence of older protagonists made its way into the story. He is also the man behind the idea of the megaphone used by Laura Bishop to make herself heard by her family, a curious way of communicating that his own mother used! With the combined efforts of the two accomplices, the story assumed the form of a Robinsonade set against the backdrop of an enchanted elopement, with a massive police search in parallel, with reinforcements from the children's parents and a scout patrol. As in *The Royal Tenenbaums* (2001), a narrator intervenes here and there to provide some context—no longer a voice-over, but a character addressing the camera. The influence of Mark Twain is evident in this film, in which Anderson explores the great American outdoors for the first time.

Paradise Lost

Even though the narrative states that the precise date of the events that take place is 1965, Anderson intuitively felt that the action should be set in a timeless location that would represent a vanished past. Such a setting exists, namely Naushon Island, off the coast of Providence, Massachusetts, on the East Coast of the United States. The filmmaker visited the island several times on his way to visit friends. He retained the image of a place untouched by the ravages of modernity: no cars, houses dating from another century with their rustic interiors, a wild and somewhat desolate nature, an old lighthouse on the island's high point...The director therefore wanted all the exteriors of the film, particularly the Bishop family home, to be imbued with this retro ambience. Location scouts had their work cut out for them (see below).

CASTING

The big challenge for Wes Anderson, as with *Rushmore* fourteen years earlier, was to bring out of the shadows not one but two totally unknown young actors, on whose shoulders the film would largely rest. The search, conducted by several of the casting director's collaborators in the four corners of the United States, lasted over six months. Each child auditioned had to play a specific scene, which was then filmed on video so that Anderson could view the most conclusive tests. Both Jared Gilman and Kara Hayward, the lucky ones (both twelve years old at the time of casting and filming), were recalled several times before learning that they had been selected.

Freeze Frame

Suzy is constantly browsing through books for teenage girls that she has stolen from the library. For the film's DVD extras, Wes Anderson created six very short animated stories from these mysteriously titled tales, introduced by the narrator (Bob Balaban): "Shelly and the Secret Universe," "The Francine Odysseys," "The Girl from Jupiter," "The Disappearance of the 6th Grade," "The Light of the Seven Matchsticks," and "The Return of Auntie Lorraine." A frustrated gymnast, a tired lion, a menacing hydra, and a witch hunter make up a gallery of strange characters whose poetry is reinforced by the abstract text chanted by a monotone voice-over.

Like Professionals

Anderson took the two apprentice actors under his wing for the purposes of a specific preparation. He instructed them to learn the script and their dialogues by heart, and had them rehearse regularly to familiarize themselves with their characters and understand their motivations. This groundwork was accompanied by a battery of instructions that had to be scrupulously respected. Kara had to work on her stamina for the film's many outdoor exploration scenes (walking through the forest, crossing a stream...). Jared, who plays an exceptional scout, had to learn to how to handle a canoe and cook on a fire. Anderson had another particular requirement: the two children had to write to each other. Their characters begin their relationship with purely epistolary exchanges, represented in the film's many flashbacks. Jared and Kara willingly lent themselves to the exercise, but did so instinctively by email, which annoyed the director when he discovered this. Having been forced to exchange handwritten letters, they finally came to appreciate what this was all about. Kara, for example, pushed perfectionism to the point of sticking a label with "Suzy Bishop" and her fictitious address on each piece of correspondence. Through self-sacrifice, their fictional characters became second nature to them.

A Striking Revelation

Jared Gilman and Kara Hayward are not the only children in the film, which features many—mainly extras for the scout camp. Another young actor stands out from the crowd. Lucas Hedges plays Redford, Sam's sworn enemy. Initially considered by Wes Anderson for the lead role (the fourteen-year-old was two years too old), Hedges, son of writer-director Peter Hedges and actress Susan Bruce, takes on the role of a dirty bully, which he gives unexpected depth. His name in the film is a direct allusion to Robert Redford, a golden boy presented in the film as a caricature of arrogance, viciousness . . . but also undeniable charm. His accomplished performance would later lead to a fine

Kara Hayward on the roof of Rhode Island's Conanicut Island Light, an inactive lighthouse converted into a residence for the crew during the filming of *Moonrise Kingdom*.

Edward Norton's first foray with Wes Anderson as Scout Master Ward in *Moonrise Kingdom*. More collaborations would follow.

Most exteriors were shot on Prudence Island in Narragansett Bay, Rhode Island.

Like Edward Norton, Frances McDormand (second from left) and Bruce Willis (far right) were newcomers to the world of Wes Anderson.

Moonrise Kingdom was Tilda Swinton's first film with Wes Anderson.

career, notably under the direction of his father in *Ben Is Back* (Peter Hedges, 2018).

A Great Renewal

Moonrise Kingdom (the name given to the bay where the hunted children take refuge) was an opportunity for Anderson, five years after his last live-action film, to renew his cast. With the exception of mascot Bill Murray (who plays Suzy's irritable father), all the film's adult actors were entering the director's world for the first time. Most of them had been acquaintances or even friends for a long time. Such is the case with Frances McDormand, whom he had in mind very early on to play Murray's fickle wife. With Edward Norton—a pilot, rafting enthusiast, and handyman in real life—the dialogue had also been going on for a long time. Wes Anderson was waiting for the right moment to offer him a role. He was offered the role of Scout Master Ward. The same applies for Tilda Swinton, with whom the director had exchanged occasional emails in the past. She was to don the stern uniform of the social worker who wants to put Sam in a reformatory. Bruce Willis, on the other hand, was a complete stranger to Anderson, who saw in him the ideal embodiment of authority—tired, not to mention bitter. The director, who did not consider anyone else for the role, appreciated the star's exemplary demeanor during filming, despite the absence of trailers for the actors and the constraint of staying together, collectively, without straying far from the set. Finally, to play the narrator, Anderson chose Bob Balaban, a solid supporting actor who would become indispensable to him (he can be seen in *The Grand Budapest Hotel* [2014], *Isle of Dogs* [2018]), *The French Dispatch* [2021], and *Asteroid City* [2023]).

The Conanicut Island Light house, where Bill Murray felt very much at home.

FILMING AND PRODUCTION

Before filming could begin, Wes Anderson had to find the wild, isolated location with old New England–style buildings that he dreamed of. Perhaps Cumberland Island, off the coast of Georgia, with its long sandy beaches and dense forest? Not New England enough and its autumn colors were all wrong. Perhaps Comfort Island, an islet between New York State and Canada, with its unique, imposing Victorian mansion and gray walls? The director was tempted, but hesitated. He had also spotted two locations on the internet that fascinated him: Ten Chimneys, a vast Wisconsin estate patiently built by a couple of actors during the first half of the twentieth century, and Clingstone, a cedar-shingled house built on the top of a tiny rocky island in Narragansett Bay, Rhode Island. Anderson finally opted for Conanicut Island Light in Rhode Island, a former lighthouse converted into a private residence, located on Conanicut Island, opposite the Newport marina and not far from Clingstone. This beautiful red building was used for the overall plans of the Bishops' house, while the archipelago of Narragansett Bay will be used for the exteriors.

Old Style

For the interior of the Bishops' house, Anderson broke with his rule of shooting on an existing set: it was built entirely in the studio on the site of an old

Jason Schwartzman (top) and Edward Norton (middle) as Scout masters, kings of resourcefulness.

Moonrise Kingdom was filmed in the dominant green and ochre colors that have become so emblematic of Wes Anderson's cinema.

warehouse near Newport. This enabled him to arrange the space as he saw fit (see below), as he had done for the cross section of the boat in *The Life Aquatic* (2004). Art director Gerald Sullivan and decorator Kris Moran were responsible for designing the Bishops' home. They drew on a wealth of period photographs, supplied in part by Anderson, and on the homes they visited in preparation. They re-created a playroom inspired by a house on Cumberland Island. They even went so far as to borrow items from members of the film crew! If the director happened to spot a piece of scenery, a piece of furniture, or a knickknack he liked, the team was tasked with finding one.

Guest House

At Anderson's request, the production team rented a house in Newport for the director, cinematographer Robert Yeoman, editor Andrew Weisblum, Edward Norton, and Bill Murray. According to Yeoman, this was a convivial way of working and strengthening ties: "Every night we would have dinner and many other cast and crew members would join us. The editing room was there so it was convenient to look at dailies and cuts of the movie at night."[1] The cinematographer and director can also review the next day's work plan at their leisure, including the axes and camera movements that Anderson has recorded in the animatics he has used since *Fantastic Mr. Fox*. "I definitely feel that Wes's experience on the animated films changed his approach to live action [after *Fantastic Mr. Fox*]. Our films took on a more cartoonlike quality."[2]

An Unreal Space

With *Moonrise Kingdom*, Anderson permits himself a few innovations and relaxes his methodology. By agreement with Yeoman, he abandoned the traditional (and heavy) Panavision cameras for Aaton Super 16 mm. The Xterà model was used for indoor scenes with adults, while the smaller, more maneuverable A-Minima was used for outdoor scenes with children. This choice was dictated by logic, as the director did not want to distract the young actors by confronting them with cumbersome equipment. The same care was taken when he saved for the end of the shoot (to give them time to get to know each other) the dance sequence on the beach in their bathing suits, which he supervised alone with Yeoman. This time, he was the one who adapted, not the others. As for

Wes Anderson prepared his young actors at length, encouraging them to develop a strong bond off set.

the interiors of the Bishops' house—particularly in the film's introduction—they do not match any architectural reality. The slow sideways dolly shots (from left to right and back again) show an endless succession of rooms, laid out side by side. These sets were designed both to accommodate the dolly tracks and to enable the actors to move around according to a choreography and millimeter precision tempo as justified by Yeoman: "The dimensions of the rooms were carefully studied to correspond exactly to the lines of dialogue in the script."[3]

Trompe L'oeil

At the end of the film, torrents of water pour down on the imaginary island of New Penzance, threatening terrible floods, and the protagonists take refuge in the local church. All scenes were shot inside Newport's Trinity Church, with the exception of the rooftop rescue where Captain Sharp comes to the aid of Sam and Suzy, who are trapped on the ledge of a turret in the pouring rain and at night. For safety reasons, a special set was built next to the house set—a concession granted by Anderson with which Yeoman was delighted. "It would have been extremely difficult and unsafe to do this on the location. The

Just for Fun

On June 18, 2012, the Funny or Die digital comedy video platform broadcast "Cousin Ben Troop," an unpublished Wes Anderson sketch. In it, Jason Schwartzman reprises his role as a scout leader, king of improvisation (he religiously marries the children in the film), authoritarian and calm at the same time, who organizes a paid screening of *Moonrise Kingdom* for his flock. It was a fun, viral way of promoting the film in the US (it was a big hit in some American cinemas at the time) ahead of its national release, scheduled for June 29.

FOR WES ADDICTS

At the Cannes press conference, Wes Anderson revealed that he had included a very personal anecdote in the film. Like Suzy, he accidentally discovered (at his father's house), during his teenage years, a book designed to help parents deal with a disturbed child. The future director, who had two brothers, always knew that this book concerned him and suffered from it, but he never discussed the issue with Melver Anderson. He later regretted having referred to it publicly.

set in the warehouse gave us complete control for camera placement, lighting, and the rain effect. [...] Plus, we could shoot it during the day! Night exteriors in the rain are always very difficult."[4] For this particular scene, the director made another departure from his artisanal principles. In postproduction, the colors were digitally reworked to give a bluish aspect to this spectacular denouement that flirts with the fantastical, with the corners of the image also darkened to link it to silent cinema.

RECEPTION

The film was presented at a world exclusive at the prestigious Cannes Film Festival on May 16, 2012, opening the festival. For Wes Anderson, this was a first and the consecration of his work begun almost twenty years earlier with the short film *Bottle Rocket* (1993). In a press release issued two months before the event, festival delegate Thierry Frémaux was full of praise for the film. "Wes Anderson is one of the rising powers of American cinema, to which he brings a very personal touch, particularly in *Moonrise Kingdom*, which once again testifies

On the left, Scout Master Ward (Edward Norton) at the foot of the tree house.
Below, the film's famous fox terrier, Snoopy.

to the creative freedom in which he continues to evolve. Sensitive and independent, this admirer of Fellini and Renoir is also a brilliant and inventive filmmaker."[5] Gilles Jacob, his historic predecessor and now president, also has a laudatory comment to make. "With Wes Anderson opening the 65th Cannes Film Festival, young American cinema will be celebrated on the Croisette."[6] More than enough compliments already!

A Creative Turning Point

Moonrise Kingdom follows very much in the footsteps of Wes Anderson's other films (the dysfunctional family, childish adults, mature children), but also stands out for its music. The influence of animated films (with *Fantastic Mr. Fox*) is noticeable in the mise-en-scène and the cartoonish spirit that characterizes this story: the Bishops' home, a sort of doll's house, and certain zany shots (the hut high above the ground, the scouts' trail dog clumsily killed by an arrow, Sam's electrocution by lightning, scoutmaster Ward's aerial leaps to save Commander Pierce at the end...) all contribute to making *Moonrise Kingdom*, well received by critics and audiences alike, a milestone in Anderson's career. With this film, the director seems to free himself from the usual narrative and aesthetic constraints to find his own way, between excessive theatricality and abstraction.

Do Not Miss the Ending!

In the middle of the end credits, a voice is suddenly heard explaining the orchestration of Alexandre Desplat's musical suite. A metronome sounds and the various instruments begin to play, one after the other: harp, pizzicato cellos, flute, piccolo, electric guitar, ukulele, classical guitar, banjo, wood blocks. The list is long and testifies to the melodic richness of the soundtrack composed by Desplat. Wes Anderson also drew heavily on works or re-orchestrations by English composer Benjamin Britten, of whom he is a great admirer, to add musical color to his film.

Protective Lenses

Magnifying Effect

Glasses and binoculars are, for Wes Anderson, a way to protect oneself from the world. They either devour or obscure the face, as evidenced by Richie in *The Royal Tenenbaums* (2001), Peter Whitman in *The Darjeeling Limited* (2007), and Sam in *Moonrise Kingdom* (2012). Glasses can protect modesty (or hide emotions) and they can shield the wearer against the outside (and establish boundaries). Binoculars, for their part, allow one to observe without being seen and to refine one's gaze on the world to better prevent dangers and unpleasant surprises. The young heroine of *Moonrise Kingdom*, who discovers her mother's infidelity in this way, uses them to scan the horizon to temporarily escape the confines of her family and dream of a better life.

Scarlett Johansson in her typical 1950s tortoiseshell glasses, the period in which Asteroid City is set.

For rebel Suzy Bishop (Kara Hayward, *Moonrise Kingdom*), binoculars are a window on the outside world.

The beautiful swan has no idea it is in the binocular sights of ill-intentioned teenagers.

For all his confidence, Max Fischer (Jason Schwartzman, *Rushmore*) hides his eyes behind thick, dark frames.

The Whitman brothers (Owen Wilson, Adrien Brody, and Jason Schwartzman, *The Darjeeling Limited*) fight over their deceased father's glasses, which the younger brother jealously wears.

Wes Anderson ponders the best—and most complex—way to prepare a shot.

Wes's Good Shots

Lessons in Cinema

Regardless of the interest he arouses, Wes Anderson is universally regarded as an important director, a creator of forms of an unprecedented kind who, to put it crudely, creates something new out of something old. Known in fact for his rejection of modernity (of technology in the broadest sense, and digital in particular), over the years he has established and improved on an atypical modus operandi that enables him to film as one did in the 1950s (on 35 mm film, with virtually no digital effects or Steadicam view stabilizers) but with a sophistication worthy of and even considerably in excess of today's productions. "There came a time when I simply decided to do what I wanted. If I want a black-and-white sequence framed wide and with handheld camera, then that's how we shoot it. Can we do this part as a cartoon? Yes, we can, and we do. When I started shooting films, the same question kept coming up: 'Can we do this or that?' Today, I no longer ask myself that question. But to achieve that, and get a coherent film, you need to be able to rely on a great team."[1]

In the Beginning . . .

Present since the feature film *Bottle Rocket* (1996, only Anderson's two animated films were lit by someone else), cinematographer Robert Yeoman is a privileged witness to Anderson's style. According to Yeoman, the thinking behind the mise-en-scène has remained virtually invariable. "Whenever we start a movie, Wes and I watch DVDs of movies that have inspired us. Some relate to our film, some

Robert Yeoman and Sanjay Sami on the set of *Asteroid City*.

do not. We just use them as a springboard for ideas. [...] We also look at paintings, still photos, and even on occasion visit an art museum together. Wes puts together a library of DVDs and books that the cast and key crew members can check out to familiarize themselves with the visual journey that we are to begin."[2] Then comes the preparation time. "On our early films Wes would draw storyboards, and we would discuss them. We would go to the actual locations and see if they would work or if we had to accommodate the storyboards for the physical space. Our production designer was usually present, and we could all discuss the plan for how we would shoot, if we needed practical lighting, and many other considerations."[3] From the outset (with the exception of *Bottle Rocket*), the two men opted for wide-format anamorphic lenses and a strong color palette, choices they more or less maintained from film to film. "Wes and I have always been drawn to the 2.35/40 frame. It allows for several actors to be in the frame at the same time and makes for interesting possibilities in blocking. We also like the look of the anamorphic lenses, how they deal with spatial relationships and the out of focus backgrounds. [...] The colors of the walls, the costumes, the props are all carefully chosen and often tested on camera during prep."[4] The increasingly saturated chromatic palette (see *Asteroid City* [2023] and its ethereal pastel tones), the benefits from special treatment in postproduction, is one of Wes Anderson's rare concessions to technology. "There are so many digital tools that allow much greater control than in the old days,"[5] continues the cinematographer. Why deprive oneself?

A Very Animated Film Shoot

The first small revolution came in 2008, during the filming of *Fantastic Mr. Fox*, from which Robert Yeoman was to benefit on his next film, *Moonrise Kingdom* (2012). "Wes started making animatics, little cartoons of each scene which depicted camera moves, blocking of the actors, and compositions. He also voices each character so that we all can get the tone and pacing of the scene."[6] This crucial tool enabled Yeoman in particular to test complicated shots devised by the filmmaker in advance, with the help of crew members who stand in for the actors. "I like to get to the set before Wes, and we light and set the shot with our crew. We take a photo of our set up and send it to him for his comments. Sometimes he will ask to see it with a different lens, or move some props, etc. When we are close to what he wants, he comes to the set and makes any final adjustments before we shoot. When he arrives he likes to start shooting as soon as possible and spend his time working with the actors. [. . .] The actors also see the animatic, so they are well aware of what the plan is."[7]

The Quest for Perfection

Many actors dream of working with Wes Anderson, whose sense of dialogue and caricature is unique. There's no question of hamming it up with him; you're at the service of his art and his vision, which means adhering to strict instructions that the filmmaker communicates with phlegm and benevolence. Bob Balaban, one of his favorite actors, unraveled the mystery. "For certain scenes with multiple characters and a single shot, where both the camera and the characters are moving, we can end up doing thirty or forty takes in which everyone has to do exactly what they need to physically and emotionally, because Wes doesn't cut ([editor's note] he uses large-capacity film magazines). [...] I've never worked with someone so good at throwing me off my game and shaking up the whole cast without them ever feeling bullied or unbalanced: on the contrary, you feel like you're in someone's picture and you're burning to realize their idea, their dream."[8] Timothée Chalamet agrees with his colleague on this point. In *The French Dispatch* (2021), "There's a shot of about four seconds, where I pin a piece of paper to the wall before walking to a jukebox. We did something like forty-five takes. At one point, I thought, 'Again, really?' But I did it. These moments are inspiring because Wes surpasses himself, his quest for excellence is extremely fine-tuned and sharp, and what might have seemed random to me, for him represented the ultimate part of a profound reflection. If banality is the enemy of art, then Wes deserves a statue for overcoming it."[9]

The Lethal Weapon

Symmetrical shots, in which the actors must find their place, are one of the great constants of Wes Anderson's cinema. The same could be said of his millimeter-accurate timed camera movements, the

French second unit director Martin Scali deep in concentration.

The cast of *The Grand Budapest Hotel* in front of a matte painting set.

complexity of which has assumed a dazzling dimension in recent years due to the ingenuity of one man: Sanjay Sami, the Indian machinist who operates the dollies in every direction, those camera mounts on rails or wheels that enable Wes Anderson to achieve limpid dolly shots, punctuated by stops and restarts. In his early days, the filmmaker was "content" to follow someone (forward or backward) or to discover a landscape (in its width or height). Since working with Sanjay Sami on *The Darjeeling Limited* (2007), Anderson has learned that he can do this simultaneously in the same shot, without resorting to digital effects. To achieve this, the machinist and key grip imagined the most sophisticated manual devices (sometimes also the simplest), making him indispensable in the eyes of the filmmaker and Robert Yeoman, who has nothing but praise for his partner. "Sanjay is a master at camera mounts and we often use a golf cart for tracking actors down a street! He has a lot of experience and is a great collaborator. I appreciate his sense of humor."[10]

The Third Man

The memorable ski sequence in *The Grand Budapest Hotel* (2014) skillfully blends several techniques. The mountain landscapes are the result of chroma keying, backgrounds inserted in postproduction on green screens in front of which the actors performed. These specific shots were finalized by the second directing team, headed since *The Grand Budapest Hotel* by a Frenchman, Martin Scali, Wes Anderson's former personal assistant, who was trained in cinema. It was a challenge, at the time, for the novice "Martin's unit" (Wes Anderson's affectionate nickname for this crack team), according to Scali: "We shot these chroma keys from a helicopter, at an altitude of three thousand meters, doors open with freezing winds at seventy kilometer per hour blowing into the aircraft!"[11] Now a fixture on Anderson's sets, Martin Scali, then barely thirty, took over this position of trust from Roman Coppola, who had assumed it on *The Life Aquatic* (2004) and *The Darjeeling Limited*. His qualities? A perfect knowledge of Andersonian grammar and a spirit of initiative appreciated by the boss. Anderson relies on Martin's unit for shots without actors (with exceptions for hand, foot, and facial expressions), inserts, additive shots (made after the actual shoot), and time-consuming shots. "On *Asteroid City*, we shot the entire train sequence, the one over which the credits roll. It took us a month and was more complicated than it sounds. As it was a miniature train, we had to calculate the perspectives according to the scenery, which wasn't necessarily all to scale. We had to create dust, make the train run on rails, and place cameras, sometimes very close to the ground, on this moving machine…It was no easy task!"[12] Martin Scali was always ready for Anderson, with whom he shares the pleasure of directing. The secret of their complicity? "Wes understood that I was an ally, that his obsession with visual precision was also mine."[13]

CASTELLO CAVALCANTI

United States, Italy • 8 min • Color • Sound: ? • 2.35 : 1

Production Dates: **September 2012**
Distribution: **November 12, 2013**
(Rome International Film Festival and online)

Producers: **Roman Coppola, Jeremy Dawson, Julie Sawyer**
Executive Producers: **Max Brun, Lisa Margulis**

Screenplay: **Wes Anderson**
Director of Photography: **Darius Khondji**
Assistant Director: **Inti Carboni**
Editing: **Stephen Perkins**
Production Design: **Stefano Maria Ortolani**
Set Decoration: **Cristina Onori**
Art Direction: **Letizia Santucci**
Musical Supervision: **Alessandro Casella, Randall Poster**
Sound: **Diego Gualino**
Costumes: **Milena Canonero**
Casting: **Alessandro Cassella, Alice Filippi, Francesco Zippel**

Starring: **JASON SCHWARTZMAN** (Jed Cavalcanti), **GIADA COLAGRANDE** (Bartender), **GIORGIO ZANCOLLA** (Bartender), **PAOLO COLUCCIO** (Cook), **SILVANO BROGLIA** (Bus Driver), **FRANCESCO ZIPPEL** (Paparazzo), **LUCA PADRINI** (Young Priest), **FERNANDO LUMACA** (Uncle Michelangelo)...

“Wes re-created the atmosphere of the Italian cinema of the 1950s–1960s.”

Darius Khondji, director of photography

SYNOPSIS

September 1955, in the peaceful Italian village of Castello Cavalcanti. The social life that traditionally takes place in the only local square in the evening is disrupted by the arrival of a car race, the Molte Miglia. Jed Cavalcanti, an American driver, loses control of his car and crashes into a statue of Christ the Redeemer, right in the middle of the local residents. The angry driver receives help from the residents but barely pays them any attention. Noting the damage to his vehicle, he decides to wait for a bus to take him home. He takes a seat on the terrace and meets the older residents. He discovers that one of them is a distant grandfather, which brings him back to his Italian origins (as evidenced by his surname) and leads him to spend more time there than planned.

GENESIS

In the early 2010s, interaction between the major Franco-Italian luxury brands and cinema intensified, for reasons of image and prestige. Louis Vuitton, for example, supplied the suitcases used in *The Darjeeling Limited* (2007).

Advertorial

Prada was reinforcing its involvement in the film industry through prestigious sponsorships. It comes as no surprise therefore that the transalpine group approached Wes Anderson with an original proposal, somewhere between the disguised promotional object and a freely inspired short film. In *Castello Cavalcanti*, a tribute to Fellini, whom the filmmaker admires, only the “Prada Racing” flocking on the back of the American driver’s fluorescent yellow racing suit identifies the luxury brand. Nothing else distinguishes this nostalgic, offbeat little film from the rest of the American director’s output.

FILMING AND PRODUCTION

Filming was scheduled to take place in the backlot of the Cinecittà studios in Rome, where it would be easy to find the kind of typical Italian village that Anderson was looking for. In the meantime, he was looking for a cinematographer to replace Robert Yeoman, who was probably absorbed by other projects—none of the people interviewed for this book can remember the reasons for this change of technician. The filmmaker instinctively thought of Darius Khondji, whose stylized, colorful lighting worked wonders for other directors, such as Danny Boyle, David Fincher, James Gray, and Wong Kar-wai.

New Lenses

The French cinematographer was delighted at the idea of collaborating with Anderson, whom he had never met but whose films he liked. The two men met in Paris and hit it off immediately. Things then moved very quickly: two days before shooting, in September 2012, they found the location where they would build the set, and then shot *Castello Cavalcanti* in two nights. Khondji has fond memories of the shoot: “As always with Wes, we shot on film with anamorphic Cinemascope lenses. However, we couldn’t get the Panavision lenses he usually uses in time. So I suggested he opt for Cooke lenses, which I like to work with, but whose lenses are very slightly different (they’re softer on

The car race Molte Miglia is an explicit reference to the Mille Miglia, an Italian endurance race.

Jason Schwartzman (center) stars as Italian race car driver Jed Cavalcanti, who crashes his car.

skin texture and color). As it happens, these lenses are historically associated with Fellini, Visconti, or Pasolini…He was so enthusiastic about the Cooke lenses that he used them again for *The Grand Budapest Hotel*."[1]

Inducted

Khondji rubbed shoulders on the set with Wes Anderson regulars: actor Jason Schwartzman, who plays the lead role; Roman Coppola, who officiates as technical director; and Milena Canonero,

In this scene, Italian commentary from the (1979) French Formula 1 Grand Prix 1 can be heard in the background.

Anderson's style remains unchanged, even with two different cinematographers (Darius Khondji and Robert Yeoman).

the costume designer. "I was very well received by his crew."[2] He was especially impressed by Sanjay Sami, the machinist who had managed the dolly mount's movements since *The Darjeeling Limited*. "He's incredibly precise, getting the dolly from one place to another at the exact speed Wes wants!"[3] With a very positive experience of their collaboration, Wes Anderson and Darius Khondji reunited a few weeks later to shoot the three "Prada Candy" spots.

These *Asteroid City* vending machines were designed by the Miniatures department, supervised by Simon Weisse.

Continuous Information

(In Case You Missed the Beginning)

Wes Anderson's films are instantly recognizable for many reasons, one of the most surprising of which is the abundance of written and spoken cues, not only the diegetic ones (i.e., those originating from the world portrayed by the film). The mainspring of this narrative profusion is comic. In *Rushmore* (1998), Anderson accentuates the offbeat nature of Max Fischer's many and strange extracurricular activities (theater, fencing, beekeeping, etc.) by creating a succession of titled playlets in fixed shots. He then used and amplified this device in *The Royal Tenenbaums* (2001), the first film to be filled with annotations and inscriptions of all kinds. Margot's secret deviations, uncovered by the private detective hired by her estranged husband, Raleigh St. Clair, are depicted in almost telegraphic style and without words: "Age 21—Rive Gauche" (she flirts with a naked girl), "Publicity Tour—Age 24" (she allows herself to be touched by a mature man), "Papua New Guinea—Age 25" (she kisses a painted warrior), and so on.

The Written Word, "For Your Information"

For Wes Anderson, the written word has a dual function: both narrative and aesthetic. As well as shedding light, usually amusingly, on something (the whimsical nature of the vending machines in *Asteroid City* (2023), ranging from drinks to real estate) or someone ("Unaccompanied minor," written on the sign carried by visiting cousin Kristofferson in *Fantastic Mr. Fox* [2009]), they dress up the image in the same way as a set element. Billboards, signs, plans, maps, labels, stamps, badges, book covers, containers (boxes, cartons), and newspapers have gradually invaded, if not saturated, Anderson's cinema. Is this a criticism of the information society? Possibly, but unlikely. More modestly, the written word is a major component of Andersonian grammar, characterized by an acute sense of derision that it tends to highlight. In *The Royal Tenenbaums*, when the child protagonists are introduced, the activities of each of them are specified, at the same

An old-school journalist at his mechanical typewriter, pipe in mouth like Monsieur Hulot.

time as they are shown on screen—"Drum set" is thus inscribed on the image of Richie playing his instrument of choice. This form of visual pleonasm is used above all to capture the imagination and elicit a smile, less so to support any kind of demonstration.

"Once Upon a Time," or the Role of the Narrator

The Royal Tenenbaums introduces a special character in Wes Anderson's universe: the narrator, the first informant. The unseen Alec Baldwin gives the narrator his warm timbre; in voice-over, in the great tradition of Hollywood cinema, he tells parts of the family story without holding back from passing judgment, with a particular tone and mood, often using irony. In *The Life Aquatic* (2004), this detached narration becomes more unpredictable. The documentary about the ship *Belafonte* and its crew, which constitutes a film—narrated by commander Steve Zissou—within the film, enables Anderson to provide details of life on board. From *Moonrise Kingdom* (2012) onward, the director, like the German-born French filmmaker Max Ophüls before him (*La Ronde*, 1950), gives the narrator a more central, embodied role. Like Monsieur Loyal in the circus, he becomes the arbiter of good taste, announcing good news and bad. During a scene, he even communicates with the protagonists and shares their misfortune! This is also the case for the half-blind mongrel in *Isle of Dogs* (2018), who starts out as a simple commentator on events, but then becomes part of the action. Conversely, an established character can become a narrator over the course of the film. The elderly bellhop Zero (*The Grand Budapest Hotel*, 2014), for example, delivers, live or in voice-over, the story of his life to the writer whom he has befriended. Henry Sugar (*The Wonderful Story of Henry Sugar*, 2023) does the same, as does columnist J. K. L. Berensen (*The French Dispatch*, 2021), a symbol of the profession of journalism that fascinates the director.

Headlines, References to Journalism

If *The French Dispatch* is a tribute to the famous American weekly magazine *The New Yorker*, which forged his intellectual identity, Wes Anderson did not wait for his tenth feature film to multiply his references to journalism. As early as *Rushmore*, Max Fischer feeds his own gazette with news from his high school. The young Tenenbaum prodigies make the headlines in economic, financial, cultural, and sports news. Many of the characters are journalists or reporters: Jane Winslett-Richardson (*The Life Aquatic*), Mr. Fox (*Fantastic Mr. Fox*), Augie Steenbeck (*Asteroid City*) and, of course, the editors of *The French Dispatch*. In *Isle of Dogs*, much of the action is covered by television, a less "noble" medium that Anderson associates with sensationalism when he reiterates from film to film his admiration for journalism, the most legitimate vehicle for conveying information in his opinion–carefully read press clippings abound. Does one need to look further for his love of the written word?

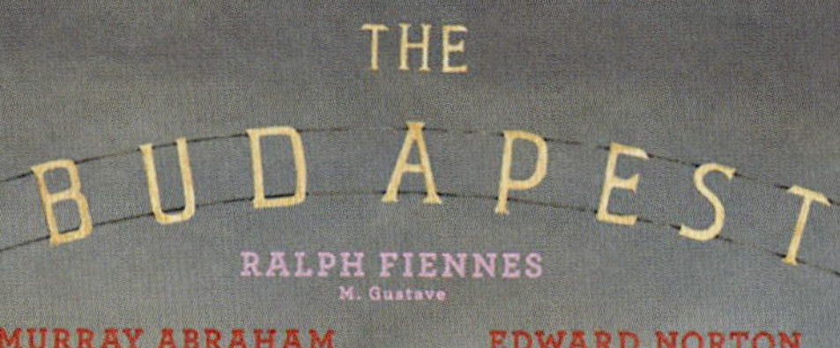
THE
GRAND BUDAPEST HOTEL
RALPH FIENNES
M. Gustave
F. MURRAY ABRAHAM
Mr. Moustafa
EDWARD NORTON
Henckels
MATHIEU AMALRIC
Serge
SAOIRSE RONAN
Agatha
ADRIEN BRODY
Dmitri
WILLEM DAFOE
Jopling
LÉA SEYDOUX
Clotilde
JEFF GOLDBLUM
Kovacs
JASON SCHWARTZMAN
M. Jean
JUDE LAW
Young Writer
TILDA SWINTON
Madame D.
HARVEY KEITEL
Ludwig
TOM WILKINSON
Author
BILL MURRAY
M. Ivan
OWEN WILSON
M. Chuck
introducing
TONY REVOLORI
Zero
in a film by
WES ANDERSON
GRAND BUDAPEST
FOX SEARCHLIGHT PICTURES Presents in Association with INDIAN PAINTBRUSH
A STUDIO BABELSBERG Production An AMERICAN EMPIRICAL PICTURE "THE GRAND BUDAPEST HOTEL"
U.S. Casting by DOUGLAS AIBEL U.K. Casting by JINA JAY Costume Designer MILENA CANONERO Original Music by ALEXANDRE DESPLAT
Music Supervisor RANDALL POSTER Editor BARNEY PILLING Production Designer ADAM STOCKHAUSEN Director of Photography ROBERT YEOMAN, A.S.C.
Co-Producer JANE FRAZER Executive Producers MOLLY COOPER CARL WOEBCKEN CHRISTOPH FISSER HENNING MOLFENTER
Produced by WES ANDERSON SCOTT RUDIN STEVEN RALES JEREMY DAWSON Story by WES ANDERSON & HUGO GUINNESS
Screenplay by WES ANDERSON 2014 Directed by WES ANDERSON
GRANDBUDAPESTHOTEL.COM

THE GRAND BUDAPEST HOTEL

United Kingdom, United States, Germany	**1 h 39**	**Color, Black and White**	**SDDS** - Datasat - Dolby Digital - Dolby Surround 7.1	**1.85 : 1**

Production Dates: **May–June 2011**
World Premiere: **February 6, 2014 (Berlin Film Festival)**
Release Dates in the United States: **March 7, 2014 (limited release); March 28, 2014**

Budget: **Approx. $25 million**
North America Box Office: **Approx. $59 million**
Worldwide Box Office: **Approx. $175 million**

Production Companies: **Fox Searchlight Pictures, Indian Paintbrush, Studio Babelsberg, American Empirical Pictures, TSG Entertainment, Scott Rudin Productions**
Producers: **Wes Anderson, Jeremy Dawson, Steven Rales, Scott Rudin**
Co-Producers: **Eli Bush, Jane Fraser**
Executive Producers: **Molly Cooper, Christoph Fisser, Henning Molfenter, Charlie Woebcken**
Associate Producer: **Octavia Peissel**

Screenplay: **Wes Anderson, based on a story by Wes Anderson and Hugo Guinness**
Director of Photography: **Robert Yeoman**
First Assistant Director: **Josh Robertson**
Second Unit Director: **Martin Scali**
Film Editing: **Barney Pilling**
Production Design: **Adam Stockhausen**
Set Decoration: **Anna Pinnock**
Art Direction: **Gerald Sullivan**
Music: **Alexandre Desplat**
Costumes: **Milena Canonero**
Makeup: **Mark Coulier, Frances Hannon**
Miniatures : **Simon Weisse**
Puppet Fabricator: **Magda Bieszczak, Andy Gent**
Graphic Design: **Annie Atkins**
Casting: **Henry Russell Bergstein, Deborah Maxwell Dion**

Starring: **RALPH FIENNES (M. Gustave), TONY REVOLORI (Zero), F. MURRAY ABRAHAM (Mr. Moustafa), JUDE LAW (Young Writer), TOM WILKINSON (Author), SAOIRSE RONAN (Agatha), ADRIEN BRODY (Dmitri), WILLEM DAFOE (Jopling), TILDA SWINTON (Madame D.), JEFF GOLDBLUM (Deputy Kovacs), HARVEY KEITEL (Ludwig), OWEN WILSON (M. Chuck), EDWARD NORTON (Henckels), MATHIEU AMALRIC (Serge X.), LÉA SEYDOUX (Clotilde), BILL MURRAY (M. Ivan), JASON SCHWARTZMAN (M. Jean)...**

"I really think that, with Wes, it's best to keep it simple. [...] And I should also say this: There was a speed element. Throughout, Wes kept saying, 'Faster, faster, faster.'"

—

Ralph Fiennes,
on the director's direction of the actor[1]

SYNOPSIS

In the late 1960s, in a Central European spa town, a writer meets the owner of a deserted hotel, Zero Moustafa. The former bellhop tells him his story. In 1932, he became assistant to M. Gustave, the head concierge of the then flourishing Grand Budapest Hotel. Authoritarian and fastidious, M. Gustave has one weakness: wealthy old women. Madame D. was his oldest conquest. On her unexplained death, he inherited a priceless painting, which infuriated the deceased's son, Dmitri. With Zero's help, the concierge steals what is owed to him. A series of incredible adventures follow, with M. Gustave going to prison and Dmitri revealing his demonic side. This burlesque comedy also features a wonderful pastry, "la courtisane au chocolat," and a perfume, "l'air de panache," poetic and whimsical bulwarks against the brutality of a changing old Europe.

GENESIS

English illustrator Hugo Guinness befriended Wes Anderson in 1998, when he moved to New York from London. From friendship, their relationship also gradually turned professional: for the American director, the artist painted the eccentric pictures that adorn Eli Cash's apartment in *The Royal Tenenbaums* (2001) and lent his voice to the villainous farmer Bunce in *Fantastic Mr. Fox* (2009). The two men had always exchanged ideas, and their imaginations were inspired when they came into contact with a friend of Guinness's, an avid traveler who had spent his life in hotels listening to concierges gossip.

The Stefan Zweig Shock

M. Gustave, the prim little chef who becomes the hero of *The Grand Budapest Hotel*, was still a long way from materializing. For the time being, Anderson, who had lived in Paris since 2005, discovered a book in a Paris bookshop that would change his life: Stefan Zweig's *Ungeduld des Herzens* (*Beware of Pity*; 1939). In the Viennese writer's only completed novel, an Austrian lieutenant finds himself chained to a rich, crippled young woman whom he seduces in spite of himself, and whom he dares not force, out of compassion. Not for the first time, the filmmaker, dazzled by this prose, seriously considered adapting a literary work. He was all the more troubled that Zweig was renowned for his dandyism and cosmopolitanism, qualities he shared with him. Another sign: every time the director strolled through the Luxembourg Gardens, he passed the bust of Zweig. Symbolically, in the final script for *The Grand Budapest Hotel*, Anderson recalls this essential discovery with the statue of the great fictional author that opens the film and the character of Agatha, Zero's beloved young pastry chef, half of whose face is covered in a birthmark (an allusion to the infirmity of the heroine in *Beware of Pity*).

Hello, Hugo?

Anderson continued his immersion in the work of Zweig. He was particularly fond of the narrative mode of the writer who relates his stories in the manner of Russian dolls, giving voice to storytellers who themselves relate tales entrusted to them. *The Royal Tenenbaums* and *Moonrise Kingdom* (2012) functioned in this way, but in a less sophisticated way than in Zweig's writings. This was an avenue the filmmaker was keen to explore, and one that would lead to the film's multilayered narrative: it begins in 1985 with a first narrator, then teleports to

Boy with Apple was painted for the film by Michael Taylor.

1968 (the time of hegemonic communism), before settling in 1932 with a second narrator—and back and forth between the eras. During this reflective process, which lasted several years and saw him abandon the project to adapt *Beware of Pity*, Anderson continued to discuss his progress, mainly by telephone, with Guinness. The two men came to speculate that a concierge, inspired by the man who had become their mutual friend, could be the hero of a film set in Zweig's time, between the wars, in Central Europe. And why should he not have a young disciple who would blindly obey him? The screenplay was beginning to take shape.

Tentacular

Anderson wrote alone, inspired by some of Guinness's insights, in particular the idea of the painting inherited by M. Gustave, which led to a number of twists and turns (*Boy with Apple* was created especially for the film by artist Michael Taylor). He also drew on his ongoing reading of Zweig and books on the two world wars, which fascinated this enthusiastic student of history, geopolitics, and philosophy. The director adhered to the interpretation of former

F. Murray Abraham (Zero as an older man, left) opposite Jude Law (Young Writer, right) in the faded decor of the Grand Budapest Hotel.

American diplomat Dean Acheson, author of a scholarly essay published in 1969, *Present at the Creation: My Years in the State Department*. "His interpretation is that there was [...] a single war of German aggression in two movements. And I thought that would suit our story, to think of things that way, even though we don't even have real Germans. I don't think that theory probably has a lot of stock in academic circles, but I liked it, certainly for our own dramatic purposes."[2] *The Grand Budapest Hotel* is indeed about an imaginary country, Zubrowka, plagued by chronic instability and haunted by the specter of war and the rise of a totalitarianism clearly demarcated from fascism. Anderson plays on the contrasts between a fairytale world, embodied by the candy-pink hotel (like the packaging for Mendl's cakes, named after the pastry shop where the gentle Agatha works) and its smiling employees, and the violent, sinister reality of the outside world. Everyone suffers from this permanent state of war, but they do what they can not to let it show. This feeling of unease eventually contaminates the story, however, when the protagonists drop their masks and reveal their true personalities.

The Only Captain of the Ship

As Anderson's ambition was to make an uplifting and moving fantasy, he revisited old American comedies from the 1930s–1940s made by Central European expatriates such as Ernst Lubitsch. *To Be or Not to Be* (1942), with its comic treatment of the war and its multiple *coups de théâtre* (which do not preclude depth and height of vision), thus exerted a major influence on him. Anderson also explored the Library of Congress website, which is teeming with photochromes (colorized black-and-white images) of early twentieth-century Europe. These incredible documents gave him a clearer picture of the visual universe he wanted to create, the most spectacular of which, inspired by existing European buildings, would be the hotel that gave the film its title. After a trial run in England by a colorist to obtain the aesthetic of photochromes, the Texan abandoned the idea. *The Grand Budapest Hotel* is the first film in which Anderson is credited as the sole screenwriter—based on a story imagined with Hugo Guinness.

CASTING

On July 16, 2012, the American media announced that Johnny Depp would be joining the cast of Wes Anderson's new film. The star of *Pirates of the Caribbean* (Jerry Bruckheimer and Walt Disney Pictures, 2003–2017) would be joining an already prestigious cast that included Anderson regulars (Jason Schwartzman, Bill Murray, Jeff Goldblum) and newcomers (Ralph Fiennes, Jude Law, Saoirse Ronan, Angela Lansbury). By the end of 2012, the list was growing. Other regulars joined the

All the film's uniforms came from the Hero Collection specialized costume workshop, based in Poland.

Tony Revolori (Zero, as a younger man) and Ralph Fiennes (M. Gustave) in a Grand Budapest Hotel compartment.

Mr. Gustave seduces many women as he embarks on a quest for fortune and priceless art.

adventure: Willem Dafoe, Adrien Brody, Owen Wilson, Edward Norton, Tilda Swinton, and Harvey Keitel. Meanwhile, F. Murray Abraham and France's Mathieu Amalric (whom Anderson admired and discovered in the small world of Paris) were carving out a place for themselves in what promised to be one of the cinematic events of the future. In the meantime, Depp had dropped off the radar. According to Anderson, there was never any question of him being in the film. The legendary Angela Lansbury (*Murder She Wrote* [1984–1996]; *Bedknobs and Broomsticks* [Robert Stevenson, 1971]), eighty-six years old at the time, had to decline the proposal due to her overloaded schedule. A little later, we learned that French actress Léa Seydoux, with whom Anderson had just shot a short film for Prada, had joined the cast to play the small role of Clotilde, an intrepid maid.

A Studious Actor

Wes Anderson, who had been friends with English actor Ralph Fiennes for a number of years, naturally considered working with him. For *Moonrise Kingdom*, he had written a role for him, but left him out of the final version. The two men had been looking for each other, waiting for the right opportunity to take on the guise of the concierge M. Gustave. Anderson was convinced that with Ralph Fiennes's haughty bearing and very British elocution, he was the ideal candidate to embody this figure of a disappearing world. Fiennes did not hesitate for a second. Keen to blend in with the character, this follower of the Actors Studio method (which involves actors letting their inner selves express themselves rather than "playing" a role) submitted his suggestions to the director. "If I remember correctly, I said something to him like, 'Wes, there's a spectrum about the way Gustave can be played. High camp, hyper, sort of crazy, or very naturalistically.' It ended up being somewhere in the middle. I think that in most of the takes that he ended up using, he went for the slightly more understated bits."[3] Among Anderson's gallery of characters, M. Gustave appears to be the most over-excited. Ralph Fiennes inoculated him with a little of his eccentricity.

Auditioned with his older brother, Tony Revolori landed the role of Zero. He has since reappeared in *The French Dispatch* and *Asteroid City*.

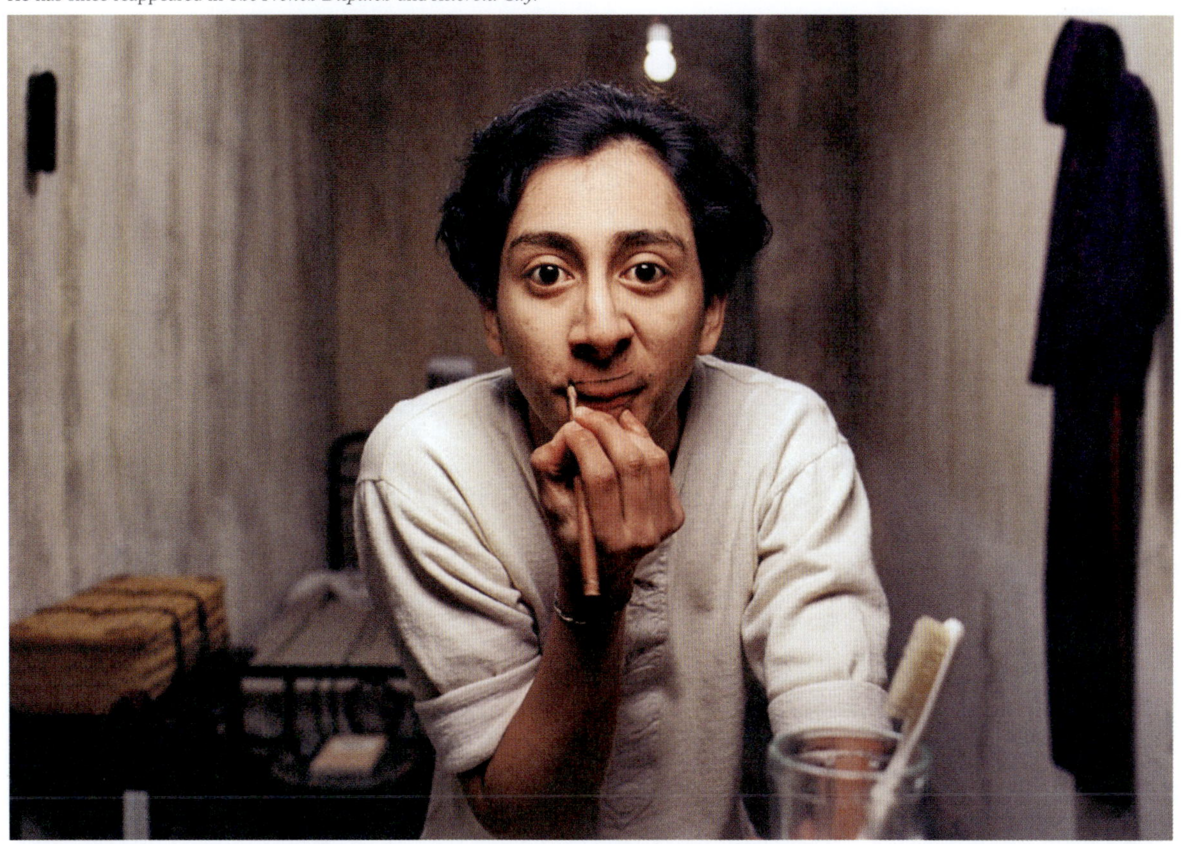

To make her look appropriately aged, Tilda Swinton (as Madame D) required five hours of makeup time prior to shooting each day.

(Top) A photochrome of the Grandhotel Pupp in Karlovy Vary, Czechia. (Bottom) A postcard painting of the real Grand Hotel Hungaria in Budapest.

Fraternal Casting

Zero Moustafa, a down-and-out nobody who ends up a millionaire by following Mr. Gustave's instructions, was the most complicated role to cast. Wes Anderson envisaged a fairly young, unknown actor with Arab features for this character. As with *Rushmore* (1998) and *Moonrise Kingdom*, the difficulty lay in finding the right novice actor. After auditions in the US, Europe, North Africa, and the Middle East, it all came together in Los Angeles, when two brothers of Guatemalan origin presented themselves to an Anderson casting director for a reading. Mario Revolori, the eldest, and Tony Revolori had a little experience: they had played small roles in film and television, but nothing of note. Their attempts were convincing. The director hesitated between them, but decided on the younger of the two. "I found out later that he saw my brother's audition first and thought it was really interesting. Then he saw mine and said, 'We're done, that's Zero!'"[4] Mario Revolori was happy for his younger brother, and went on to enjoy a successful career on screen.

A Hotel for Every Situation

Enchanted by his collective experience on *Moonrise Kingdom*, where part of the crew stayed in a rented house not far from the shooting location, Anderson this time gathered all the actors with him in a hotel in Görlitz, the eastern German border town where the main sets were located. Makeup and costume fittings were carried out on site, for the sake of efficiency. This way, when Tilda Swinton had to wait five hours to be aged (her character, Madame D., wears her eighty-four years with pride!), she felt less alone. To thank him for his contribution and for the inconvenience caused, Anderson offered a role as an extra to the owner of the hotel in question.

FILMING AND PRODUCTION

After extensive location scouting in Central Europe and Italy, Wes Anderson finally settled on Görlitz. This historic Saxon town, bordering Poland and the Czech Republic, boasts a varied architectural heritage and was chosen as the main location for the film, as were several others in the surrounding area. In order to concentrate shooting locations and spare the production expensive logistics, he crisscrossed the area by golf cart with his two faithful lieutenants, director of photography Robert Yeoman and art director Adam Stockhausen. The story does not say whether the three men discovered the Chemnitz thermal baths (for the bathing sequence between the elderly Zero Moustafa [F. Murray Abraham] and the young writer [Jude Law]), 110 miles from the hotel.

The Perfect Illusion

In Görlitz, the film crew took over the Görlitzer Warenhaus, an unoccupied five-story former shopping mall with an ideal structure, according to Robert Yeoman. "It was open in the middle with a beautiful skylight. We were able to build many of our hotel interiors including the hotel lobby with complete control. The top floor was reserved for production offices, art department, wardrobe, and make up."[5] The set decoration department set about

Photochrome of the Hotel Schafbergspitze in Austria, another inspiration for the film's setting.

transforming the place into a shimmering 1930s palace. Adam Stockhausen scrutinized every detail. For example, the klubeck, the film's imaginary currency, had to be properly minted. Meanwhile, property master Robin Miller and graphic artist Annie Atkins spent countless hours designing the famous Mendl's boxes, emblematic of the film's intentional kitsch. Once the impressive model of the Grand Budapest Hotel was completed, many little hands busied themselves concealing it behind plasterboard and false ceilings. Stockhausen's ingenious idea was to build the hotel's 1960s set on top of the 1930s one, and to shoot in reverse order, i.e. starting with the scenes set in 1968, at the time when communism had triumphed, but with a dull aesthetic. It then sufficed to dismantle and break down the false walls to make way for the first set.

An Impressive Wardrobe

As Anderson's second period film in a row, *The Grand Budapest Hotel*'s baroque excess demanded a great deal of research and finesse in its reconstruction. For the costumes, designer Milena Canonero drew her inspiration from old films and photographs from the interwar period. She also used refined materials, such as a "purple and mauve facecloth, which is a very densely woven wool used to make military uniforms."[6] Unfortunately, at a certain point, this fabric ran out. A German wool supplier came to the rescue, according to costume supervisor Patricia Colin. "He had fabrics in all shades and weights. You could have it dyed any color you wanted, and have clean edges cut, it didn't fray! A marvel."[7] For the outfits worn by the eccentric Madame D., Milena Canonero pulled out all the stops: silk velvet was used and the motifs on her yellow dress were hand-painted; the luxury brand Fendi took care of making the old aristocrat's muff, as well as the black mink trim on her cape and hat. For Patricia Colin, the film marked a turning point, so colossal was the energy deployed. "We really started to work on the costume in detail."[8]

Matte painting by Italian artist Simone de Salvatore.

Below: Willem Dafoe (left) plays the killer "creature" to Adrien Brody's sinister heir.
On the right: Officer Henckels (Edward Norton, foreground) proves to be more compassionate than others.

Resolving Complex Equations

Wes Anderson and his close collaborators found many tricks to optimize the shoot by centralizing it as much as possible. The train occupied by M. Gustave and Zero for two of the film's crucial scenes, for example, is a set built on the site of the dining room that once housed the elderly Zero and the author. To simulate the snowy landscape behind the window of their compartment, stagehands waved large white silks that were overlit from behind. On the other hand, Anderson had to be cunning when it came to the soldiers who occasionally appeared on the horizon, as he avoided as far as possible the use of green screens—on which the scene in question, previously shot on location, could be digitally integrated. The crew therefore detached the collapsible compartment and placed it on a dolly (for movement), so that Robert Yeoman could frame all the actors in the same shot. The cinematographer remembers the difficult weather conditions. "It was painfully cold in eastern Germany in the winter. Even our interiors were cold (I am thinking about our prison and the baths in particular). Also our window of light was approximately 8:30 a.m. to 4 p.m., so we did not have much time for our day exteriors. [...] Wes constantly challenges us all to work outside of our comfort zone and find unique solutions to bring to the film."[9] The same spirit of resourcefulness governed the ski chase of Jopling—Dmitri's hired killer—by M. Gustave and Zero. The sequence required a mix of live action (with the actors placed on a slope and receiving wind and smoke in their faces), frame-by-frame animation (with miniature sleds zigzagging dangerously), and green screens (on which mountain images were projected).

Highly Formatted

Absorbed in the story, viewers may not realize that there are three image formats in the film: 1:1.37 (known as square format), 1:1.85 (today's standard format), and 1:2.40 (wide format), which correspond respectively to the 1930s, 1980s, and

1960s, when they were most widely used. Robert Yeoman had his hands full. "The different aspect ratios would change compositions. It was a challenge to fit several people in the 1:37 frame!"[10] In the end, all these formats were fitted into a 1:1.85 frame, a technical feat achieved in postproduction. "I was skeptical at first that this would work, but after I saw a test during prep I realized that it was going to work perfectly. I credit Wes."[11]

RECEPTION

The Grand Budapest Hotel was unveiled with great ceremony at the Berlin Film Festival, which it opened on February 6, 2014. The press reception was enthusiastic. A few days later, the film won the Jury Grand Prix at the Berlin Film Festival, the second prestigious international distinction awarded to Wes Anderson's work—following the Cristal awarded by the Annecy International Animation Film Festival in 2010 to *Fantastic Mr. Fox*. This was the start of a tidal wave of undreamt-of proportions.

FOR WES ADDICTS

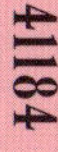

The prisoner character played by Harvey Keitel is adorned with tattoos. On his left arm, he has a mysterious tattoo consisting of three letters, "MAV." This refers precisely to the identical tattoo worn by the anarchist Père Jules in the French film classic *L'Atalante* (Jean Vigo, 1934). "MAV" is actually an acronym for "Mort Aux Vaches" (Death to Cows). Another wink: executor Vilmos Kovacs (played by Jeff Goldblum) pays tribute to Hungarian-born American cinematographers Vilmos Zsigmond and László Kovács.

Zero (Tony Revolori) and Agatha (Saoirse Ronan) in the middle of the famous Mendl's boxes designed for the film.

MENDL'S
MENDL'S
MENDL'S
MENDL'S
MENDL'S
MENDL'S
MENDL'S
MENDL'S

Sulfurous Tableaux

At one point in the story, M. Gustave and Zero replace the valuable painting bequeathed by Madame D. with a highly erotic one, inspired by the work *Lesbian Couple*, 1916, by rising star Egon Schiele, the Austrian Expressionist artist who died in 1918, at age twenty-eight. Titled *Two Lesbians Masturbating*, this one was painted by American illustrator Rich Pellegrino, a regular contributor to San Francisco's annual "Bad Dads" exhibition. This art event featured creations related to Wes Anderson's films.

Viral Marketing

Distributor Fox Searchlight was convinced of the film's potential and launched an original marketing campaign. Works of art inspired by the film's world were specially created (under the supervision of Adam Stockhausen) and auctioned off, creating an immediate buzz. Videos, posted online to explain how to bake Mendl's pastries in the style of the famous chocolate-filled "courtesan," generated a similar buzz, prompting internet users to post images of their creations; Fox used these in spots broadcast on cooking channels. On Spotify, users could access playlists dedicated to the film's secondary characters and their imaginary musical tastes. The concierge M. Ivan (Bill Murray), for example, purportedly loved English dance bands, while his young colleague M. Jean (Jason Schwartzman) would prefer rock pioneers like Buddy Holly. The icing on the cake: a faux educational site centered on the invented country of Zubrowka provided cultural "information" on this flourishing republic before it descended into war.

A Total Triumph

Anderson's loyal audience, which had expanded to include young people since *Fantastic Mr. Fox* and *Moonrise Kingdom*, responded massively, joined by a cohort of new admirers. Indeed, *The Grand Budapest Hotel* had a unifying effect like never before: not only was it the director's biggest North American success (ahead of *The Royal Tenenbaums*); it was also a triumph worldwide, where Anderson was increasingly establishing himself as a must-see filmmaker. The impressive total takings ($175 million, i.e., almost 30 percent of all Wes Anderson films to date!) rewarded the hard work and tenacity of this extraordinary artist, who had succeeded in imposing his singular style without ever conceding any-

Wes Anderson gives Tony Revolori and Ralph Fiennes their final direction for the film's grand, final sequence.

thing to fashion or the system. *The Grand Budapest Hotel* is an exemplary illustration of a method patiently established with regular collaborators and reinforced by the unfailing support of producers such as Scott Rudin, in the early days, and of Steven Rales, since *The Darjeeling Limited.* The five BAFTAs (the annual British awards) and four Oscars (for music, sets, costumes, and makeup/hair) that the film won in 2015 attest to the new dimension Anderson had taken on.

The theatrical world of *Asteroid City*, with its naive artificiality.

The Vintage Look

A Passion for the Handmade

Margot's zebra wallpaper and the Twiggy look in *The Royal Tenenbaums* (2001), the Cousteau beanies in *The Life Aquatic* (2004), the retro orange palette in *The Darjeeling Limited* (2007), the old-fashioned scout outfits in *Moonrise Kingdom* (2012), the Art Deco style of *The Grand Budapest Hotel* (2014), the patchwork of aesthetic influences (from the 1950s to the 1970s) in *The French Dispatch* (2021)...Throughout his prolific career, Wes Anderson has defined a unique, unmistakable visual universe that draws its inspiration from the past and old-fashioned working methods, a past digested and transformed by the director-dandy—always impeccably dressed in a tweed jacket—who benefits from the expertise of carefully selected technicians and craftsmen. From preparatory drawings to sets, graphic design, costumes, and miniatures, we may decipher, with the main players involved, the Anderson method with its famous vintage rendering.

SKETCHBOOKS

Turlo Griffin is a conceptual artist and illustrator who has worked regularly for Wes Anderson since *Fantastic Mr. Fox* (2009), a film for which he created a large number of environments on his drawing board (such as the beech tree in which the foxes live, their living room, and the canvases that adorn his walls). It is he who gives the director's vision its first incarnation and initial variations.

Preparatory Sketches

The process Griffin encountered on *Fantastic Mr. Fox* had not changed much since, whether on animated or live-action films. "Usually, I would get a storyboard frame, or series of them, plotting out all the angles of a certain scene, with direction from Nelson Lowry or Adam Stockhausen via Wes, along with the carefully chosen references. Then I go about making it look real, lived in, and solid. [...] I might start small with a fully realized thumbnail sketch, because a large, detailed pencil drawing can take a while, so it's good to have worked out beforehand what you're going to do. I'll take the finished drawing, scan it in, and work it up in photoshop. [...] There will be back-and-forths of notes from Wes. Sometimes it will need to be redone, with several versions, but on occasions, he's approved the first draft."[1]

Atmosphere, Atmosphere

The working story lines plotted out enable the illustrators to orientate their creations more precisely, as they enjoy more freedom than one might imagine. "We would normally get very specific direction for what period the film should look like. There's usually a folder of impeccably researched vintage photos that are really helpful in showing how he wants it to end up. We take little bits from here and there, never copying something completely, and we always have to do further research ourselves."[2] The retro-futuristic world of *Isle of Dogs* (2018) is thus based on the 1960s idea of the future in films such as *You Only Live Twice* (Lewis Gilbert, 1967). From there one must extrapolate, knowing that nothing is set in stone. For *Fantastic Mr. Fox*, visually anchored in the 1970s, Griffin received an anachronistic request from the Texan director: "The animals' HQ in the sewer was based on Churchill's underground war bunker!"[3] The unpredictable director pushes artists out of their comfort zones. "When you work on a Wes Anderson project, you're pretty much surrendering your personal style to his own. I can only offer my artistic expertise to make it look as good as I can. [...] The final result will be somewhere you would never have got to by yourself alone."[4]

NUMBERS AND LETTERS

Born in Japan to a French father and Japanese mother, Erica Dorn has a degree in graphic design. She was working in branding and illustration in London when she was asked to work on *Isle of Dogs*. Over the years, she has become head of the graphics department on Wes Anderson's films, responsible for lettering in the broadest sense (which may include calligraphy and typography), a crucial task that contributes to the antiquated aesthetic sought by the filmmaker.

Density

Like Griffin, Dorn begins her work well in advance of the shoot, taking as her starting point the references that Anderson passes on to her. "He gives us access to film archives from the 1950s and 1960s, often in black and white, which are part of his inspiration. [...] For *Isle of Dogs*, it was mainly the films of Yasujirō Ozu and Akira Kurosawa. For *The French Dispatch*, it was films by Jacques Tati, Jean Renoir, Jacques Becker, Jean-Luc Godard, Henri-Georges Clouzot...The list goes on. Sometimes it's just for a scene; other times, for the colors or the atmosphere."[5] Dorn and her team hand-draw and paint all the texts and graphics for the films, sometimes collaborating with the set decoration team, sometimes with the costumes team, and sometimes with the accessories team. "The graphics have to fit into the world imagined by Wes and Adam Stockhausen. It has to be recognizable and legible, which is sometimes difficult because Wes likes to place a lot of text in the image."[6]

A Common Language

Dorn does not limit herself to simple lettering. Her department can, for example, design floor tiles in false perspective (each tile has a unique shape!) or create vintage wallpaper and fabric. For Dorn, the filmmaker's retro tastes are a matter of instinct. "He systematically rejects anything that seems too digital, too contemporary, or otherwise too 'pastiche.' He is drawn to artisanal aesthetics. When it's handmade, imperfections emerge naturally—like the spaces between words. But it can't be too messy either! It's a delicate balance to be struck."[7] With experience, Erica Dorn has come to anticipate Wes Anderson's wishes. "We have a common language that took me a while to learn [...] His preferences became my preferences."[8]

The retro-futuristic world in *You Only Live Twice* inspired *Isle of Dogs*.

Wes Anderson on the *Asteroid City* train seat, on display at the Musée Cinéma et Miniature in Lyon, France.

CORRECT ATTIRE REQUIRED

A close friend and first collaborator of Italian costume designer Milena Canonero, costume designer Patricia Colin entered Wes Anderson's world in 2004 for the American Express commercial. An admirer of the complicity between Anderson and Canonero ("they form a fascinating duo"[9]), the Frenchwoman was well placed to know that costume is an essential part of the Anderson aesthetic.

The "Wes Look"

Even before preparation begins, the costumes department assesses the needs of the current project to set a budget, as rationally as possible. According to Colin, "Wes and Milena don't like to throw money away."[10] They buy and recycle in a sensible way. "I live in a big house in the country where I store all the haberdashery we have left over after each film for use in the next. It sounds silly, but haberdashery costs a fortune, so we save a lot that way."[11] Canonero does not compromise on materials, which must correspond to the period of the film and the references given. The same goes for costume cuts. "I wouldn't say that his films have a vintage look, they have a Wes look! The way he likes his clothes to be worn is all his own, as are certain styles and materials that he loves: safari suits, velvet, terry cloth."[12]

Handmade

For each film, the costumes department buys existing outfits for the extras. They rarely rent, as Anderson prefers to keep everything. He creates his clothes from scratch for the main actors, but sometimes it is necessary to tailor clothes for simple silhouettes. This happened on *The Grand Budapest Hotel* when the crew could not find the right clothes for the hotel staff and the monks. To this costly exception, an alternative was found: "Milena and Wes increasingly like to create their own fabrics, which we have printed or hand-painted."[13] Tilda Swinton's dresses in *The Grand Budapest Hotel* and *The French Dispatch*, as well as many of the outfits for *Asteroid City* (2023), were designed in this way.

REDUCED-SIZE MODELS

A world specialist in miniature sets and props (his Berlin workshop is inundated with requests), German-born Simon Weisse has been working with Wes Anderson since *The Grand Budapest Hotel*, where he designed the famous palace façade. His various creations have become indispensable to the director, who loves their artificiality. "It's becoming more and more important in his films, because Wes has realized that you can do a lot with these miniatures."[14] From simple little objects here and there, to the train in *Asteroid City*, to entire districts in *The French Dispatch*, the range of possibilities is virtually infinite.

Bigger or Smaller

A trick almost as old as cinema itself, miniatures almost did not survive the emergence of less expensive and more "realistic" digital effects. It was not until a visionary filmmaker like Wes Anderson turned to it that it became fashionable again. "Wes is attracted to miniatures purely as an artistic choice. It brings a very special aesthetic touch to his cinema."[15] Simon Weisse and his teams work mainly on 1/35th and 1/18th scale models (the façade of *The Grand Budapest Hotel*, for example), but they do occasionally think bigger. "The train in *Asteroid City* was an incredible 1/8th scale. The locomotive was over two meters long. With the carriages, we were approaching forty meters! We had to build it that big, otherwise it would have looked like the little train you'd have at home. For my part, I wanted to adopt the English standard, which is 1/22nd scale, but Wes and Adam Stockhausen insisted on the predefined scale! In the end, the hardest part was transporting the huge individual parts to the Madrid region where Wes filmed."[16] The filling machines (for gas, cocktails, and other oddities) in *Asteroid City* are another special case, since they are full scale.

In the Detail

The miniatures, which require standard materials (wood, plastic, metal, plaster), have the ideal patina for blending into the vintage world of Wes Anderson, who keeps a constant eye on their slow evolution, both before and after shooting. "When a pre-model is almost finished, I send him an image to validate,

Top and bottom: Vintage harmony between costumes, colors, and sets for *The Grand Budapest Hotel*.

because he's only interested in what it looks like on screen. He doesn't need to travel to see things in real life. He rarely comes back to the overall concept, but focuses on the details. If there's writing on a miniature store, for example, he'll (in agreement with the graphics team) fine-tune the font, the spacing between the letters...He's often exactly right!"[17] Then, during postproduction, a special team films the designed objects before they are integrated into the edited shots.

Top and bottom: Facade cladding for a real set on *The French Dispatch*.

BEHIND THE WALLS

Wes Anderson's main collaborator (along with director of photography Robert Yeoman), production designer Adam Stockhausen now relies heavily on Frenchman Stéphane Cressend, his right-hand man on set since *The French Dispatch*. "I'm in charge of setting up the team, building the sets, putting them in place, painting them, liaising with the various decorating departments (which include set designers and props) and coordinating with other departments such as special effects and stunts."[18] The perfect right-hand man.

To the Nearest (Quarter) Inch

Like the other artistic directors, Cressend relies on a considerable amount of information provided by Stockausen and Anderson: "Lighting notes, links to references, to certain films, etc."[19] The set decoration team then set to work using classic materials. "We work mainly from wooden frames that we cover with different materials, with imitation stone plaster, faux wood…We also have a lot of metal constructions made with our locksmiths, as well as polystyrene or resin elements that the sculpture department molds in large numbers."[20] How does Anderson's obsession with symmetry affect the sets? "This is not a constraint for us, because everything is designed in advance. On the other hand, the placement of sets can be complicated. In *The French Dispatch*, for the shootout sequence in a square between the police and the bandits, we had to shift a massive fountain (four meters by three, with a cast-iron element in the center) by a quarter of an inch! Adam is constantly on set for this reason, making decisions like this in consultation with Wes. Once all these small modifications have been made, the composition of the frame is impressively accurate."[21]

Complications

To create the filmmaker's retro universe, the set decoration team hunts extensively (antique shops, secondhand dealers, thrift shops, abandoned buildings…) and carries out many transformations. "For *The French Dispatch*, we found a printing works that had been closed since 1975, with all its equipment inside. Its old stocks of paper were then used by the graphic designers to create the antiqued letters."[22] Wes Anderson's fierce determination to use digital technology as little as possible can lead to logistical constraints. "For *Asteroid City*, we had to sculpt seven thousand cubic meters of polystyrene to create moun-

Top and bottom: Decor department craftsmen put the finishing touches to a gigantic *Asteroid City* panel under Wes Anderson's watchful eye.

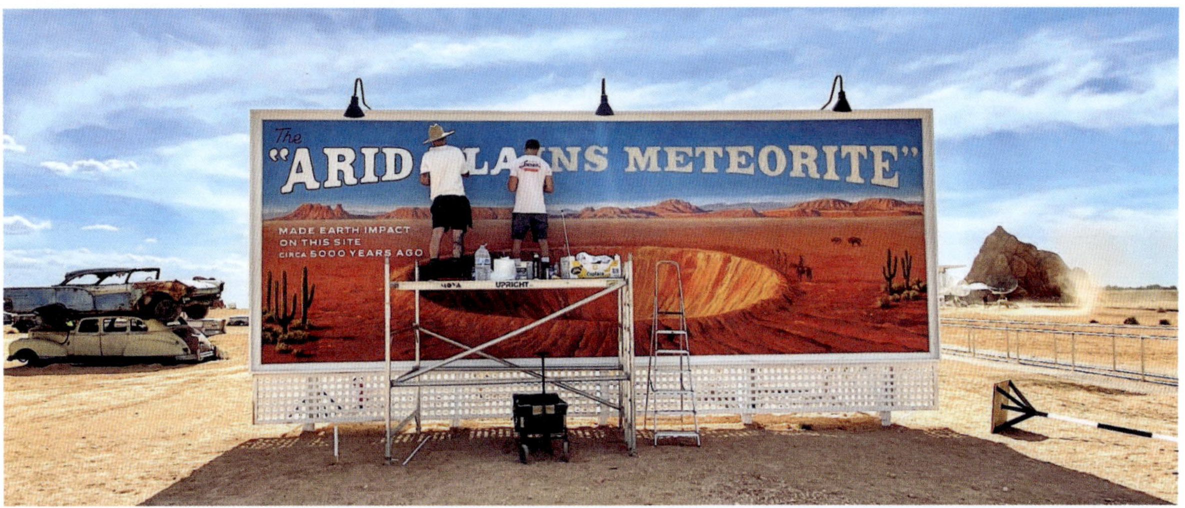

tains in the distance, in false perspective! Our reference was Monument Valley. The whole thing was placed on the horizon on a perimeter five hundred meters wide and eight hundred meters long. For three months, I heard the Spanish set decoration team (and the subcontractor responsible for laser-cutting our countless blocks of polystyrene to represent the difference in altitude of the mountains) repeat to me: 'But why, in 2021, aren't we using digital effects for this?' [Laughs] The result would undoubtedly be more perfect. I think that, irrespective of Wes's preference for the handmade, there was a very strong idea in *Asteroid City* of a theatrical universe, with the fake side that this implies. There's a naïve, figurative side to it. The same goes for the crater, which we could have done completely on green backgrounds."[23]

(L to R) Bill Murray and Owen Wilson await Wes Anderson's direction on the set of *The French Dispatch*.

ILE D'YEU
LA ROCHELLE

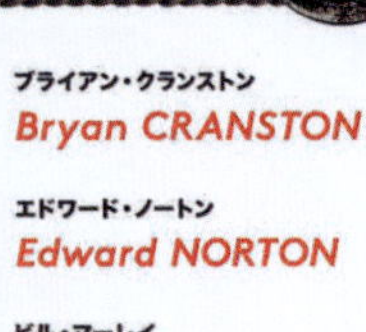

ブライアン・クランストン
Bryan CRANSTON

エドワード・ノートン
Edward NORTON

ビル・マーレイ
Bill MURRAY

ジェフ・ゴールドブラム
Jeff GOLDBLUM

犬 Isle ヶ of 島 Dogs

ランキン・こうゆう
Koyu RANKIN

リーブ・シュレイバー
Liev SCHREIBER

ボブ・バラバン
Bob BALABAN

スカーレット・ヨハンソン
Scarlett JOHANSSON

野村訓市
Kunichi NOMURA

渡辺謙
Ken WATANABE

グレタ・ガーウィグ
Greta GERWIG

フランシス・マクドーマンド
Frances McDORMAND

コートニー・B・ヴァンス
Courtney B. VANCE

フィッシャー・スティーブンス
Fisher STEVENS

村上虹郎
Nijiro MURAKAMI

ハーヴェイ・カイテル
Harvey KEITEL

ティルダ・スウィントン
Tilda SWINTON

伊藤晃
Akira ITO

高山明
Akira TAKAYAMA

F・マーリー・エイブラハム
F. Murray ABRAHAM

野田洋次郎
Yojiro NODA

夏木マリ
Mari NATSUKI

オノ・ヨーコ
Yoko ONO

フランク・ウッド
Frank WOOD

ウェス・アンダーソン監督
Directed by Wes ANDERSON

FOX SEARCHLIGHT PICTURES and INDIAN PAINTBRUSH present an AMERICAN EMPIRICAL PICTURE by WES ANDERSON "ISLE OF DOGS" Casting by DOUGLAS AIBEL, CSA Lead Animators ANTHONY ELWORTHY, KIM KEUKELEIRE, and JASON STALMAN Animation Director MARK WARING Animation Supervisor TOBIAS FOURACRE Animation Producer SIMON QUINN Editors RALPH FOSTER and EDWARD BURSCH Supervising Editor ANDREW WEISBLUM, A.C.E. Music Supervisor RANDALL POSTER Music by ALEXANDRE DESPLAT Head of Puppets Department ANDY GENT Visual Effects Supervisor TIM LEDBURY Production Designers ADAM STOCKHAUSEN and PAUL HARROD Director of Photography TRISTAN OLIVER Co-Producer OCTAVIA PEISSEL Executive Producers CHRISTOPH FISSER, HENNING MOLFENTER, and CHARLIE WOEBCKEN Produced by WES ANDERSON, SCOTT RUDIN, STEVEN RALES, and JEREMY DAWSON Story by WES ANDERSON, ROMAN COPPOLA, JASON SCHWARTZMAN, and KUNICHI NOMURA Screenplay by WES ANDERSON

ISLE OF DOGS

2018

United States, Germany, United Kingdom, Japan • 1 h 41 • Color • Dolby Digital • 2.39 : 1

Production Dates: **September 2015–November 2017**
Release Dates in the United States: **March 17, 2018 (South by Southwest); March 23, 2018 (limited release); April 13, 2018**

Budget: **?**
North America Box Office: **Approx. $32 million**
Worldwide Box Office: **Approx. $65 million**

Production Companies: **Indian Paintbrush, American Empirical Pictures, Scott Rudin Productions, Studio Babelsberg, 20th Century-Fox Animation**
Producers: **Wes Anderson, Jeremy Dawson, Steven Rales, Scott Rudin**
Co-Producers: **Eli Bush, Octavia Peissel**
Executive Producers: **Christoph Fisser, Henning Molfenter, Charlie Woebcken**
Associate Producers: **Ben Adler, John Peet**

Screenplay: **Wes Anderson, based on an original story by Wes Anderson, Roman Coppola, Jason Schwartzman, and Kunichi Nomura**
Director of Photography: **Tristan Oliver**
Editing: **Andrew Weisblum**
Director of Animation: **Mark Waring**
Production Design: **Paul Harrod, Adam Stockhausen**
Art Direction: **Curt Enderle**
Music Supervisor: **Randall Poster**
Music: **Alexandre Desplat**
Head of Puppets: **Andy Gent**
Graphic Design: **Annie Atkins, Erica Dorn**
Visual Effects Supervisor: **Tim Ledbury**
Casting: **Douglas Aibel, Kunichi Nomura**

Starring: **BRYAN CRANSTON (Chief), EDWARD NORTON (Rex), LIEV SCHREIBER (Spots), GRETA GERWIG (Tracy Walker), SCARLETT JOHANSSON (Nutmeg), F. MURRAY ABRAHAM (Jupiter), JEFF GOLDBLUM (Duke), BILL MURRAY (Boss), BOB BALABAN (King), TILDA SWINTON (Oracle), KOYU RANKIN (Atari), KUNICHI NOMURA (Mayor Kobayashi), AKIRA TAKAYAMA (Major Domo), FRANCES MCDORMAND (Interpreter Nelson)...**

“I was bred as a show dog, I was groomed for that purpose. It wasn’t my choice, I don’t consider it my identity.”

—

Nutmeg to Chief

SYNOPSIS

In a futuristic Japan, the mayor of Megasaki orders the exile of all dogs to Trash Island (a former industrial site transformed into a gigantic open-air waste dump) due to a truffle-related flu virus that threatens humanity. To set an example, the authoritarian Kobayashi banishes Spots, the guard dog of his adopted orphan nephew, Atari. Despite fierce opposition from Professor Watanabe of the Science Party, who is on the verge of finding a serum, the deportation of the canine race begins. Six months later, Atari crashes on Trash Island in a makeshift plane. All he can think about is finding his beloved pooch. In a bad way, he is almost devoured by the aggressive Chief, before being rescued and helped by his pack, which was touched by the child’s vulnerability. From Megasaki, the sinister Koboyashi prepares an offensive against the Isle of Dogs to recover Atari, whom he believes to be in danger, while students organize themselves to expose the mayor’s dubious maneuvers.

The puppets for *Isle of Dogs* were designed by the Arch Model Studio, founded by Andy Gent.

GENESIS

The experience gained on *Fantastic Mr. Fox* (2009) convinced Wes Anderson that volume animation fits perfectly into his world. He thought that a second feature film using this technique could be an enjoyable enterprise. At the end of 2014, at a master class organized by the Lisbon and Estoril Film Festival, he confided that he was toying with the idea of adapting *L'oro di Napoli* [*The Gold of Naples*] (Vittorio de Sica, 1954), a classic Italian sketch film, in stop motion. For this fervent fan of transalpine cinema, the project was not as far-fetched as it seemed. After all, Anderson has just paid the genre a heartfelt tribute in the short film *Castello Cavalcanti* (2013), produced by the luxury brand Prada, of which he is an ambassador.

A Mysterious Project

The idea fizzled out. Was it indeed ever tangible? Anderson's imagination is so fertile that one project can oust another in a split second, during a discussion with his inner circle (Jason Schwartzman and Roman Coppola) or on a hunch. In October 2015, eleven months after the unsuccessful announcement of the adaptation of *The Gold of Naples*, several American media outlets revealed that Anderson was now devoting himself to the preproduction of an animated film inspired by Japanese cinema, starring dogs. The mystery deepened. It is only fair to point out in the press that canines do not always have the best outcomes in his films: a beagle was crushed to death in *The Royal Tenenbaums* (2001), a mongrel trotted around with one leg amputated in *The Life Aquatic* (2004), an enraged stag sowed terror in *Fantastic Mr. Fox* (2009), and a fox terrier succumbed to an arrow in *Moonrise Kingdom* (2012).

A Homage to Japan

On December 21, 2016, a video posted on YouTube showed Anderson talking about shooting his next stop-motion film in England. Entitled *Isle of Dogs*, it was to feature a host of stars, including actor Edward Norton, because the pawed and furry protagonists would be talking. It would be several more months before the first trailer was unveiled, on September 21, 2017. This is a dystopia, an imaginary tale set in a totalitarian society, in this case a futuristic Japan that

The dog Boss is voiced by Bill Murray.

shows an aversion to dogs. It comes as no surprise that Anderson chose to set his story in a Japanese environment; he makes no secret of his deep love for the Land of the Rising Sun and the diversity of its cinema, from the urban thrillers of Akira Kurosawa to the retro-futuristic monster and steampunk films, via the intimate dramas of Yasujirō Ozu. *Isle of Dogs* also refers aesthetically to the clean lines of Japanese printmaking embodied by its two revered masters, Hokusai and Hiroshige. In addition to Jason Schwartzman and Roman Coppola, the Texan filmmaker consulted Kunichi Nomura, a Japanese friend and author, to help anchor his story in a credible alternative reality. With Nomura's help, his film contrasts technology and nature, honor and corruption, lonely heroes and blind masses—all issues that have always troubled the Pacific archipelago.

A New Method

As with *Fantastic Mr. Fox*, Wes Anderson turned to illustrators and to the indispensable puppet creator Andy Gent at an early stage. "Wes told me: 'I'd like to send you the script and see what you think. Before that, I want you to watch this short film, a YouTube clip,' and after I'd watched that, 'read the script.' The clip he sent was of traditional Japanese drummers. I watched that, read the script, and texted Wes with enthusiasm. 'We have much, much to discuss,' he replied. (Laughs)."[1] For the first time, Gent discovered the vast database in which the director collects his notes and references so that he can share them with his artistic departments. Illustrator Félicie Haymoz happily seized upon this mine of information. "One archive contained the films that Wes Anderson wanted to draw inspiration from: Studio Ghibli titles, Kurosawa films, and even *Citizen Kane* [Orson Welles, 1941]. Paul Harrod [one of the two art supervisors] had also collected numerous magnificent Japanese advertisements from the 1960s."[2] Two major Japanese actors, Toshirō Mifune and Tatsuya Nakadai, were used as models for the characters of Mayor Kobayashi and Professor Watanabe.

CASTING

At the beginning of the film, just after the prologue, a note to the viewer, typical of the filmmaker's trademark idiosyncrasy, states that "The humans in this story speak only in their native tongue (occasionally translated via bi-lingual interpreter, foreign-exchange-student, or electronic device). All barks have been rendered into English." An immediate consequence of this: when not translated by a third party, the Japanese dialogues are not subtitled. Wes Anderson prefers the viewer, whose attention is not focused on the text, to listen to the characters express themselves in their own language and perceive their emotions. This poetic license adds an eerie dimension

Show dog Nutmeg is voiced by Scarlett Johansson.

to the story, some passages of which will remain eternally encrypted for non-Japanese speakers.

Not the Same People

With the exception of his lucky mascot Bill Murray (who voices Boss, one of the dogs in the pack), Anderson relies on a voice cast entirely different from that of *Fantastic Mr. Fox*, whose performances he records before the actual filming, in keeping with a rule commonly applied in animation. This important step enabled him to meet actors with whom he would later work again, such as Bryan Cranston (Chief), Scarlett Johansson (Nutmeg, an entrancing show dog), and Liev Schreiber (Spots). For the role of Tracy, the strong-willed character who leads the student revolt against Mayor Kobayashi, he hired Greta Gerwig, the girlfriend of his old friend Noah Baumbach. For the actress—and future director of *Barbie* (2023)—this was her first voice for an animated film, for which she also provided the French version (she is bilingual). The roles of the Japanese characters are entrusted to actors fluent in the language. The intrepid Atari is played by Koyu Rankin, a young Canadian of Japanese origin who was eight years old at the time of filming. The role of Mayor Kobayashi was offered to writer Kunichi Nomura. Despite his youth, his deep voice matched that of the mayor in the imagination of his director friend.

FILMING AND PRODUCTION

The voices were recorded in 2015, just before filming began in the autumn of the same year. The operation was identical to that which was specified by Wes Anderson for *Fantastic Mr. Fox*: he issued his instructions remotely to his teams, who once again set up shop at 3 Mills Studios, a stone's throw from the actual Isle of Dogs, the real name of an area in East London bounded by the River Thames. While the animators methodically filmed the first shots, frame by frame, in the sets and with the puppets already designed, each artistic department continued its task, while dealing with a number of imponderables.

The Art of the Written Word

A French Japanese artist-graphic designer and illustrator based in London, Erica Dorn was called in by one of the producers, Jeremy Dawson, during the production process. "He was looking for a Japanese person to assist the graphics team headed by Annie Atkins. [...] I then spent a two-week trial period with Paul Harrod and his teams before actually being hired. [...] In particular, there were a lot of Japanese graphic elements to be processed for the sets that Paul and Adam Stockhausen [the other art supervisor] had imagined. Entire cities had to be filled with signs, packaging, lettering, motifs... I had to integrate them as closely as possible with reality. [...]

As a fan of Japanese filmmaker Akira Kurosawa, Wes Anderson had to pay tribute to samurai.

Most of the signs and brands in the film are hand-drawn, as we wanted to remain faithful to the historical images and works we were referring to."[3] More surprisingly (although are we really surprised with Wes Anderson?), Erica Dorn was in charge of personalizing the English subtitles… The team imagined and redesigned by hand a more personal version of the LL Brown font, to be more in harmony with the film's graphical environment.

> 41184 **FOR WES ADDICTS** 41184
>
> **Wes Anderson went beyond simply peppering his film with references to Japanese cinema. Tracy, for example, with her abundant curly red hair, is clearly inspired by the character played by Kerry Fox in *An Angel at My Table* (Jane Campion, 1990). The chapter "The Search for Spots" alludes to *Star Trek III: The Search for Spock* (Leonard Nimoy, 1984). The slide named Pagoda on which Atari slides is a self-citation: Pagoda was the first name of the character played in *The Royal Tenenbaums* by Kumar Pallana, Wes Anderson's favorite actor, who died in 2013.**

Greater Flexibility

While Andy Gent had been very closely supervised by the director on *Fantastic Mr. Fox*, he was given a great deal of freedom to create the puppets for *Isle of Dogs*. "Wes said: 'Because you know the process of fur and how it works, we just need to start sculpting things and see where it takes us.'"[4] Erica Dorn has a similar recollection. "I executed […] the large drawing etched in rust that tells the story of the dogs on the island. I had presented my sketch to Wes, thinking that it would have to be reworked, but he immediately approved it."[5] Of course, there were times when the director was uncompromising. For example, the sushi delivered to Professor Watanabe had to be prepared with the same care as the great Japanese chefs would employ. The puppets had to use knives correctly and cut the fish as meticulously as a real sushi chef. The animation director, Brad Schiff, and three of his collaborators spent two months finalizing this minute of film!

More and More

Compared to *Fantastic Mr. Fox*, *Isle of Dogs* required almost twice as many resources. One thousand puppets were made by hand—half for the dogs, half for the humans—and five different sizes (from very small to very large) were needed for each puppet. This phenomenal project prompted Andy Gent to set up a special workshop in early 2015 at 3 Mills Studios, which was transformed into a kennel for the occasion: the production went so far as to bring in puppies to inspire the craftsmen. For Gent and his collaborators, it was not a question of reproducing dog breeds identically but rather, as Anderson had wished, of focusing on their attitudes. Depending on their activities and the time of day, the dogs would express sadness or joy, which would be translated by the puppeteers and animators into an inflection of the ears, a squinting of the eyes, or a quivering of the hair. Only the film's robot dogs were created digitally, using 3D printers. In Anderson's view, this departure from the artisanal rule was justified by the very nature of these machines of death.

Made to Measure

The human puppets also required very precise adjustments. To give their skin a realistic and expressive appearance, the painters used translucent resins, which, for example, made the face of the hero, Atari, luminous. Another challenge was dressing the main and secondary characters, as well as the many extras. Maggie Haden, a costume designer specializing in miniatures, had never had so many puppets to deal with! In particular, she had to be patient in convincing a renowned London tailor to design Mayor Kobayashi's slim-fitting get-up. "This costume had to be perfectly cut, with very straight lines, which is difficult to achieve on such a small scale. We had a lot of film references for this rather neat gangster look, so we knew what we wanted to achieve. But our tailor almost gave up. It took us almost three months to achieve the desired result."[6]

And Then There Was Light

Despite a slight disagreement over *Fantastic Mr. Fox*, the Texan director could not do without the services of Tristan Oliver, the director of photography who had made a specialty of lighting dolls and miniature sets since his apprenticeship at Aardman in the 1990s. For his part, the English technician was fully aware of Anderson's singular vision. In short, it matched his taste. For *Isle of Dogs*, 240 complex sets (ranging from the garbage landscapes and disused sites of Trash Island to the glittering cityscape of Megasaki) and numerous puppets with different characteristics had to be brought to life—a headache amplified by Anderson's demands for the same image quality as in his live-action films (i.e., great depth of field and uniform sharpness that crushes perspective). "In itself, it's not very difficult to light fur, but it's more complicated if you want to render it without relief. Hair will refract light [...]. It can sometimes assume an incandescent appearance, because it has a very high level of radiance, which diffracts light. So sometimes we softened the fur to the point of making it look like down!"[7] Pushed to his limits, Tristan Oliver once again achieved the impossible.

More than 200 sets were created for *Isle of Dogs*'s many landscapes.

Wes Anderson's trademark ochre in *Isle of Dogs*.

波潟
出でし月かも
長月の
紅葉踏みわけ
富士の高嶺に
今はた同じ
天の原
吹くからに

Greta Gerwig lent her voice to Tracy, the student protester in *Isle of Dogs*.

The sushi-making sequence required two months of work for just one minute of film.

RECEPTION

Between 2014, the year *The Grand Budapest Hotel* was released, and 2018, the world had changed. The Black Lives Matter and #MeToo movements occupied media space, and the protest they carried with them (against racial discrimination and violence against women) spread to all sociocultural fields. *Isle of Dogs* felt the impact of this. When it was released in the United States on March 17, 2018, a month after Anderson was awarded the Silver Bear for Best Director at the Berlin Film Festival, voices were raised against what some saw as cultural appropriation. In other words, Wes Anderson has been accused by influential media of appropriating a (Japanese) culture that is not his own, and of giving his (white) vision of a thousand-year-old country reduced to a few patriarchal, authoritarian clichés. Alexandre Desplat's magnificent music, which mixes traditional taiko drums with Western brass, does not help matters.

The End of the Debate?

Interviewed by *Time* magazine a month after the film's release, Erica Dorn gave her artist's and Japanese view of the controversy. "Cultural appropriation isn't really a concept in Japan. Japan is becoming an inspiration for artists, filmmakers and fashion outside the country, and Japanese culture generally is all about assimilating and mixing with other cultures. Wes chose Japan [as a setting for this movie] and I think people in Japan will be really excited to see that."[8] The proof is in the pudding: *Isle of Dogs* was adapted as a manga by respected cartoonist Minetarō Mochizuki in 2019, extinguishing a controversy that no one had anticipated.

Preparatory casts for Tracy's puppet.

An Uncertain Future

Twice nominated for an Oscar in 2019 (in the categories of Best Animated Feature and Best Score), *Isle of Dogs* generated more ticket sales than *Fantastic Mr. Fox* without achieving remarkable box office receipts. Was this Anderson's last foray into animation? Given the time-consuming and costly nature of this type of project (higher than live-action), it is uncertain whether director will return to it. We can only regret this, as the playground and possibilities are so infinite and conducive to the most incongruous deliriums. Anderson's two animated films have also enabled him to introduce new tools each time (animatics and the database), which have considerably lightened and facilitated his work and that of his collaborators. All good reasons for prolonging the audience's enjoyment.

Freeze Frame

At the start of the film, Atari, having just been accepted by the Trash Island dogs, has lunch with them while sitting on a raised metal beam. This image is a direct homage to the famous photograph *Lunch atop a Skyscraper*, taken in 1932 by Charles Clyde Ebbets, of workers perched on what would become the Rockefeller Center building.

Dmitri (Adrien Brody, foreground) in *The Grand Budapest Hotel* is the archetypal domineering villain.

Little Masters

From Tyrant to Mentor

Beneath its minimalist exterior and behind its delicate varnish, apparent flourishes, reassuring symmetry, and charming miniatures, Wes Anderson's world conceals a more or less subdued violence, culminating in *Isle of Dogs* (2018), an anguished dystopia in which mutts, penned and mutilated, remind us of our inhumanity. The sinister mayor Kobayashi, with his stern expression and massive figure swathed in an impeccable cream suit, is likened to a populist leader who instills terror in the population to get them to accept the mass eradication of dogs, carriers of a dangerous canine flu. A bloodthirsty tyrant ready to sacrifice Atari, the nephew he took in when his parents died, Kobayashi is the ultimate illustration of Anderson's interest in authority figures, legitimate or improvised, who abound in his work and are often the vectors of action.

In His Own World

It all began with Dignan, the magnificent oddball determined to become a bandit in *Bottle Rocket* (1993). A self-proclaimed expert in stratagems, he convinces his two friends, Anthony and Bob, to follow him in his delusions, to which they agree without batting an eyelid, just to please him. The would-be dictator does not necessarily start out with bad intentions: he may be seeking to satisfy a narcissistic need, but he truly believes in the righteousness of his schemes. His notion of reality is highly subjective, and it comes naturally to him to impose it upon others. Even the slightest resistance from his audience can be enough to make him tense up and turn authoritarian, the aftereffects of his megalomania. This is the case with Dignan when Anthony and Bob ironically comment on one of his plans of action, but also with Francis

Whitman (*The Darjeeling Limited*, 2007) when his younger brothers question his leadership; he imposes a definite roadmap, strict instructions, and a clumsy paternalism. Shaking up the order established by the putative leader and reversing the balance of power are among the main plot strings pulled by Wes Anderson and his writers.

Uniformization

Max Fischer (*Rushmore*, 1998), Chas (*The Royal Tenenbaums*, 2001), Steve Zissou (*The Life Aquatic with Steve Zissou*, 2004), M. Gustave and Dmitri (*The Grand Budapest Hotel*, 2014), Simone (*The French Dispatch*, 2021) and Grif Gibson (*Asteroid City*, 2023) have one thing in common: they all wear a uniform (or something similar, like Chas's bright red tracksuit), a distinctive mark of their hold on the group, which sometimes adopts the same look as a sign of obedience—the yellow jumpsuit imposed on his acolytes by Dignan for the final heist in *Bottle Rocket*; the Steve Zissou branded clothes donned by members of the *Belafonte* crew; the all-black outfits worn by those close to the sinister Dmitri. The case of Simone, the matron of the "Concrete Masterpiece" segment in *The French Dispatch*, is edifying in this respect. The first time we see her, she poses in the simplest of garb for prisoner-painter Moses Rosenthaler. Literally naked and vulnerable, she seems to be under the control of the wild-eyed artist. Then, a curt slap on his hand breaks the illusion, and in the next shot, we see her dressed in her guard's uniform: Simone is the one who exercises power, without question, and not the other way around.

Helping Hands

What would tyrants be without their underlings, subordinates, and henchmen? It is through these people that the master's message is conveyed, through them that actions are carried out—the brutal murders committed by Jopling, Dmitri's hired killer in *The Grand Budapest Hotel*, are the bloodiest representation of this. Placed on the front line, the subordinate is also the designated whipping boy. Poor Brendan (*The Darjeeling Limited*) is exploited by his employer Francis Whitman, who, despite his brothers' criticism of his behavior, fails to see the harm. Max Fischer is equally lacking in tenderness toward Dirk, his young disciple, whose admiration for him is blind and unquestioning. But beware of rebellion! If the satrap's armor cracks, the underlings can turn as quickly as they were converted. Dirk Calloway is ruthless toward Max, who has disappointed him, as are Steve Zissou's trainees and Major-Domo, Mayor Kobayashi's Frankenstein creature. Ironically, Anderson himself is surrounded by assistants in his daily and professional life. This is all just a short step from self-mockery.

In *Isle of Dogs*, Mayor Kobayashi is ready for any populist maneuver.

Awareness

In Wes Anderson's work, tyranny is not inevitable. One day's despots often become the next day's mentors. M. Gustave, the concierge in *The Grand Budapest Hotel*, is the best example. Presented as the archetypal tyrant, obnoxious to the little people on the staff and servile to the powerful, he holds young bellboy Zero under his thumb before becoming convinced of his usefulness and developing increasingly paternal feelings toward him. From then on, he sets out to give him the education that Zero, an orphan of immigrant origin, never had, and protect him from the effects of the fascism taking hold in the film's imaginary country. Max Fischer, Chas Tenenbaum, Steve Zissou, Francis Whitman, and, to a lesser extent, Mayor Kobayashi also learn that passing on knowledge is more rewarding than domination.

GARDIENNE
GARDIENNE

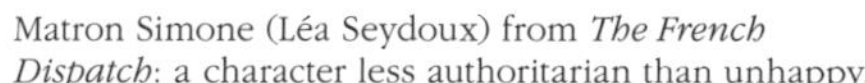

Matron Simone (Léa Seydoux) from *The French Dispatch*: a character less authoritarian than unhappy.

149e Série, N° 12

200 Old Francs

THE FRENCH DISPATCH

OF THE LIBERTY, KANSAS EVENING SUN

SEARCHLIGHT PICTURES and INDIAN PAINTBRUSH present an AMERICAN EMPIRICAL PICTURE by WES ANDERSON
"THE FRENCH DISPATCH OF THE LIBERTY, KANSAS EVENING SUN" U.S. Casting by DOUGLAS AIBEL, CSA
French Casting by ANTOINETTE BOULAT U.K. Casting by JINA JAY Music Supervisor RANDALL POSTER Music by ALEXANDRE DESPLAT
Costume Designer MILENA CANONERO Editor ANDREW WEISBLUM, ACE Production Designer ADAM STOCKHAUSEN
Director of Photography ROBERT YEOMAN, ASC Line Producer FRÉDÉRIC BLUM Co-Producer OCTAVIA PEISSEL Executive Producers SCOTT RUDIN
ROMAN COPPOLA HENNING MOLFENTER CHRISTOPH FISSER CHARLIE WOEBCKEN Produced by WES ANDERSON
STEVEN RALES JEREMY DAWSON Story by WES ANDERSON & ROMAN COPPOLA & HUGO GUINNESS & JASON SCHWARTZMAN

Screenplay by WES ANDERSON **COMING SOON** Directed by WES ANDERSON

THE FRENCH DISPATCH

United States, Germany • 1 h 47 • Color / Black and white • Dolby Digital • 1.37 : 1 / 2.40 : 1

Production Dates: **November 17, 2018–March 23, 2019**
World Premiere: **July 12, 2021 (Cannes Film Festival)**
United States Release Date: **October 22, 2021**

Budget: **approx. $25 million**
North America Box Office: **approx. $16 million**
Worldwide Box Office: **approx. $46 million**

Production Companies: **American Empirical Pictures, Indian Paintbrush, Studio Babelsberg, TSG Entertainment**
Producers: **Wes Anderson, Jeremy Dawson, Steven Rales**
Co-Producer: **Octavia Peissel**
Executive Producers: **Roman Coppola, Christoph Fisser, Henning Molfenter, Charlie Woebcken**
Line Producer: **Frédéric Blum**
Associate Producers: **Ben Adler, John Peet**

Screenplay: **Wes Anderson, based on a story by Wes Anderson, Roman Coppola, Hugo Guinness, and Jason Schwartzman**
Director of Photography: **Robert Yeoman**
First Assistant Director: **Ben Howard**
Second Unit Director: **Martin Scali**
Film Editor: **Andrew Weisblum**
Production Designer: **Adam Stockhausen**
Set Decorator: **Rena DeAngelo**
Art Director: **Stéphane Cressend**
Music Supervisor: **Randall Poster**
Music: **Alexandre Desplat**
Sound: **Jean-Paul Mugel**
Costumes: **Milena Canonero**
Makeup: **Frances Hannon**
Miniatures: **Simon Weisse**
Graphic Design: **Annie Atkins, Erica Dorn**
Casting: **Douglas Aibel (United States), Antoinette Boulat (France), Luise Eigner (Germany), Jina Jey (United Kingdom)**

Starring: **BENICIO DEL TORO (Moses Rosenthaler), ADRIEN BRODY (Julian Cadazio), LÉA SEYDOUX (Simone), TILDA SWINTON (J. K. L. Berensen), FRANCES MCDORMAND (Lucinda Krementz), TIMOTHÉE CHALAMET (Zeffirelli), LYNA KHOUDRI (Juliette), JEFFREY WRIGHT (Roebuck Wright), MATHIEU AMALRIC (the commissaire), STEPHEN PARK (Nescaffier), BILL MURRAY (Arthur Howitzer Jr.), OWEN WILSON (Herbsaint Sazerac), CHRISTOPH WALTZ (Paul Duval), CÉCILE DE FRANCE (Mrs. B.) GUILLAUME GALLIENNE (Mr. B)...**

“We started testing the black-and-white film in prep and really liked the look.”

Robert Yeoman,
Director of Photography[1]

SYNOPSIS

On the death of its creator, *The French Dispatch*, a supplement to an American magazine based in France, suddenly ceased publication. As a tribute, a final issue was printed, featuring four articles written by the magazine's top writers, all linked to their home town of Ennui-sur-Blasé. These essays are set to pictures. “The Cycling Reporter” shows reporter Herbsaint Sazerac cycling through the streets of the town, describing its sociocultural evolution over the course of the century. In “The Concrete Masterpiece” art critic J. K. L. Berensen recounts how a troubled painter, in prison for murder, arouses the interest of a rogue art dealer and forms an ambiguous relationship with an icy matron. Lucinda Krementz covers a student demonstration for her article “Revisions to a Manifesto.” She is torn between the two leaders of this revolution, her young lover and a woman who is jealous of her. Finally, in “The Private Dining Room of the Police Commissioner,” writer Roebuck Wright bears witness to the kidnapping of a policeman's son, who had invited him to sample the cuisine of the famous chef Nescaffier.

GENESIS

In 2008, while working on *Fantastic Mr. Fox*, Wes Anderson was approached by American producer Brian Grazer to adapt the French comedy *Mon meilleur ami* (Patrice Leconte, 2006). Grazer may have seen in this story of a misanthropic art dealer who invents a friend—in response to a challenge from his business partner—a potential that the American director could exploit in his own style. Taking advantage of the time afforded by the protracted filming of his animated feature, Anderson worked on a version that was fairly faithful to the original: the names were changed, the action was set in New York, and a naïve cab driver was still used as a decoy. The stake in the bet (a priceless vase) became the collection of a painter by the name of Moses Rosenthaler, from which the hero hoped to profit following a vast speculative venture. *The Rosenthaler Suite*, the project's working title, never saw the light of day. Nevertheless, it remained in the archives of Anderson, who has a habit of never quite putting aside what he has written.

Contradictory Information

Ten years on, Anderson, who had directed *Moonrise Kingdom* (2012), *The Grand Budapest Hotel* (2014), and *Isle of Dogs* (2018), three of his biggest successes, was one of the leading American independent directors. Going to see a Wes Anderson film was becoming a must for moviegoers the world over. In the summer of 2018, rumors began to circulate that he would be tackling a musical filmed in France. Brad Pitt was then announced as a possible candidate. In the autumn, producer Jeremy Dawson denied virtually all of this! In an article in the *Charente Libre* newspaper, he refused to confirm any names, and dismissed the idea of a musical. "It's a film set in France at different times, [...] a story about writers, with links to Kansas, in the US."[2] Why speak out in *Charente Libre*? Because filming was due to take place in Angoulême, where the planned arrival of Wes Anderson and a host of stars, starting in November 2018, was generating a feverish excitement that would not abate over the following months.

Example of a false façade concealing an existing Angoulême setting.

Elisabeth Moss, star of television and cinema, plays the small role of Alumna.

Bill Murray (Arthur Howitzer Jr.) and Pablo Pauly (the waiter) in front of the newspaper's railway in *The French Dispatch*.

A Declaration of Love

The rumors continued into 2019, some true, some false. The mystery surrounding Anderson's feature films was not a strategy, but simply a reflection of his discreet nature and his nostalgia for a time when the content of a film was not already "played out" before its release. The director was fond of sophisticated, literary, humorous press, such as that which appeared in the pages of the *New Yorker* magazine, which he has been collecting since he was old enough to cultivate himself. In September 2019, a press release from distributor Searchlight Pictures informed audiences that his next film would be set in the editorial offices of an American newspaper, *The French Dispatch*, in a fictional twentieth-century French town. In a veritable love letter to journalists, Anderson would bring to life a collection of stories that appeared in the paper, paying homage to the *New Yorker*, a publication he respects, and to the country that adopted him.

Twisting Reality

The French Dispatch is a film of sketches, in four distinct parts, which are enactments of articles by American reporter-writers sent to Ennui-sur-Blasé, the film's imaginary location. The second of these sketches, titled "The Concrete Masterpiece," is a reappropriation of Anderson's adaptation of *Mon meilleur ami*, written ten years earlier. He retained the character's name—the painter Moses Rosenthaler—and the subplot about the turpitudes of the art market, to conceive a totally original story about a captive artist who is rescued from anonymity by an aesthete swindler. Even though he is the only one credited as screenwriter, Anderson once again relies on artist and writer Hugo Guinness, Roman Coppola, and Jason Schwartzman to develop a fantasy universe where poetry and abstraction are increasingly prevalent. As with the authors of the *New Yorker*, it is not so much a question of reporting information as of twisting it into novelistic, offbeat narratives. "Revisions to a Manifesto," the third sketch, recalls the events of May 1968 from the biased point of view of a fortysomething American journalist infatuated with a young student protester.

Eternal France

Anderson is increasingly fond of embedded narratives, brutal ellipses, and mixtures of genres, colors, formats, and shots (real or animated). He allows himself every option, like Moses Rosenthaler, the unpredictable visual explorer, or Jean-Luc Godard, whose shadow looms large over *The French Dispatch*, Anderson's most political and freewheeling film. It is also, of course, the most French of all, with its Angoulême setting (depicting a France frozen in an eternal past), its archetypal characters (the gourmet policeman in "The Private Dining Room of the Police Commissioner"), and its cinematic references (Tati, Clouzot, Renoir, Truffaut). Composer Alexandre Desplat sums it up perfectly. "This film is made up of visions of France that have been somewhat reworked because they went through Wes's brain. So you could say it's France,

Angoulême was chosen to represent a fictional French town that would resemble both the provinces and Paris.

but a poetic France, rich in details and references that sometimes aren't true, but seem to be. Is this the real France? No, but in a way, it's French."[3]

CASTING

As with every new film, Anderson draws mainly on the cast of actors he has built up over the years and makes a few adjustments. The choice of the captivating Timothée Chalamet (the Franco-American plays the student Zeffirelli, leader of the revolt) is dictated, for example, by the romantic and revolutionary aspect of the "Revisions to a Manifesto" segment. The arrival in his world of Benicio Del Toro—with whom Wes Anderson dreamed of filming and to whom he entrusted the role of Moses Rosenthaler—is in itself an event. The Puerto Rican–born American (winner of an Oscar for Best Supporting Actor in Steven Soderbergh's *Traffic* [2000]) is one of those highly charismatic actors with an imposing presence and strong interiority who, like Ralph Fiennes, have been adding an extra dimension to Wes Anderson's films since the mid-2010s. Lightness and melancholy are always present, but to these are added an unprecedented baroque touch and bestiality. The rumblings of violence, which had long been contained or caricatured, are increasingly in evidence. After the diabolical Jopling (played by Willem Dafoe in *The Grand Budapest Hotel*) and Major Domo (the right-hand man of tyrannical Mayor Kobayashi in *Isle of Dogs*), the tortured painter Moses Rosenthaler is the illustration of this trend.

Laid Bare

Some have noted the uncanny resemblance (corpulence, long beard, deep gaze) of the character played by Benicio Del Toro to the Chinese artist Ai Weiwei, known for his militant and provocative works. It's a pure coincidence, according to Anderson, who had in mind instead the French-Swiss actor Michel Simon—the tramp from Jean Renoir's *Boudu sauvé des eaux* (1932). This reference inspired Benicio Del Toro. Boudu is an anarchist whose offbeat behavior shatters the bourgeois family who took him in; in another segment, the

French actors Denis Ménochet (a prison guard) and Léa Seydoux (Simone) flank American Benicio Del Toro (Moses Rosenthaler) in the "Concrete Masterpiece" segment.

quiet Moses Rosenthaler provokes incomprehension and impatience from everyone except the enigmatic Simone, the matron played by Léa Seydoux. For the Frenchwoman, who poses nude for the painter from the very first scene, the role represents a challenge, but her confidence in Anderson is such that she accepted it without second thoughts. "I don't know if I can say that I submit to a director's gaze. I'm a bit like Simone. I offer my nudity, my femininity too, but I'm always in control of what I give. I've never felt that anything was stolen from me. From the moment I do something, it's a choice on my part."[4]

Broken Faces

Leading actors in the cast include Lyna Khoudri, Mathieu Amalric, Guillaume Gallienne, and Cécile de France, rounding out the film's large French-speaking contingent, which is made up exclusively of extras from Angoulême. Not all of them (nearly a thousand!) were easy to recruit, given the specific nature of Anderson's requirements. Second unit director Martin Scali, who was exceptionally asked to help with the casting, has fond memories of the experience. "Wes really wanted some of the faces to be 'Fellinian *à la française*,' like the subjects of Eugène Atget's photographs. It had to be very *France populaire*. It wasn't easy for me: I was the only one in Angoulême casting broken faces, in fact. I'd stop people in the street and ask them if they had any brothers or sisters, so I could reconstruct particular families. They were often homeless people, people in bistros who didn't have very easy lives."[5] In *Wes in Town*, the book of illustrations inspired by the filming in Angoulême, the authors list a number of precious testimonials from extras transfigured by this unique experience.

Acrobatic Painting

Moses Rosenthaler's final fresco in "The Concrete Masterpiece" was designed by Sandro Kopp, a German New Zealander artist and companion of Tilda Swinton. He had less than three months to create ten gigantic murals whose very thick texture did not hold well to the walls, forcing him to work very quickly, most of the time horizontally, to avoid drips.

FILMING AND PRODUCTION

Having considered filming in several locations that, when artificially combined in the editing process, would represent an imaginary French metropolis (inspired by Paris, Lyon, and other cities with great historical potential), the production team chose Angoulême. The préfecture of Charente has the advantage of being perfectly preserved and offering, in a tightly packed area, natural settings that suit Anderson's retro vision. He crisscrossed France by car, visiting a dozen towns before settling on Angoulême, seduced by its hilltop location, winding steps, and roads. This vertical accumulation of buildings, as found in Montmartre or Ménilmontant, was an ideal cinematographic location for him. He simply added cobblestones to the streets.

Everyone Involved

The art department, headed by Adam Stockhausen, was responsible for taking over the city's interiors and exteriors and "dressing them up" as required. Angoulême's town council and residents were enthusiastic about the project. They were well aware that such an event would not be repeated any time soon. Stéphane Cressend, the French set supervisor, was delighted with this active and spontaneous collaboration. "The chess tournament [from the 'Revisions to a Manifesto' segment] was shot in the town hall's village hall. [. . .] For the squares [in the town] there were many set additions—fake facades, in particular."[6] The production also employed local people (for the extras) and local industry. Local craftsmen, for example, designed the pottery that the prisoners in the "Concrete Masterpiece" segment made in their workshops. These same prisoners also wore the famous charentaises, woolen slippers with felt soles, a local specialty ordered in large numbers for the filming because, in addition to the characters, the entire film crew wore them, too. It was particularly cold during filming, which took place from November to March. Lodging in the same hotel (a practice instituted by the director), the actors and postmasters dined in their charentaises. One can imagine Wes Anderson putting them on his feet when he went

Timothée Chalamet (Zeffirelli) is thwarted in the "Revisions to a Manifesto" segment.

Two women (Lyna Khoudri as Juliette and Frances McDormand as Lucinda Krementz) for one man (Timothée Chalamet as Zeffirelli).

into the editing room, set up in the hotel—with the conference room serving as a space for makeup and costume fittings.

Improvised Studio

During their research in the region, Wes Anderson and his collaborators discovered a huge disused felt factory, which they transformed into a studio capable of housing several nonexistent sets, such as the prison and its secure paint shop for "The Concrete Masterpiece." This provided an unexpected solution for the producer, who was also able to set up a production workshop, a model workshop, and several film sets. Stéphane Cressend points out that "the café and radio station [from 'Revisions to a Manifesto'], the journalists' apartments, and *The French Dispatch* editorial office are also studio constructions."[7] For cinematographer Robert Yeoman, lighting the penitentiary (and its multiple cells) and its studio proved a particularly complicated assignment. "In the prison Wes wanted to hold focus very close and far from the camera, which requires a lot of light. I wanted to create a soft top light, which entailed bouncing huge lights into a white cloth which covered the ceiling, then diffusing the light further for the required softness."[8] Rosenthaler's art studio occupied a large set, lit by skylights emanating from the roof. To obtain constant light, it would have been necessary to install supporting lights, but the structure was too fragile to lend itself to this kind of DIY. So Robert Yeoman had three large "softsuns" installed outside the studio, hanging from cranes, overhanging the roof in question, "so we could keep a consistent look throughout the day [and after dark]."[9]

All Dressed Up

With its 130 different sets, *The French Dispatch* established a record: more sets than in any other

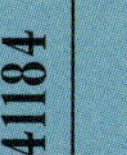

FOR WES ADDICTS

In the "Revisions to a Manifesto" segment, the students visit Le Sans Blague café, where a jukebox plays Christophe's hit "Aline," covered by Jarvis Cocker. Wes Anderson had planned for the French singer to duet with the former Pulp frontman. Unfortunately, Christophe passed away on April 16, 2020, and was unable to take part in this potentially mythical recording. Released on September 14, 2021, this revisited "Aline" benefited from an animated video directed by Anderson.

Jeffrey Wright, presenter and narrator of the "The Private Dining Room of the Police Commissioner" segment.

Wes Anderson film. The same goes for the costumes, which numbered around a thousand (in addition to the actors, each extra wore a unique costume), an unprecedented figure according to head costume designer Patricia Colin, who, along with designer Milena Canonero, experienced a demanding but rewarding shoot. "You need a volume of around 1,300 costumes to make a thousand different ones in the end. [...] It's a long process to get what you see on screen, and a fitting can take several hours to get the right result. [...] It also creates a close bond with the extras: they're chosen, and they're taken care of as if they were a lead role. On the set Wes knows them, calls them by their first names, and they're very happy."[10] As the film was shot mainly in black and white, Milena Canonero had to think differently about the shades and textures of the clothes, in conjunction with the makeup/hair department. In particular, she was inspired by the effects achieved (in black and white) on specific colors by the filmmakers of yesteryear. Looking back, Patricia Colin retains an indelible memory of the experience, as well as an amusing anecdote. "Our costume room was in a former retirement home. We were preparing the patina in the morgue, and it was cold, winter. There was a long corridor with rooms, some of whose walls were covered with strange drawings. [...] Some people will even tell you they saw ghosts!"[11]

A Very Animated Sequence

The film's fourth segment, "The Private Dining Room of the Police Commissioner," ends with a three-minute 2D animated sequence that pits the protagonists against each other in a car chase. Anderson commissioned French animation director Gwenn Germain to design the sequence, drawing inspiration from Franco-Belgian comics, in particular the "clear line" (simple lines, flat colors) as defined by Hergé and Edgar P. Jacobs, in *Tintin* and *Les Aventures de Blake et Mortimer* (The Adventures of Blake and Mortimer), respectively.

Mathieu Amalric (the Commissaire, right) and Hippolyte Girardot (Chou-fleur, left) are among the many French actors in the cast.

Saoirse Ronan, who plays a junkie showgirl, reunites with her director from *The Grand Budapest Hotel.*

An occasional actor, screenwriter Wally Wolodarsky (bottom) has mainly played small roles for Wes Anderson.

(L to R) Elisabeth Moss (Alumna), Owen Wilson (Herbsaint Sazerac), Tilda Swinton (J. K. L. Berensen), Fisher Stevens (an editor) and Griffin Dunne (a legal advisor).

Roebuck Wright (played by Jeffrey Wright) unblinkingly types his paper in front of his boss's lifeless body.

RECEPTION

Originally scheduled for the 2020 Cannes Film Festival, *The French Dispatch* proved to be one of the major casualties of the COVID-19 pandemic sweeping the world in the first quarter of the year. The Cannes event was canceled and the film's release date changed several times on both sides of the Atlantic. The world was turned upside down, as was the film world's calendar.

Fever Abated?

It was therefore necessary to wait until Cannes 2021 to finally discover Wes Anderson's tenth feature film. At the official screening on July 12, *The French Dispatch* received a long standing ovation, lasting over six minutes, commensurate with the anticipation it had generated. The COVID parenthesis had just closed, and life was returning to more or less normal. Highly cerebral and sophisticated, packed with insider references, this is perhaps its author's most complex and least accessible film. Wes Anderson's love of France shines through in every shot, however, and helped the film to become the filmmaker's fourth-highest-grossing film in that country. In the rest of the world, on the other hand, the results were rather disappointing. The postpandemic period no doubt had something to do with that.

A Nostalgic Sequence

In Angoulême, people were having a hard time getting over the end of the filming. From October 21, 2021, to January 2, 2022, a free exhibition, "The French Dispatch—Behind the Scenes," enabled the nostalgic members of the Angoulême populus to immerse themselves in the world of Wes Anderson. The exhibition was set up by Pascal Lefort, who appeared in the film and took a large number of photographs on the various film sets. In addition to his photos, the exhibition also featured sets, original plates from the book *Wes in Town*, and an animated sequence created for the occasion by 3.0 Studio, a local animation company. Finally, there was a room where one could listen to a loop of tracks from *Chanson d'Ennui Tip-Top*, Jarvis Cocker's album of covers. Together with Anderson, the British artist revisited the French repertoire of the 1960s to accompany the soundtrack of *The French Dispatch*.

The French Debrief

As soon as filming of *The French Dispatch* was completed at the end of March 2019, a number of Angoulême residents expressed their dismay at the planned disappearance of the film's sets and transformed locations. Among them was Jim Jourdane. This man of images, who had practiced many visual professions, quickly planned to leave a mark of the passage of Anderson and his collaborators. And what could be better than an illustrated book, made in the home of the International Comic Strip Festival, where there is an artist on every street corner. Jim Jourdane and Julie Gore, an illustrator friend, easily enlisted the help of ten other talented artists to collaborate on *Wes in Town: A Filming in Angoulême* (Makisapa, 2021).

Jourdane and his cohorts worked tirelessly to be ready for the release of *The French Dispatch*, scheduled for May 2020, with the film's premiere at the Cannes Film Festival. But COVID, which kept everyone at home beginning March 2020, postponed the theatrical release by a year. This was to be a blessing in disguise for the book: originally conceived as seventy pages, it had doubled in size. In addition to offering an inventive rereading of the filming and Wes Anderson's universe, *Wes in Town* shed retroactive light on the workings of a major production through the vivid accounts of extras, shopkeepers, and technicians involved in this film.

The Sans Blague Café in *The French Dispatch*'s third segment, "Revisions to a Manifesto."

French Touch

A Heady Perfume

Having fallen in love with France because of French cinema, Wes Anderson became an extreme Francophile, substantiated by his move to Paris, where he had been spending most of each year since the mid-2000s, and by the celebrated filming, in Angoulême, of *The French Dispatch* (2021), the culmination of this French passion that he had been cultivating on screen since his early days. For him, fantasy has become reality.

A Seminal Love of Film

During his formative years in high school, and then at university, Anderson was an avid watcher of films, and not only of American films. An admirer of the great international masters, notably Japanese, Indian, and Italian (Akira Kurosawa, Satyajit Ray, Federico Fellini), he gradually developed a particular fascination for French cinema, born out of the impact of his discovery of *Quatre Cents Coups* (François Truffaut, 1959). The freedom of tone, the rebellious youth, the generational conflict, the dysfunctional family, the existential despair, the break with the cinematic classicism of the time, the authors' doctrine (protection and independence) that the film embodied were all motifs and founding acts that spoke intimately to him. Almost all of his work

The French Dispatch is full of little distractions, like this pack of Gaullist cigarettes.

bears the imprint of this. In the wake of this, Wes Anderson watched, read, and listened to everything to do with France. He learned that the members of the Nouvelle Vague (Truffaut and Godard were his favorites) worshipped Jean Renoir and Robert Bresson, whose filmographies he explored. From Renoir and Bresson, he moved on to Max Ophüls (*Madame de...* [1953] is one of his favorite films), Louis Malle (a maverick whose *Le Souffle au cœur* [1971] and documentaries on India left a lasting impression on him), Henri-Georges Clouzot (one of the great French stylists, whose pessimism and darkness, among other things, fascinated him), Maurice Pialat, Claude Sautet...For Anderson, this influence is more personal than theoretical or aesthetic, more a matter of appreciation than imitation. Although the deliberate lack of expressivity of his actors can be likened to the films of Godard or Bresson, there is none of the glibness and militancy of the former, nor the atonic distance characteristic of the latter. Most of the time, Anderson is more modestly content with quotations for film lovers. When in *The Life Aquatic* (2004) Steve Zissou lecherously addresses his second-in-command in reference to the seductive journalist—"Not this one, Klaus"—he is explicitly referring to a scene from *Jules et Jim* (François Truffaut, 1962) in which the former exhorts the latter ("Not that one, Jim, okay?") not to seduce Catherine, whom they both covet.

Two Myths, Two Influences

In *Bottle Rocket* (1996), his first feature film, Wes Anderson could not resist hanging a large photo of Jacques-Yves Cousteau on the wall for one shot. At the time, in the late 1990s, no one paid much attention to this reference to France: the French oceanographer was at least as big a star in his native country as he was in the United States, where, in 1973, he founded the Cousteau Society, an association for the protection of nature. His documentaries, recounting his expeditions in largely fictionalized form, enjoyed an international television audience and fascinated the Anderson brothers when they were children. In short, Cousteau was a long-standing obsession, a mythical figure that Wes Anderson, after invoking him again in *Rushmore* (1998), then reinvented in *The Life Aquatic* through the melancholic character of Steve Zissou. The latter's name is a hidden allusion to another French legend: the photographer Jacques-Henri Lartigue. Indeed, "Zissou" was the nickname of Maurice, his older brother, a daredevil and inventor, whom "JHL" immortalized in many famous fantasy shots. Some of them, which appear in *Rushmore*, provide a regressive pleasure that establishes an immediate correspondence with Anderson's universe. Acknowledging his debt to these two models, the director thanks them in the credits of *Rushmore* (for Lartigue) and *The Life Aquatic* (which ends with the words: "In memory of Jacques-Yves Cousteau and with gratitude to the Cousteau Society, which was not involved in making this film").

Musicality

The spirit of France can be found in the soundtracks of many of Wes Anderson's films, both in terms of dialogue and musical choices. In *Rushmore*, when the schoolteacher tells him she is not attracted to him, Max Fischer retorts in French with the cliché "C'est la vie," perfectly comprehensible for Anglo-Saxon audiences. But most of the time, these dialogues remain purely confidential. Only a French viewer can directly perceive "Port-au-Patois" or "Hôtel Citroën," enigmatic places evoked with an irresistible accent in *The Life Aquatic*. The sounds of Molière's language seem to hold such an appeal for Anderson that he associates them with a form of poetic imagination, as in the scene from *Fantastic Mr. Fox* (2009) where the hero, seeking to communicate with a mythical wolf, addresses him in French (in the original English version) as follows: "Pensez-vous que l'hiver sera rude?" [Do you think it will be a harsh winter?] Even more definitely, Anderson associates French with a form of retro musicality that he loves, and which finds its natural extension in the choice of titles for his film soundtracks: In *Rushmore*, Miss

The 400 Blows (*Les quatre cents coups*) is one of Wes Anderson's favorite films.

Cross plays Yves Montand's "Rue Saint Vincent" (1960) on her cassette player; Joe Dassin's "Les Champs-Élysées" (1969) resonates during the closing credits of *The Darjeeling Limited* (2007); young Sam and Suzy dance to Françoise Hardy's "Le Temps de l'amour" (1962) in *Moonrise Kingdom* (2012). The director also draws on instrumental pieces composed by Frenchmen such as Georges Delerue ("Une Petite Île" [1971] and "Le Grand Choral" [1973] in *Fantastic Mr. Fox*) and guitarist Django Reinhardt ("Manoir de mes rêves" [1943] can be heard in muted tones at the end of *Rushmore*).

Dandyism

In 2007, fourteen years before *The French Dispatch*, the short film *Hotel Chevalier*, a prequel to *The Darjeeling Limited*, formalized Wes Anderson's romance with France, already more than palpable in *Rushmore* and *The Life Aquatic*. Shot entirely at the Hotel Raphaël, in Paris's 16th arrondissement, it enables the filmmaker to film in situ, in the capital of pleasure and love, the end—or the renewal—of a complicated relationship between two damaged beings, two Americans who do not have the same relationship with France. He seems to be a Francophone and Francophile (a double of Anderson?), while she scoffs at his tastes. "What's this music?" she says as she enters the room. The music is "Where Do You Go To (My Lovely)" (Peter Sarstedt, 1969), an English song paying homage to France...the lyrics refer to cabaret dancer Zizi Jeanmaire, the Latin Quarter, the Côte d'Azur, and jazz guitarist, singer, and composer Sacha Distel. Anderson reproduces this subtle *mise en abyme* in *The Darjeeling Limited*, when the same male character pulls out of his briefcase an imaginary perfume called Voltaire #6—La petite mort, a way of reconnecting to the Parisian episode to the mourning of an impossible love and to the orgasm in the figurative sense. In general, anything to do with luxury, culture, and thought is, for the director, synonymous with the French. Margot (*The Royal Tenenbaums*, 2001) wears the famous Birkin bag designed by Hermès, journalist Jane Winslett-Richardson (*The Life Aquatic*) reads excerpts from *Du côté de chez Swann* (Marcel Proust, 1913) to the baby in her womb, Mr. Gustave (*The Grand Budapest Hotel*, 2014) demands the fragrance L'air de panache, and journalist Augie Steenbeck (*Asteroid City*, 2023) works as a photojournalist for French Press International.

Gwyneth Paltrow (Margot Tenenbaum) sports the famous Hermès Birkin bag in *The Royal Tenenbaums*.

A Very Blue, White, and Red Team

Wes Anderson's move to Paris undoubtedly heightened his Francophile leanings and led to a simultaneous Frenchification of his professional entourage. Among his closest associates were Octavia Peissel, producer (associate or co-producer) since *Moonrise Kingdom*; Martin Scali, his former personal assistant turned second-unit director (starting with *The Grand Budapest Hotel*); and, of course, Alexandre Desplat, his regular composer since *Fantastic Mr. Fox*. Other French personnel occupied key positions on Anderson's organizational chart. The Franco-Japanese Erica Dorn, who entered the director's circle at the time of *Isle of Dogs* (2018), became head of the graphics department, where she was mainly surrounded by French collaborators. Stéphane Cressend, the great coordinator of the set decoration team since *The French Dispatch*, was now a direct assistant to Adam Stockhausen, the influential artistic supervisor. Patricia Colin, the head lighting designer who worked hand in hand with Italian designer Milena Canonero, began her collaboration on Wes Anderson's 2004 American Express advertisement. More recently, tailor Nathalie Paillon and milliner Karine Niederman also joined this little family. Finally, one could mention the case of Simon Weisse, a German born in France, who was responsible for miniatures, completely bilingual, and strongly attached to France. And this is a non-exhaustive list...

Don't Cut

Land Lines

You will never see a character with a smartphone in a film by Wes Anderson, who conscientiously erases all traces of modernity from his outdated images. He prefers landline telephones and phone booths—if possible from before the 1980s. The object itself is not necessarily very aesthetic, but its anchorage in a bygone era and the prehistoric gestures it elicits contribute to the museum-like mannerism that characterizes the director's work. With a few exceptions, its use is reserved for notables, employees, and depressed characters—like Margot in *The Royal Tenenbaums* (2001). The immobility it implies stands in stark contrast to the perpetual motion of Andersonian cinema.

Augie Steenbeck (played by Jason Schwartzman) phones his father-in-law (Tom Hanks) in the middle of the desert in *Asteroid City*.

Bill Murray (Mr. Ivan) sporting his mustache and speaking into his concierge handset in *The Grand Budapest Hotel*.

Gwyneth Paltrow (Margot Tenenbaum) and the pink telephone in *The Royal Tenenbaums*.

In *Rushmore*, Max Fischer's life depends on a phone call.

Young Chas Tenenbaum (Aram Aslanian-Persico) is a budding businessman in *The Royal Tenenbaums*.

Alexandre Desplat has composed six soundtracks for Wes Anderson, as of the first printing of this book.

Alexandre Desplat The Metronome

Heart of Music

Alexandre Desplat, the French maestro, honored as a Chevalier de la Légion d'Honneur in 2011 for his film scores, navigates between France, England (Stephen Frears, Tom Hooper) and the United States (David Fincher, Terrence Malick, George Clooney). It was on the other side of the Atlantic that he had his first decisive encounter with Wes Anderson around 2007. Since *Fantastic Mr. Fox* (2009), he has created the haunting music for the Texan filmmaker's films, earning him one of his two Oscars in 2015 for the soundtrack to *The Grand Budapest Hotel* (2014)—the other one being for Guillermo Del Toro's *The Shape of Water* (2017) in 2018. The two men have been together ever since. Characterized by an uninterrupted dialogue (favored by their Parisian proximity) and a shared taste, their collaboration is one of the most fruitful of the twenty-first century from an aesthete's perspective.

First Contact

"A mutual friend, director Stephen Gaghan, with whom I collaborated on *Syriana* (2005), introduced me to Wes. We chatted and he mentioned a project that might interest me. He got back to me almost a year later. At the time, he was in Paris editing *Fantastic Mr. Fox* and showed me some excerpts. From there, I started working on the music. He wanted a big symphony orchestra, but I felt it didn't work with the delicate aesthetic of the film and the adorable little dolls. So I proposed a miniature symphony orchestra, consisting of a single instrument per section: a flute, a horn, a trumpet, a trombone, a first and second violin, a cello, a double bass, etc. No timpani or overly sonorous big timpani sound, but small toy instruments such as the glockenspiel (a kind of metal xylophone), banjo, mandolin, Jew's harp, recorder, or sound-making objects that almost fit within the hand."[1]

Follow the Guide

"Wes's music is, on the whole, deeply melancholy, but underneath a playful, joyful surface. It's highly legible, sparsely orchestrated, deliberately melodic, with rhythms that are often haunting or frenetic. [...] It's there to contribute a whimsy, an original purity that comes from childhood, a bit like Nino Rota's music for Fellini. [...] With each film, the crucial question arises concerning which instruments to use. It's practically the first thing Wes asks me. It's like a game between me and him, like two kids trying to decide which toy to play with! For my part, I try to broaden the possibilities, to help him discover new sounds, always connected to his tastes. [...] Take *Isle of Dogs* [2018], for example: we had to create a collective unconscious of Japanese music, while bypassing it at the same time. In my opinion, this meant using typical instruments, but also an orchestra of saxophones, recorders, and whistles. Or through the use of very deep male choruses, inspired by Noh theater, with which I had a lot of fun. As an anecdote, there's a particular scansion where the singers say, in very low tones, 'yo-ko-o-no.' It's a tribute to Yoko Ono, who does the voice of a secondary character! I don't think anyone made the connection, but we liked this 'private joke' tribute."[2]

A Simple, Effective Modus Operandi

"We start putting ideas together at a very early stage, as soon as the script comes out of the oven. For *Asteroid City* [2023], for example, I wrote some of the music before the shoot. Wes was able to have it on set and play the original theme during the takes. Otherwise, most of the time, I watch the film more or less finalized, thinking about themes, motifs, and orchestrations. We meet for the first time to listen to them, and from this initial meeting, a selection is made. He leaves with them, and I keep on looking. [...] We make rapid progress together. As it happens, we're neighbors in Paris, and Wes visits me regularly to exchange ideas. He has an exceptional musical memory. I remember when I was working on *The Grand Budapest Hotel*, he came to my studio one morning, and I played him the themes I was working on. A week later, he whistled me one of the tunes he'd heard on that day. [...] In this case, it was a question of finding a catchy melody with typical Central European instruments, such as the cimbalom [hammered dulcimer] and the balalaika [Russian long-necked lute-like instrument], again avoiding the trap of the symphony orchestra; it was about maintaining a clownish energy without losing depth."[3]

Positive Emulation

"Like all great directors, Wes loves control. If you're lucky enough to develop a long-term collaboration with a filmmaker, you inevitably adopt their tone and colors. I'm an Andersonian, just as I'm an Audiardian. [...] One of my assets in his view, I think, is that I know all his references very well. I was able to suggest music that had a certain familiarity with what he liked. [...] On *Moonrise Kingdom* [2012], for example, we had to take inspiration from Benjamin Britten [a British composer], whom Wes reveres, but at the same time distance ourselves from it. So I went back to *Fantastic Mr. Fox*, to this idea of a miniature ensemble, but with more scope and melancholy. [...] In the end, everything starts from an ongoing dialogue with Wes, who in turn relies on the music editor to recalibrate and recut what I write. In a way, he's having fun with my database. I have no objection to this, in fact it's quite satisfying. When you compose music and motifs, and all these pieces work at every point in the film, it's because you've succeeded in getting to the heart of the story, and the universe the director wanted to create."[4]

A Slow Build

Alexandre Desplat, a flautist by training, was captivated by the music of *Star Wars* (George Lucas, 1977), written by John Williams. An epiphany that determined his vocation. In his early days, in the mid-1980s, he composed for television, film, and theater, before working for Jacques Audiard on *Regarde les hommes tomber*, in 1994. His work with the director earned him two of his three Césars—in 2006 for *De battre mon cœur s'est arrêté* (2005) and, in 2013, for *De rouille et d'os* (2012). Finally recognized in France, he tried his luck abroad, and was a resounding success: the British-Luxembourg film *The Girl with the Pearl Earring* (Peter Webber, 2003) received two nominations for its music at the Golden Globes and BAFTAs (the British equivalent of the Césars).

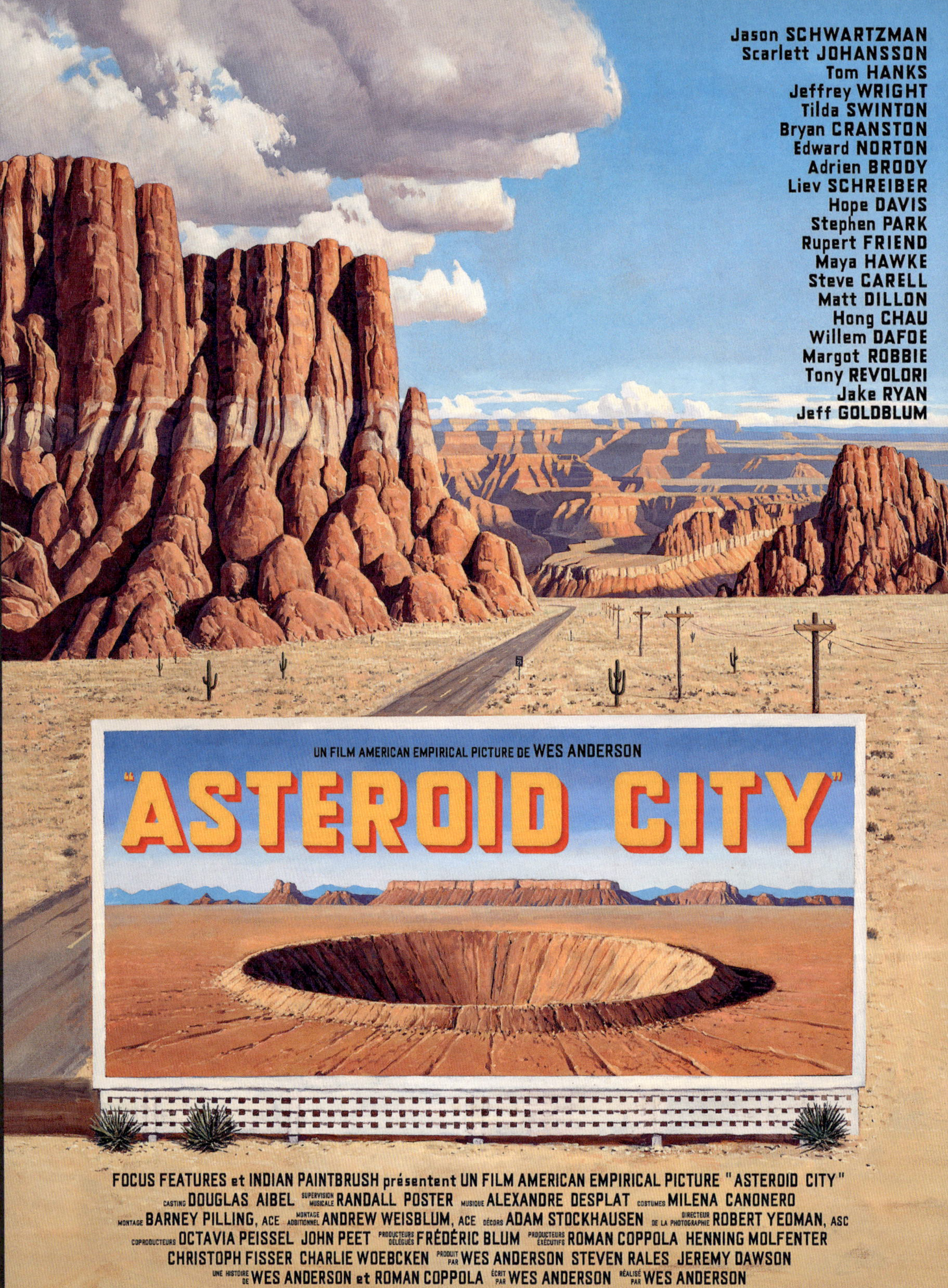
Jason SCHWARTZMAN
Scarlett JOHANSSON
Tom HANKS
Jeffrey WRIGHT
Tilda SWINTON
Bryan CRANSTON
Edward NORTON
Adrien BRODY
Liev SCHREIBER
Hope DAVIS
Stephen PARK
Rupert FRIEND
Maya HAWKE
Steve CARELL
Matt DILLON
Hong CHAU
Willem DAFOE
Margot ROBBIE
Tony REVOLORI
Jake RYAN
Jeff GOLDBLUM
UN FILM AMERICAN EMPIRICAL PICTURE DE WES ANDERSON
"ASTEROID CITY"
FOCUS FEATURES et INDIAN PAINTBRUSH présentent UN FILM AMERICAN EMPIRICAL PICTURE "ASTEROID CITY"
CASTING DOUGLAS AIBEL SUPERVISION MUSICALE RANDALL POSTER MUSIQUE ALEXANDRE DESPLAT COSTUMES MILENA CANONERO
MONTAGE BARNEY PILLING, ACE MONTAGE ADDITIONNEL ANDREW WEISBLUM, ACE DÉCORS ADAM STOCKHAUSEN DIRECTEUR DE LA PHOTOGRAPHIE ROBERT YEOMAN, ASC
COPRODUCTEURS OCTAVIA PEISSEL JOHN PEET PRODUCTEURS DÉLÉGUÉS FRÉDÉRIC BLUM PRODUCTEURS EXÉCUTIFS ROMAN COPPOLA HENNING MOLFENTER
CHRISTOPH FISSER CHARLIE WOEBCKEN PRODUIT PAR WES ANDERSON STEVEN RALES JEREMY DAWSON
UNE HISTOIRE DE WES ANDERSON et ROMAN COPPOLA ÉCRIT PAR WES ANDERSON RÉALISÉ PAR WES ANDERSON
FOCUS FEATURES
INDIAN PAINTBRUSH
BANDE ORIGINALE DISPONIBLE CHEZ abkco RECORDS
LE 21 JUIN AU CINÉMA
@UniversalFR
AsteroidCity-LeFilm.com #AsteroidCityLeFilm
UNIVERSAL

ASTEROID CITY

United States, Germany	1 h 45	Color / Black and white	Dolby Digital	1.37 : 1 / 2.39 : 1

Production Dates: **August–October 2021**
World Premiere: **May 23, 2023 (Cannes Film Festival)**
Release Dates in the United States: **June 16, 2023 (limited release); June 23, 2023**

Budget: **approx. $25 million**
North America Box Office: **approx. $28 million**
Worldwide Box Office: **approx. $54 million**

Production Companies: **Focus Features, American Empirical Pictures, Indian Paintbrush, Studio Babelsberg**
Producers: **Wes Anderson, Jeremy Dawson, Steven Rales**
Executive Producers: **Roman Coppola, Christoph Fisser, Henning Molfenter, Charlie Woebcken**
Co-Producers: **John Peet, Octavia Peissel**
Line Producers: **Frédéric Blum, Fernando Victoria de Lecea**
Associate Producer: **Molly Rosenblatt**

Screenplay: **Wes Anderson, based on a story by Wes Anderson and Roman Coppola**
Director of Photography: **Robert Yeoman**
First Assistant Director: **Atilla Salih Yücer**
Second Unit Director: **Martin Scali**
Film Editor: **Barney Pilling**
Production Designer: **Adam Stockhausen**
Set Decorator: **Kris Moran**
Supervising Art Director: **Stéphane Cressend**
Music Supervisor: **Randall Poster**
Music: **Alexandre Desplat**
Sound: **Valentino Giannì, Wayne Lemmer, Chris Scarabosio**
Costumes: **Milena Canonero**
Makeup: **Julie Dartnell**
Lead Graphic Designer: **Erica Dorn**
Miniatures: **Simon Weisse**
Miniatures: **Douglas Aibel**

Starring: **JASON SCHWARTZMAN (Augie Steenbeck), SCARLETT JOHANSSON (Midge Campbell), TOM HANKS (Stanley Zak), JEFFREY WRIGHT (General Gibson), TILDA SWINTON (Dr. Hickenlooper), BRYAN CRANSTON (host), EDWARD NORTON (Conrad Earp), ADRIEN BRODY (Schubert Green), HOPE DAVIS (Sandy Borden), STEPHEN PARK (Roger Cho), RUPERT FRIEND (Montana), STEVE CARELL (Motel Manager), MATT DILLON (Mechanic), JEFF GOLDBLUM (the Alien)...**

“I spent nine months designing all the [fake] mountains for *Asteroid City*.”

Turlo Griffin,
concept artist and illustrator[1]

SYNOPSIS

It's 1955. A TV presenter (in black and white) reveals the behind-the-scenes story of playwright Conrad Earp's new play, *Asteroid City*, to be staged in New York. The characters come and go: a war photographer, Augie Steenbeck, and his gifted son, Woodrow; an actress, Midge Campbell, and her daughter, Dinah… We learn more about the actors who play them in the course of the story, which is cut in two. Then it is time for color and the film based on the play just presented. It features the same characters landing in Asteroid City, a tiny town lost in the middle of the desert in the southwest of the United States, where nuclear testing is taking place in the distance. Augie Steenbeck, Midge Campbell, and other parents accompany their children to a scientific convention, where these little geniuses, inventors of more or less extravagant contraptions, are invited to demonstrate their abilities. Soon, something extraordinary happens. A flying saucer lands unexpectedly in the crater (where a meteorite is said to have crashed) that is the pride of the town! Is the world in danger?

Bryan Cranston plays the phlegmatic presenter and narrator of *Asteroid City*.

GENESIS

Early 2020. The world discovered two words it would not forget in a hurry: "COVID" and "lockdown." Forced to postpone the release of *The French Dispatch* (scheduled for the 2020 Cannes Film Festival, which did not take place), Wes Anderson did not allow the prevailing gloom to get the better of him. As an auteur, time was his ally, and fortunately so, as he was about to have plenty of it! Roman Coppola, his longtime associate, was in the same situation, and obviously available to continue working on the next project. He knew full well that with Anderson, storytelling is never linear. It proceeds by cross-referencing ideas, poetic visions, and thematic aspirations. During preliminary discussions in 2019, a number of themes took shape: theater, the Cold War, the desert, the paranoia of American society...These broad outlines naturally situate the action of the film in the 1950s, a period of both great economic prosperity (the "American way of life" was experiencing its peak growth, with household appliances making stay-at-home mothers happy) and irrational fears (of communism, nuclear power, and extraterrestrial invasions).

Dramatic Events

In 1947, future filmmaker Elia Kazan—along with producer Cheryl Crawford and director Robert Lewis—founded the Actors Studio in New York, a theater school poised to revolutionize the art of acting. From 1951 onward, actor Lee Strasberg took up the torch (Kazan had moved to Hollywood) and developed "the Method," a new approach in which the actor draws on his personal memory and emotions to play a role. A product of this school, the Paul Newman–Joanne Woodward pairing inspired in Wes Anderson and Roman Coppola (who would be credited as co-writer of the original story) a plot revolving around a play being staged, with all the emotional and artistic issues that implies. The two partners were also thinking of Sam Shepard, a playwright who fascinated them and whose semi-experimental theater was marked by the consequences of war (in the broadest sense) on men and their loved ones. They were also interested in another key figure of the 1950s: Arthur Miller. In addition to his links with Kazan (who directed his first play, *Death of a Salesman*, in 1949), the playwright is famous for his marriage to Marilyn Monroe—who also enrolled at

Jake Ryan had a small role as Woodrow, Augie Steenbeck's eldest son, in *Moonrise Kingdom*.

the Actors Studio in 1955. Anderson and Coppola put all these references through the sieve of their unbridled imagination to come up with a story—narrated by a TV presenter—of the backstage drama of a New York theatrical production. Four main characters emerged: an omnipotent author, a tortured director, an actor well versed in "the Method," and a preoccupied platinum blonde.

Mise en abyme

Armed with this theatrical backbone, Anderson and Coppola decided to couple it with a fictionalized version of their author's play *Asteroid City*. A clever parallel montage, of which the director is a master, takes the viewer from the New York rehearsal scenes to their film adaptation, set in the Arizona desert. This second strand of the film takes up a little more space and develops the secondary characters, less prominent in the "theater" part. We discover that the play tells the story of a scientific convention attended by precocious geniuses (accompanied by their parents) near a crater and nuclear tests that can be seen behind the hills in the distance. This film-within-a-film enables Anderson to tackle themes close to his heart, such as family (parenthood, siblings), grief (the main character, father of three little girls and a teenager, has just lost his wife), and childhood.

Science Frictions

The 1950s also saw the intensification of the Cold War and the fear of nuclear conflict, which gave rise to widespread anxiety in the United States. It fostered the emergence of McCarthyism, the policy of tracking down suspected communists in society, which would have a considerable impact on the film industry—Elia Kazan was infamous for denouncing his comrades. The average American was also inundated with literary, television, and film works that tackled the subject in more or less roundabout ways. The growing success of science fiction stems from this particular context. In *The Day the Earth Stood Still* (Robert Wise, 1951) and *The Thing from Another World* (Howard Hawks and Christian Nyby, 1951), the classic villains, are replaced by fantastic creatures from outer space aboard flying saucers, metaphors for an imminent invasion from outside (the Soviet Union). As pop culture enthusiasts, Anderson and Coppola saw this as an opportunity to pay homage to a genre that had nurtured them. In addition to the scientific convention, *Asteroid City* the play (and therefore the film, if one follows the logic) would feature the unexpected irruption of a UFO and one of its strange occupants, leading to an improvised quarantine by panicked military personnel. An obvious reference to the classic *Close Encounters of the Third Kind* (Steven Spielberg, 1977), which Anderson and

A mushroom cloud testifies to the existence of nuclear testing not far away.

Coppola cherish, along with *2001: A Space Odyssey* (Stanley Kubrick, 1968). In the end, despite all its influences, *Asteroid City* still resembles nothing so much as a Wes Anderson film: unique, unclassifiable (Comedy? Drama? Science fiction? Art film?), with a strong sense of fantasy and poetry, it enables viewers to look at the world differently.

CASTING

Asteroid City offers an abundant gallery of characters, dominated by the play's two lead actors (Jones Hall and Mercedes Ford) and their film doubles (Augie Steenbeck and Midge Campbell), played by Jason Schwartzman and Scarlett Johansson, respectively. All were required to play two roles under strict sanitary conditions (in the summer of 2021, extreme precautions were still the norm). The actors were chosen for their ability to blend easily into Wes Anderson's world, instinctively understand its nuances, and know its routines and demands. With a few exceptions (Hope Davis, Steve Carell, Matt Dillon, Margot Robbie, and the kids), most of the stars selected had already worked with the director.

A Sad Parallel

At no point did the question of casting the male lead arise for Anderson. "This film was written for Jason [Schwartzman]. It is a type of character he has never played before, and it draws on aspects of his personality that we know and what we think he is capable of doing."[2] Schwartzman, close to the director and to Coppola (his cousin), was obviously informed of the news before the rest of the cast. He was overwhelmed by the news and feverishly followed the progress of the writing process, which coincided with the

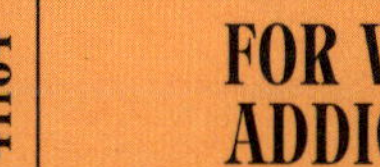

FOR WES ADDICTS

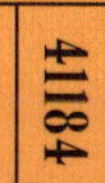

For the first time since *Rushmore*, Bill Murray had to turn down a Wes Anderson film, constrained by the COVID virus he contracted just before shooting began. He was replaced on short notice by Steve Carell, who took his place as the manager of the motel where the participants in the scientific convention are staying. Carell had earlier filled in for the unavailable Murray on *Little Miss Sunshine* (Jonathan Dayton and Valerie Faris, 2006).

How better to illustrate the loneliness of these two people, at the same time so far away and yet so close?

A convention brings together budding scientific geniuses in the crater of *Asteroid City*.

emergence and subsequent spread of the pandemic. In these troubled times, such a proposal was like a breath of fresh air. Grateful, and perhaps anxious (he had not played a major film role for a long time), he took his characters very seriously, especially that of Augie Steenbeck, the war photographer devastated by the recent death of his wife and unable to break the news to his children. This situation awakened a painful family memory: faced with the same tragedy, his paternal grandfather had left his two sons (including the actor's father, Jack Schwartzman) in the dark for several weeks.

A Studious Actor

Dedicated and diligent, Jason Schwartzman searched for the best way to create a sad, inexpressive face. Seeing how his wife's speech was impeded by a moisturizing face mask, he decided to apply one himself and film himself delivering his lines! His experiments eventually led him to fit a tiny mouthguard over his molars to block his jaw. Scarlett Johansson did not go as far as Jason Schwartzman to slip into the skin of Mercedes Ford, the platinum-blond actress in the play (a Marilyn Monroe clone) who turns into a depressed brunette star and overwhelmed mother (under the name Midge Campbell) in the film adaptation. A few years after lending her voice to a proud show dog in *Isle of Dogs* (2018), she knew what Anderson wanted from her: sex appeal tinged with melancholy.

The Club of Five

Accustomed to casting children and teenagers (in *Rushmore* [1998] and especially *Moonrise Kingdom* [2012]), Wes Anderson had no particular problems finding the five young actors who would play—mainly—the geniuses of the film within the film. The role of Woodrow, Augie Steenbeck's eldest son, is played by Jake Ryan, who had already appeared in *Moonrise Kingdom*—he was the heroine's dark-haired little brother. Grace Edwards (Dinah, Midge Campbell's daughter), Sophia Lillis (Shelly), and Ethan Josh Lee (Ricky), all at least eighteen at the time of filming, had careers behind them before being cast. Only Aristou Meehan (Clifford) had no previous solid experience. Although Meehan had applied for auditions, Anderson and his collaborators spotted him in videos he had posted on YouTube that showed off robotic arms he had made that were similar to octopus tentacles. Following a tried-and-tested method on *Moonrise Kingdom*, Wes Anderson encouraged these five hopefuls to spend time together off the set to strengthen the bonds between them. Lodging next to each other, they shared meals and activities, creating their own bubble, away from the "adults."

Waiting for signs from outer space . . .

Woodrow's three little sisters are not afraid of aliens.

Wes Anderson directs Jason Schwartzman and a newcomer to his world, Tom Hanks (as Stanley Zak) in *Asteroid City*.

FILMING AND PRODUCTION

Initially, it was strongly envisaged that the sun-drenched city of *Asteroid City* would be recreated in a backlot at Cinecittà, where Wes Anderson had shot part of *The Life Aquatic* (2004). The idea was abandoned for a specific reason explained by Stéphane Cressend, the French set supervisor: "Wes doesn't like what we call 'company moves,' the English term for moving from one set to another. This is why he finally chose to shoot in Chinchón, Spain, rather than in Cinecittà as originally planned, because the hotel in Rome was a long way from the studios. He likes to travel to the set in a golf cart!"[3]

Safe Distances

Chinchón, a small town with a listed historic center, located fifty kilometers southeast of Madrid, offered all the necessary features: wide open spaces in the immediate vicinity (where Asteroid City was to be built on a vast field that would be leveled and sandblasted to resemble the desert), clear skies in summer, and all the hotel facilities one could wish for. According to Stéphane Cressend, these logistical conditions were ideal. "In Chinchón, an old convent converted into a hotel was completely privatized. Wes, the actors, the producers and all the site managers stayed there."[4] Regardless of these management issues, Wes Anderson and Adam Stockhausen, the artistic designer, pulled off a tour de force by preparing the film in the middle of a pandemic, remotely! In constant contact with the Spanish team on location, they had to consider all the possibilities open to them before putting together a small team to travel to the filming location and supervise the construction of the three main sets: the motel where the families and their offspring stay, the bar-restaurant where Augie Steenbeck meets Midge Campbell for the first time, and the service station where the grumpy garage owner, played by Matt Dillon, works.

Daylight

Anderson's references to his collaborators are numerous, as usual. Cinematographer Robert Yeoman, for example, revisited *Bad Day at Black Rock* (John Sturges, 1955) and *Paris, Texas* (Wim Wenders, 1984) for their treatment of vast desert spaces and light. "Wes was eager to not use movie lights for the day scenes. To light the interiors, I asked to build skylights in the buildings [like the diner or motel office]. We covered the skylights with a heavy diffusion material so the interior had a soft, even light. It gave us a perfect balance between the exposure of the inside and outside. It also enabled Wes to stage the scenes without worrying about the placement of any lighting gear."[5] The saturated pastel tones of the image, which make the film look like a graphic novel come to life, do not owe everything to nature. The result is a combination of the various artistic choices made by Wes Anderson and Adam Stockhausen (on sets and costumes) and the use of digital tools during color grading, that final stage of harmonizing colors and light.

A Renewed Sense of Purpose

On the front line with the sets team, the costumes department pulled out all the stops to support the film's retro feel. Under the direction of designer Milena Canonero, several original motifs were hand-painted by textile artists. This trend, which had been favored since *The Grand Budapest Hotel*, was becoming increasingly pronounced, according to French costume designer Patricia Colin. "We went even further in working with fabric prints! [...] We created author Conrad Earp's robe, Stanley Zak's golf pants [Augie Steenbeck's father-in-law], Roger Cho's Hawaiian shirt [one of Genie's parents], Midge Campbell's robe with desert flowers."[6] This outpouring of creativity was accompanied by an intensive hunt for more classic outfits. This laborious quest ended, for Patricia Colin, with an unexpected Holy Grail. "I found a pair of original 1950s Levi's jeans at one of my vintage retailers, which you can't find anywhere! And not at all expensive! It was like discovering a golden nugget."[7]

Nueva York

For the practical reasons mentioned above, Anderson insisted on filming the New York sequences in black and white in Spain (including those with the presenter, live from his TV set). In Chinchón and the surrounding towns, theaters of various sizes abound. The crew took over some of them, transforming them into sets to suit his taste. For Robert Yeoman, working conditions were logically altered. Not only did he have to rethink his framing to accommodate the change in format (these sequences were shot in square format, rather than the scope format used for the film-in-film section), but also his lighting, switching from color to black and white. "I added more backlights and edge lights to separate the actors from the background. We also used more hard lights [instead of soft lights], as they looked better on the black and white film stock."[8] Despite the difficulties, the aesthetic continuity between the two parts was perfectly achieved.

Freeze Frame

Several stages were involved in the conception of the film's alien, animated frame by frame. Dressed in a special jumpsuit, Jeff Goldblum, on small stilts to reach nearly seven feet tall (he is six foot four), was first filmed moving around and mimicking the space creature. The resulting footage was then used by French animator Kim Keukeleire to bring to life the nearly three-foot-tall doll, designed by puppet maker Andy Gent.

The young geniuses attempt a forbidden connection with the outside world.

RECEPTION

Asteroid City was previewed at the Cannes Film Festival on May 23, 2023. Critics were divided. Some called it "Wes Anderson in top form"[9] or "an exhilarating triumph of pure style"[10]; others said it was "a desert of déjà vu"[11] or "a who's who of actors, a 1950s fever-dream look, and no point whatsoever."[12] Box office results were much better than those of *The French Dispatch*, but not the rebound expected. Despite its obvious qualities (photography, music, acting), the film failed to receive a single Golden Globe nomination, let alone an Oscar nomination. Had Anderson's resolutely arty turn in the last two films reached a dead end?

The Future?

Wes Anderson's films are often criticized for "running on empty," trapped in his staging devices and more or less entrenched existential obsessions. The director is certainly no great believer in the "great divide," but he has always been able to vary his perspectives and evolve his vision when the time was right (shooting in India, use of animation). After *The Grand Budapest Hotel*, his biggest success, he could have become a specialist in historical illuminations. Instead, he opted for a sharper (some would say nerdy) style of filmmaking, even if it meant bewildering critics and audiences alike. A definite trend or an experimental parenthesis? Only time will tell.

No Wrong Notes

Composer Alexandre Desplat's main challenge with *Asteroid City* was to avoid the cliché of a science fiction score—given the mystery of the alien's presence. "When I discovered the animation, the landscapes of the American West, with their gas pumps and old abandoned billboards, their archaic electrical cables tossed about by the wind, their gaunt ghost town facades, symbols of a time stopped, inspired me to create a sound world and a main motif based on two notes played in the high register of the piano and repeated endlessly, blending in with the noise of these cables buffeted by the sandy winds. I built the whole score around these two notes."[13]

Edward Norton (Conrad Earp, the play's author) concentrates before a scene that will be shot in black and white.

On either side of the camera, Wes Anderson and his director of photography, Robert Yeoman.

In *The Royal Tenenbaums*, Danny Glover (right) plays Henry Sherman, Etheline Tenenbaum's suitor, and Al Thompson plays Walter Sherman, Henry's son.

At the Theater This Evening

Behind the Scenes

The erudite Wes Anderson has a keen interest in literature. In his films, his characters devote a great deal of time to reading, and books occasionally invade the screen. The book as an object, directly linked to culture, the civilized world, and order, reassures him. The theater enables him to quench his thirst for knowledge and his passion for directing.

Challenged in primary school by a teacher eager to channel his unruliness, Anderson had written and directed plays as part of his extracurricular activities. He drew on this memorable experience for the script of *Rushmore* (1998), which features the eccentric theatrical creations of Max Fischer, directly inspired by his own. To underline the importance of the stage in his life, the film ends with a spectacular play, full of noise and fury, in which Max, dressed like Tom Cruise in *Top Gun* (Tony Scott, 1986), leather jacket on his back and sunglasses on his nose, improvises as a Vietnam War hero.

Reclaiming Artificiality

Each chapter of *Rushmore* opens with a rising curtain, Wes Anderson's way of demystifying cinematic realism in his second film by likening it to theatrical artificiality. In the same spirit, frames within frames (windows, screens, car interiors, train cabins, etc.), which refer to the scenic space as seen from the auditorium, began to abound in his cinema. He would never renounce this profession of faith, which he has continued to refine. *Moonrise Kingdom* (2012) marks another milestone. The character of the narrator, who addresses the camera, breaks through the famous fourth wall (an imaginary wall separating the audience from reality) dear to the German playwright Bertolt Brecht and his epic theater, an obvious source of inspiration for Anderson: the minimalist acting of the actors, frozen in a single expression of absence and incredulity, encourages both distancing and reflection on the part of the spectator. The director never forgets to remind the viewer of this, for example in *The Grand Budapest Hotel* (2014), when the older Zero reverts to his youth, the light suddenly dims in the reception room where he is sitting. One can almost hear the three knocks...

Between a Film and a Statement

As Martin Scali, his loyal French second unit director, asserts, Wes Anderson has, in *The Wonderful Story of Henry Sugar* (2023), "taken another step forward in the theatricalization of his mise-en-scène, in the choreography of the scenes, their sequence."[1] This Roald Dahl adaptation stands out for the transparency of its theatrical device: entire sections of the set are lifted or slid away, replaced by others arriving in the opposite direction, while the main character continues to act as if nothing had happened, speaking directly to the camera. Occasionally, stagehands appear on screen, pulling curtains here, moving a table there. For this art film, the director claims to have been inspired by *Swimming to Cambodia* (Jonathan Demme, 1987),[2] a curious feature-length film, somewhere between fiction and documentary, in which the American actor Spalding Gray recounts his experience of Cambodia during the filming of *The Killing Fields* (Roland Joffé, 1984), in which he played a secondary role. Seated in front of a table, on which two microphones are placed, Gray addresses an imaginary audience whose reactions can be heard. Half in a trance, the actor delivers both amusing anecdotes and sordid accounts of the massacres perpetrated by the Khmer Rouge. From a distance, *Swimming to Cambodia* looks like the recording of an extraordinary stage performance, but on closer inspection, it is actually a cinema film. Lighting effects, framing, and music all contribute to the tension created by this long monologue, which resonates both deeply and poetically.

Spalding Gray in *Swimming to Cambodia.*

Toward Abstraction

This intimate quest for an art film, borrowing as much from theater as from the experiments of the American avant-garde and the New Wave (Godard comes to mind), is not entirely new. *The French Dispatch* (2021) already showed its colors, with its narrative contortions, unpredictable use of black-and-white, intellectual dialogues, and numerous closed-door scenes. Wes Anderson followed up with *Asteroid City* (2023), a dizzying *mise en abyme* about a film within a film, itself adapted from a play, with a narrator explaining its intricacies to the viewer. Increasingly, the Texas director's feature films resemble Russian dolls in which different levels of narrative are superimposed—with variations in genre and aesthetic. Twenty-five years after *Rushmore*, Anderson is no longer afraid to engage with the artificiality of his cinema: in fact he embraces it wholeheartedly.

The Rat Catcher

The Swan

COLLECTION ROALD DAHL

United States • **41 min / 17 min 17 min / 17 min** • **Color** • **Dolby Digital** • **1.66:1 / 1.33:1 / 1.33:1 / 2.35:1**

Production Dates: **January–February 2022**
World Premiere: **September 1, 2023 (Venice Film Festival)**
Worldwide Release on Netflix: **September 27, 2023** ***(The Wonderful Story of Henry Sugar)*****, September 28, 2023** ***(The Swan)*****, September 29, 2023** ***(The Rat Catcher)*****, September 30, 2023** ***(Poison)***
Budget: **?**

Production Companies: **Netflix, American Empirical Pictures, Indian Paintbrush**
Producers: **Wes Anderson, Jeremy Dawson, Steven Rales**
Co-Producers: **Alice Dawson, John Peet, Octavia Peissel**
Associate Producer: **Molly Rosenblatt**

Screenplay: **Wes Anderson, based on the short stories of Roald Dahl**
Directors of Photography: **Robert Yeoman, Roman Coppola** ***(The Swan)***
First Assistant Director: **Adam Somner** ***(The Wonderful Story of Henry Sugar)***
Second Unit Director: **Martin Scali** ***(The Wonderful Story of Henry Sugar)***
Film Editors: **Barney Pilling, Andrew Weisblum**
Production Designer: **Adam Stockhausen**
Set Decorators: **Anna Pinnock, Cathy Featherstone**
Art Directors: **Kevin Timon Hill** ***(The Wonderful Story of Henry Sugar)*****, Claire Peerless** ***(The Swan, The Rat Catcher, Poison)***
Music Supervisor: **Randall Poster**
Sound: **Wayne Lemmer, Chris Scarabosio**
Costumes: **Kasia Walicka Maimone**
Makeup/Hair: **Frances Hannon**
Graphics: **Erica Dorn** ***(The Wonderful Story of Henry Sugar)***
Miniatures: **Simon Weisse** ***(The Wonderful Story of Henry Sugar)***
Special Effects: **Chris Reynolds** ***(The Wonderful Story of Henry Sugar)***

Starring: **RALPH FIENNES (Roald Dahl / Policeman / Rat Man), BENEDICT CUMBERBATCH (Henry Sugar / Makeup Artist / Harry Pope), DEV PATEL (Dr. Chatterjee / John Winston / Timber Woods), BEN KINGSLEY (Imdad Khan / Croupier / Dr. Ganderbai), RICHARD AYOADE (Dr. Marshall / Yogi / Editor), RUPERT FRIEND (Narrator / Claude), ASA JENNINGS (Peter Watson)…**

"We had an Indian costume designer lady who scoured the markets for us in Bombay."

Patricia Colin,
costume supervisor, regarding
The Wonderful Story of Henry Sugar[1]

SYNOPSIS

Writer Roald Dahl tells the viewer four short stories. In *The Wonderful Story of Henry Sugar*, a well-to-do gentleman of leisure learns the secret of Imdad Khan, "the man who can see without his eyes," a famous fairground entertainer himself mentored by an Indian yogi master. Henry Sugar uses this knowledge to win with impunity at the casino, before his conscience catches up with him. *The Swan* follows the harassment of a thirteen-year-old boy by two other schoolboys, who end up driving him to the edge. In *The Rat Catcher*, a man presents himself to two others as an infallible rodent exterminator. Unfortunately, his trap does not work. He then reveals his true nature. Lying in bed, forced to stay put, *Poison*'s character waits for someone to remove a dangerous snake coiled around him, threatening to kill him at any moment. A young man and an old doctor work together to save his life.

Benedict Cumberbatch and Ben Kingsley sit at the table in front of Wes Anderson.

GENESIS

This collection is the result of a fortuitous combination of circumstances. Wes Anderson, an admirer of Roald Dahl from an early age, had always dreamed of adapting *The Wonderful Story of Henry Sugar*, his favorite tale by the author, published in the collection of the same name (*The Wonderful Story of Henry Sugar and Six More*, 1977). This desire resurfaced in the early 2000s, when he stayed at the Dahl home to prepare *Fantastic Mr. Fox* (2009), his first foray into the Welsh writer's gritty, childlike universe. He then spoke to Felicity Dahl, Roald's widow, who was delighted by the prospect of a new collaboration. However, it would take another twenty years for the project to take shape, in the wake of the acquisition of the company that managed the rights to the writer's catalog, in September 2021, by the streaming giant Netflix.

Netflix Joins the Dance

Netflix, who wanted to develop a Roald Dahl cinematic universe (like Disney with Marvel), contacted a number of directors for this purpose, including Wes Anderson, known for his closeness to the British author's heirs. The latter was quick to respond, only too happy to resurrect *The Wonderful Story of Henry Sugar*, a project he had left to mature without finding the right treatment. Netflix's proposal was a godsend for one essential reason: the streaming giant could afford to release a medium-length film on its platform (the format the director ultimately wanted), unlike the cinemas. Furthermore, Netflix commissioned not one but four short films from Anderson, who drew on two short story collections to adapt the stories that interested him. While *The Swan* is one of the tales that accompany *The Wonderful Story of Henry Sugar* in the British edition mentioned, *The Rat Catcher* and *Poison* come from the anthology translated into French as *Bizarre! Bizarre* (1962).

Acting while Narrating

For a long time, Anderson struggled to adapt *The Wonderful Story of Henry Sugar*, a story that fascinated him as much as the words Dahl used to tell it. How could this dual interest—narrative and literary—be translated to the screen? Why not ask the actors to act out the scenes while describing them to the audience (as well as occasionally featuring Dahl, who introduces the stories and comments on them)? This basic principle, applied to the other three stories, led to the choice of medium and short formats, as Anderson was unsure whether this particular storytelling method would work for the duration of a feature-length film.

While Benedict Cumberbatch plays Henry Sugar in *The Wonderful Story of Henry Sugar*, Ralph Fiennes plays both Roald Dahl and a policeman.

CASTING

Another principle defined by Wes Anderson for this collection: allowing actors to play several characters in the different segments. "I like[d] the idea, right off the bat, of having a little company play the whole film."[2] To implement his plan, the director called upon regulars Ralph Fiennes (who takes on three roles, including Dahl) and Rupert Friend (two roles, including the narrator of *The Swan*). The latter was particularly delighted by the opportunity. "I grew up completely obsessed with Dahl. I actually had his obituary on my bedroom door. I was so saddened when he died [in 1990]. This film was a dream come true."[3] Fiennes, an obsessive stickler for detail, immersed himself in the archives on the author made available by the family to assimilate the rituals he observed before writing.

Invigorating

The four other actors sharing the bill had never worked with Anderson, who was keen to direct them: Benedict Cumberbatch (who plays Henry Sugar, among other roles), Ben Kingsley ("the man who can see without eyes," a croupier, a doctor), Dev Patel (two roles in *The Wonderful Story of Henry Sugar* and another in *Poison*), and Richard Ayoade (a doctor, a yogi, an editor). For Cumberbatch, working with Anderson extended beyond the strictly professional sphere. "I would have him over my house every night, and we'd watch the great masters of cinema together—Powell and Pressburger, David Lean and Kurosawa. And we'd have these incredible meals and intellectually rigorous conversations, but he's loose and funny and generous and great company. It was so invigorating."[4]

FILMING AND PRODUCTION

Wes Anderson also laid down precise rules for filming and artistic design. These short films would be shot in 16 mm (like the BBC dramas of the 1970s–1980s), in square format (with the exception of *Poison*, filmed in Scope due to the occasional use of multiple screens), and—a rarity for the director—in the studio. The main staging concept he came up with involved building most of the sets on a gigantic set transformed into a convertible theater stage. With a surface area of over a thousand square meters, Stage 1 at Maidstone Studios (located in Kent, southeast of London) would fit the bill. The backlot was to be used for some exteriors, such as those for *The Swan*,

Will the rodent be caught by the rat catcher played by Ralph Fiennes (middle)?

shot entirely in the adjacent parking lot and in natural light.

Mission (Almost) Impossible

Anderson's big idea for *The Wonderful Story of Henry Sugar* (the longest segment, on which Netflix was basing its entire promotion) was to have the characters move—without cutting—through landscapes and sets that fade away as they pass, to make way for others, artificially moved by stagehands who will appear on screen. Miniature buildings and props, false perspectives, and lighting effects also contribute to the desired theatrical effect. Some shot compositions border on the surreal: an actor may find themself in the middle of a set, with a miniature building in the foreground (which will

(L to R) Dev Patel as Timber Woods, Benedict Cumberbatch as Harry Pope, and Ben Kingsley as Dr. Ganderbai in *Poison*.

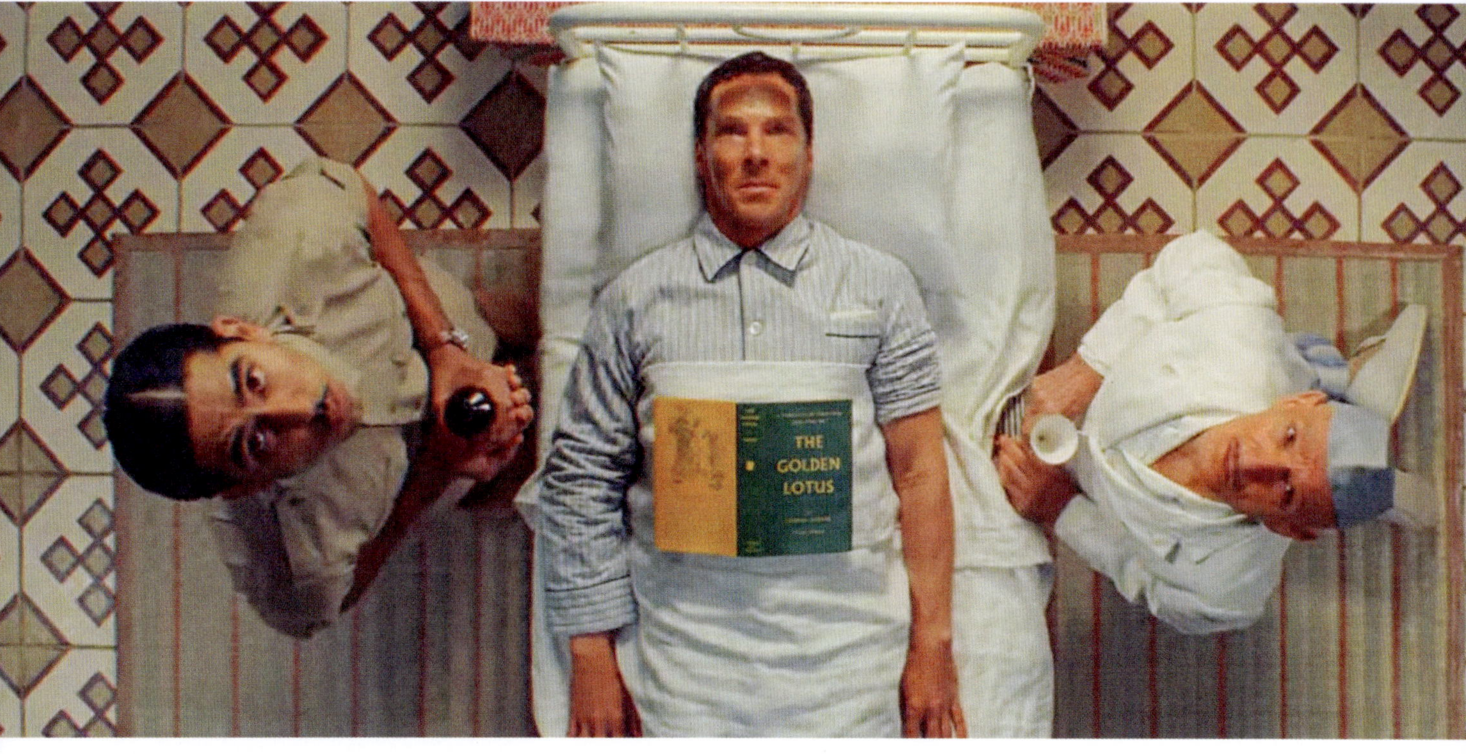

appear "normal" if the right lens and camera angle are used) and a full-scale environment in the background. It was up to the actor and technicians to ensure that the whole thing flowed smoothly. This new challenge was a major one for cinematographer Robert Yeoman, who had seen it all with Wes Anderson. "The shots were complicated. [...] There were a lot of moving parts which required coordination between the actors, tricky camera moves, constant dimming of lights and the movement of the sets within the shot."[5]

The Writer's Hut

Throughout the four segments, Roald Dahl (played by Ralph Fiennes) is shown in the famous hut where he wrote—which was built behind his main residence. Wes Anderson and his collaborators reconstructed the hut almost identically, with a few original objects graciously loaned here and there by the Dahl Museum. The interior design team, led by Adam Stockhausen, did, however, "cheat" a little: "The space is sized and proportioned specifically for our lens and angles."[9]

Precision Mechanics

Second-unit director Martin Scali, here exclusively in charge of the "line-up" (an operation that consists, in parallel with shooting, of going with the second camera to another set or another axis of the same set to prepare the next shot), was once again impressed by the fiendish precision of Anderson's direction. "We had to time the opening and closing of sets, the passage of characters. [...] I have the impression that Wes is more and more inspired by himself. Everything is becoming more and more constructed and precise, with an overtly espoused theatricality. His signatures (symmetry, the accumulation of information within a shot, dolly shots) are reinforced."[6] Adam Stockhausen, who has designed and overseen the art direction of Anderson's films since *Moonrise Kingdom* (2012), agrees. The making of the fake jungle in *The Wonderful Story of Henry Sugar* was edifying in this respect. "It's sort of an illustrated jungle come to life, so none of the plants were real or pretending to be," Stockhausen is quoted as saying in an IndieWire article. Writer Sarah Shachat continues, "But it took a lot of experimentation to get the right level of sculptural and painted vines and flowers in order to create the overall effect of the magic-lantern-esque foliage" (a magic lantern is a historical projection device that reflected images drawn on a painted glass plate).[7]

The Swan song for Rupert Friend (narrator, on the floor) and Asa Jennings (Peter Watson).

RECEPTION

While his last two feature films, *The French Dispatch* (2021) and *Asteroid City* (2023), received mixed reviews from critics, Wes Anderson managed to turn the tide of opinion in his favor with *The Wonderful Story of Henry Sugar*, which premiered at the Venice Film Festival on September 1, 2023. Most observers welcomed the director's return to form and the renewal achieved with this medium-length film, whose extreme inventiveness escaped no one. The other three short films were also subsequently praised.

Precision Mechanics

As Netflix doesn't publish details on its viewership, it is difficult to know if this Roald Dahl collection was a success. Wes Anderson's audacity paid off, however. *The Wonderful Story of Henry Sugar* won the Oscar for Best Live-Action Short Film in 2024. Wes Anderson received his first personal Oscar on that occasion, knowing that the four statuettes awarded to *The Grand Budapest Hotel* in 2015 were for his collaborators (for music, sets, costumes, and makeup and hair). Ironically, the director and his faithful producer Steven Rales were absent from the great annual Hollywood gathering as they prepared for Anderson's twelfth feature film, which was to begin filming the day after the ceremony.

FOR WES ADDICTS

The setting and lighting for *The Swan* were provided by friend and loyal collaborator Roman Coppola, replacing Robert Yeoman. "I had been booked on another film, so Roman took over as our cinematographer." A successful rescue as much as an amusing coincidence: in English, the short film is called *The Swan*, but it just so happens that the title of the second film directed by Roman Coppola is *A Glimpse Inside the Mind of Charles Swan III* (2013).

Wes Anderson at the 2023 Venice Film Festival for the presentation of *The Wonderful Story of Henry Sugar.*

The Wes Influence

International Prestige

Wes Anderson is not only a first-rate filmmaker, but also a multifaceted artist whose art extends into the four corners of the screen. His universe, connected to architecture, design, graphics, animation, history, and pop culture, makes him a rich personality who fascinates beyond his films. Since the announcement of the retirement of Quentin Tarantino (who has stated that his tenth film, currently in production, will be his last), it is even safe to assume that the Texan director is currently the one who is making the biggest mark on the creative world and, more or less visibly, on our daily lives, as evidenced by the famous Instagram account Accidentally Wes Anderson or the hashtag #WesAndersonTrend on TikTok, which encourages members of this network to put themselves in situations evoking his productions. This brilliant creator of shapes also designed the Bar Luce at the Prada Foundation in Milan, and decorated the Cygnus carriage on the famous British Belmond Pullman train, offering British passengers a unique experience. In short, Wes Anderson touches on everything.

Wes at the Museum

Proof of his international influence in France, the Musée Miniatures et Cinéma de Lyon (Cinema and Miniature Museum in Lyon), whose mission is to introduce the public to special effects, crafts, and techniques specific to the seventh art,) opened a permanent space in October 2023 dedicated to the art of cinema through the lens of Wes Anderson. Models, miniatures, objects, costumes, and accessories make up the collection, developed in

The *Accidentally Wes Anderson* exhibition in London, features photos taken by anonymous people in tribute to the director's world.

partnership with the American director. It was a successful gamble for the museum, which had already engaged in dialogue with the filmmaker back in 2015 with a first exhibition devoted to his extraordinary world. The instigator was Simon Weisse, chief model maker on *The Grand Budapest Hotel* (2014), who subsequently became a regular collaborator with the Texan genius. In particular, it was he who designed the model of the façade of the famous hotel (fourteen feet wide and nine feet high), a "character" in the film in its own right, and the highlight of the Lyon exhibition. A great success (sixty thousand visitors in three months), the exhibition also featured miniature set elements from *Fantastic Mr. Fox* (2009), and it enabled the museum's directors to establish a relationship of trust with Anderson. The event, which even had an impact beyond French borders, drew attention to this magical place, located in a Renaissance building listed as a UNESCO World Heritage Site, and to this unique collection featuring the animatronic queen of the *Aliens* saga (James Cameron, 1986), Charlie Chaplin's original walking stick, Alfred Hitchcock's VistaVision camera, and a host of iconic film-related objects.

Win-Win

While the production team of *The Grand Budapest Hotel* had since reclaimed the famous model of the façade, Wes Anderson bequeathed other objects to the Cinema and Miniature Museum, giving them a second life. The advantages are obvious: preservation in such a place avoids storage problems or, worse, outright destruction. Director Julien Dumont, a film enthusiast with many strings to his bow (he is also a producer and director), is delighted that the museum can exhibit in miniature, among other things, the funicular station from *The Grand Budapest Hotel*, the abandoned amusement park from *Isle of Dogs* (2018), and the forced perspective rails from *The Swan*, one of the four short stories that Anderson adapted in 2023 for Netflix. All of these pieces are wonderfully enhanced by the museum's scenography, not to mention the storyboard extracts that shed further light, undoubtedly more abstract for the layman, on the making of films. The permanent space dedicated to the world of Wes Anderson alone occupies two of the museum's nine large rooms. The first, for example, gives visitors the impression of becoming actors in *Asteroid City* (2023), as they face the life-size train compartment where, in the film, Scarlett Johansson—in a splendid black-and-white sequence—scans a letter. Will the American actress appear out of nowhere and continue reading, one wonders, as this cinematic artifact is transposed into the real world? As for the costumes of the concierge from *The Grand Budapest Hotel* and the creature from *Asteroid City*, do they still bear the traces of their use by Ralph Fiennes (Mr. Gustave) and Jeff Goldblum (the alien)? In the second room, of identical size, exclusive making-of videos from Anderson's various films are shown, in which some of the filmmaker's collaborators explain their work. This more in-depth pedagogy provides an ideal complement to this unique genre immersive experience, somewhere between the cabinet of curiosities *(Wunderkammer)* that is close to the *auteur*'s heart, and the time capsule.

A Good Mutual Understanding

The Cinema and Miniature Museum and Wes Anderson should be able to actively pursue their collaboration in the future. His visit on October 15, 2023, for the inauguration of the permanent space dedicated to him, gave the director the opportunity to clearly express his renewed interest in exploiting his universe: "It is unusual to be able to install the characters and locations of a film in a medium-sized permanent exhibition space—but that is one of the advantages of working with puppets and miniatures...*Isle of Dogs*, *Fantastic Mr. Fox*, *Asteroid City*, to name but a few: the great Musée Cinéma et Miniature exhibits them, along with magnificent objects that trace the entire history of cinema."[1] For Lena Weisse, the museum's communications manager, the aim now is to continue to build on the partnership begun in 2015. "We're getting to know more and more of his close collaborators to see with them what can be recovered. Some of them have kept molds, others, the first versions of the costumes."[2] The range of possibilities is all the greater in that Anderson seems willing to spread his art, and takes into consideration all the proposals that come his way, or independently of him.

Delliberately Wes

In 2017, a man by the name of Wally Koval embarked on an adventure as outlandish as Steve Zissou's in *The Life Aquatic* (2004): with his wife, he decided to set off to discover places inspired by the Wes Anderson universe of which he is a fan, and to bring back photos of them! The couple set up the Accidentally Wes Anderson account on Instagram, posting their best shots. Soon, a community of enthusiasts joined AWA, the cool acronym for the account. Seven years later, AWA has almost two million subscribers and a considerable number of contributors. Wally Koval had the great idea of asking his followers to submit suitable photos, along with precise comments on the places they visited. Over the years, the database has grown considerably, so much so that in 2020, the Kovals were able to put together a book of the best images from all corners of the globe. After the Instagram account, the book *Accidentally Wes Anderson* was born—a second one is in preparation. Anderson was not unmoved by this flattering initiative. He even prefaced the book with his characteristic humor: "There must be about 200 locations here, which should keep me busy for several decades, but I plan not to let any of these experiences escape me, especially the Croatian pancakes stand. [...] I now understand what it means to be accidentally myself. Thank you. I am still confused what it means to be *deliberately* me, if that is even what I am, but that is not important."[3] Some Wes Anderson in the text!

The Cabinet of Doctor Wes

At the end of 2018, a few months after the release of *Isle of Dogs*, Wes Anderson was back in the news with an art exhibition curated by him and his wife, Lebanese illustrator and novelist Juman Malouf. At the invitation of Vienna's prestigious Kunsthistorisches Museum, which gave them carte blanche and access to its abundant collection, the flattered couple chose to offer the public something very much their own: a cabinet of curiosities, bringing together the most unusual pieces made available by the institution—some four hundred objects, paintings, sculptures, and other accessories. Indeed, the filmmaker and his wife share a pronounced taste for the absurd. After all, Malouf collaborated on some of her husband's films. In *Fantastic Mr. Fox*, she lent her voice to a secondary character; for *Moonrise Kingdom* (2012), she imagined one of the books carried by the heroine in her flight; she also drew protagonist sketches for *The Grand Budapest Hotel*. So it comes as no surprise that the exhibition is titled "Spitzmaus Mummy in a Coffin and Other Treasures." Walking through the eight rooms of the exhibition, the intrigued visitor would have thought they were in a Wes Anderson film, with its walls painted in the filmmaker's fetish colors (green, yellow, red), symmetrically organized showcases, judiciously hung canvases, blending of genres, associations of ideas, telescoping of opposing emotions...The exhibition was a great success and was subsequently hosted in Milan, in autumn 2019, in the sumptuous setting of the Prada Foundation.

Next page spread:
Robert Yeoman and Wes Anderson scrutinize Margot Robbie in *Asteroid City*.

The British Belmond Pullman train carriage, entirely decorated by Wes Anderson.

PREMI
DEA
SIST
A PLA
MONT

LIGHTING CREW
SHOWS

GLOSSARY

Animatic: a briefly animated video based on storyboard drawings and synchronized with provisional voices, sound effects, and music. In essence, an animated storyboard.

Animatronics: term combining "animation" and "electronics." This is a technique for animating models or artificial creatures using cables, hydraulic cylinders and levers, robotics, radio-controlled systems, or computer-configured commands.

Backlot: series of dummy sets for a film studio (streets, façades, residential areas, bodies of water, exotic locations) located on the outskirts of the covered sets and intended for location shoots but more easily controlled than real-world sites.

Blocking (of actors): movement and placement of actors within the frame.

Calibration (color correction and grading): a harmonization process that involves fine-tuning the chromatic balance and density of shot images. It can also be used to amplify or reduce certain details. This process takes place during postproduction.

Chroma keying: background filmed beforehand and added in postproduction to depict a setting or detail that did not exist in the original shot, commonly used for green screen compositing.

Company moves: moving from one set to another.

Dolly: wheeled platform on which a camera is mounted. It is often placed on rails, enabling stable and fluid lateral camera movements.

Forced perspective: an artisanal method of artificially amplifying depth of field or simulating size differences between characters or objects. This is achieved by playing with the size of the backgrounds, camera placement, and the distance/closeness of the subjects concerned.

Matte painting: painting on glass representing a set, which is either complete in itself or intended to enlarge or modify a real set. Spaces left empty are used to project scenes filmed separately, but in such a way as to blend in perfectly with the painting. The combination of the two elements is then filmed to create the illusion that an action is taking place inside the set.

Score: the original music created specifically for a particular film.

Set decorator: person responsible for finding elements (objects, furniture, wallpaper, etc.) to enrich sets according to the director's stylistic choices. They work in close collaboration with the props designer and set designer.

Steadicam: a mechanism consisting of articulated arms, bearings, and counterweights to which a camera is attached and which is harnessed to a camera operator. The camera operator retains the freedom of movement of the mounted camera while taking steady, fluid shots as with a dolly (see *Dolly* entry), all without being hampered by the weight of the camera. It was invented in 1972 by Garrett Brown, who was himself a Steadicam operator on numerous feature films, such as *Bound for Glory* (Hal Ashby, 1976), *Marathon Man* (John Schlesinger, 1976), *Rocky* (John G. Avildsen, 1976), *The Shining* (Stanley Kubrick, 1980), *Wolfen* (Michael Wadleigh, 1981), *Return of the Jedi* (Richard Marquand, 1983), *Indiana Jones and the Temple of Doom* (Steven Spielberg, 1984), and *Casino* (Martin Scorsese, 1995).

Stop-motion: an animation process in which a fixed object (model, character) is photographed and its position changed very slightly from one shot to the next. The movement is generated by the scrolling of images assembled one after the other, in a similar way to cartoons.

Storyboard: a series of drawings based on the script, representing the different shots of a film at the preproduction stage. Camera and actor movements are indicated, enabling a work plan to be drawn up and a budget to be estimated.

Traveling shot: a term used to describe the movement of the camera, forward, backward, laterally, vertically, or even circularly. This movement is facilitated by the use of rails, cranes, or Steadicam-type handheld cameras (see *Steadicam*).

Wes Anderson, in 1998, during the filming of *Rushmore*.

NOTES

BOTTLE ROCKET (1993) (p. 16)

1. Pamela Colloff, "The New Kids—Wes Anderson and Owen Wilson," *Texas Monthly*, May 1998.

BOTTLE ROCKET (1996) (p. 21)

1. "Bottle Rocket: Production Information" (press kit), n.d., http://www.rushmoreacademy.com/academy/films/bottlerocket/bookstore/production_info_presskit.pdf, 2. Audio commentary on *Bottle Rocket* DVD.
3. Audio commentary on *Bottle Rocket* DVD.
4. Audio commentary on *Bottle Rocket* DVD.
5. "Bottle Rocket: Production Information" (press kit), n.d., http://www.rushmoreacademy.com/academy/films/bottlerocket/bookstore/production_info_presskit.pdf, 5.
6. Interview with Robert Yeoman, October 2023.
7. Interview with Robert Yeoman, October 2023.
8. Interview with Robert Yeoman, October 2023.
9. Interview with Robert Yeoman, October 2023.
10. Interview with Robert Yeoman, October 2023.
11. Audio commentary on *Bottle Rocket* DVD.
12. Simon Houpt, "A Mighty Successful Failure," *Globe and Mail* (Toronto), December 23, 2004, https://www.theglobeandmail.com/arts/a-mighty-successful-failure/article22733176.

RUSHMORE (p. 39)

1. "Rushmore" (press kit), October 1, 1998, http://rushmore.shootangle.com/academy/films/rushmore/library/rushmore_press_kit.pdf, 6.
2. "Rushmore" (press kit), October 1, 1998, http://rushmore.shootangle.com/academy/films/rushmore/library/rushmore_press_kit.pdf, 8.
3. Interview with Robert Yeoman, October 2023.
4. Interview with Robert Yeoman, October 2023.
5. Interview with Robert Yeoman, October 2023.
6. Interview with Robert Yeoman, October 2023.
7. Interview with Robert Yeoman, October 2023.
8. Matt Zoller Seitz, *The Wes Anderson Collection* (Abrams, 2013), 92.
9. Interview with Robert Yeoman, October 2023.
10. Interview with Robert Yeoman, October 2023.

BILL MURRAY (p. 52)

1. Charlie Rose, January 29, 1999.

THE ROYAL TENENBAUMS (p. 59)

1. Interview with Robert Yeoman, November 2023.
2. "The Royal Tenenbaums" (press kit), November 20, 2001, http://rushmore.shootangle.com/academy/films/tenenbaums/library/royal_tenenbaums_presskit.pdf, 11–12.
3. "The Royal Tenenbaums" (press kit), http://rushmore.shootangle.com/academy/films/tenenbaums/library/royal_tenenbaums_presskit.pdf, 13.
4. "The Royal Tenenbaums" (press kit), http://rushmore.shootangle.com/academy/films/tenenbaums/library/royal_tenenbaums_presspre.pdf, 11.
5. Interview with Robert Yeoman, November 2023.
6. Interview with Robert Yeoman, November 2023.
7. Interview with Robert Yeoman, November 2023.
8. "The Royal Tenenbaums" (press kit), http://rushmore.shootangle.com/academy/films/tenenbaums/library/royal_tenenbaums_presskit.pdf, 18.
9. Interview with Robert Yeoman, November 2023.
10. ABC News, October 8, 2001.

THE LIFE AQUATIC WITH STEVE ZISSOU (p. 79)

1. *Les Inrockuptibles* (France) magazine, March 9, 2005.
2. "The Life Aquatic with Steve Zissou" (press kit), June 2007, https://rushmoreacademy.com/wp-content/uploads/2007/06/The.Life.Aquatic.press.kit.pdf.
3. Interview with Robert Yeoman, December 2023.
4. Interview with Robert Yeoman, December 2023.
5. Interview with Robert Yeoman, December 2023.
6. "Nina Jacobson: How to Make a Hit in Hollywood," *Without Fail* (podcast), October 22, 2018, https://gimletmedia.com/shows/without-fail/94h8w9, at 9:55.

THE WES CONNECTION (p. 92)

1. Matt Zoller Seitz, *The Wes Anderson Collection* (Abrams, 2013), 123.
2. Marcos Uzal, "Wes Anderson 'J'ai toujours voulu faire un film sur les déchets, j'aime leur complexité,'" *Libération*, April 10, 2018.
3. Toma Clarac, "Wes Anderson's Japan," *Vanity Fair* (France), April 10, 2018, https://www.vanityfair.fr/culture/ecrans/story/wes-anderson-raconte-les-influences-japonaises-de-lile-aux-chiens/1799.
4. Wes Anderson on Stefan Zweig and The Grand Budapest Hotel, New York Public Library, February 27, 2014, https://www.youtube.com/watch?v=4jk1s74i8r8.
5. "The Wonderful Story of Henry Sugar" (press kit), 5–6.
6. "7 Perfectly-Scored Wes Anderson Scenes," *Rolling Stone*, March 5, 2014, https://www.rollingstone.com/music/music-lists/7-perfectly-scored-wes-anderson-scenes-20640.

HOTEL CHEVALIER (p. 100)

1. Chris Lee, "A Tantalizing Taste of 'Darjeeling,'" *Los Angeles Times*, September 24, 2007.
2. Chris Lee, "A Tantalizing Taste of 'Darjeeling,'" *Los Angeles Times*, September 24, 2007.
3. Interview with Robert Yeoman.
4. Interview with Robert Yeoman.

THE DARJEELING LIMITED (p. 105)

1. Interview with Wes Anderson, January 2024.
2. "Darjeeling Limited" (press kit), https://www.rushmoreacademy.com/academy/films/darjeelinglimited/traindata/TDL.Press.Kit.pdf.
3. "Darjeeling Limited" (press kit), https://www.rushmoreacademy.com/academy/films/darjeelinglimited/traindata/TDL.Press.Kit.pdf, 12.
4. Interview with Robert Yeoman, December 2023.
5. Interview with Robert Yeoman, December 2023.
6. Interview with Robert Yeoman, December 2023.

MARKETING CULTURE (p. 118)

1. Interview with Darius Khondji, December 2023.

FANTASTIC MR. FOX (p. 123)

1. Interview with Turlo Griffin, November 2023.
2. Interview with Turlo Griffin, November 2023.
3. Interview with Turlo Griffin, November 2023.
4. Interview with Turlo Griffin, November 2023.
5. *La Septième Obsession*, special issue 5 dedicated to Wes Anderson, p. 119.
6. Interview with Andy Gent, October 2023.
7. Interview with Andy Gent, October 2023.
8. Chris Lee, "Fur Flies on 'Mr. Fox,'" *Los Angeles Times*, October 11, 2009, https://www.latimes.com/archives/la-xpm-2009-oct-11-ca-mrfox11-story.html.
9. Matt Zoller Seitz, *The Wes Anderson Collection* (Abrams, 2013), 251.

A HIGHLY ANIMATED WORLD (p. 136)

1. Interview with Andy Gent, October 2023.
2. Interview with Andy Gent, October 2023.
3. Interview with Andy Gent, October 2023.
4. Interview with Andy Gent, October 2023.
5. Interview with Andy Gent, October 2023.
6. Interview with Andy Gent, October 2023.
7. Interview with Andy Gent, October 2023.
8. Interview with Andy Gent, October 2023.
9. Interview with Andy Gent, October 2023.

MOONRISE KINGDOM (p. 145)

1. Interview with Robert Yeoman, December 2023.
2. Interview with Robert Yeoman, December 2023.
3. Interview with Robert Yeoman, December 2023.
4. Interview with Robert Yeoman, December 2023.
5. "Moonrise Kingdom by Wes Anderson Is the Opening Film of the 65th Festival de Cannes," press release, Festival de Cannes, March 9, 2012, https://www.festival-cannes.com/en/2012/moonrise-kingdom-by-wes-anderson-is-the-opening-film-of-the-65th-festival-de-cannes.

6. "Moonrise Kingdom by Wes Anderson Is the Opening Film of the 65th Festival de Cannes," press release, Festival de Cannes, March 9, 2012, https://www.festival-cannes.com/en/2012/moonrise-kingdom-by-wes-anderson-is-the-opening-film-of-the-65th-festival-de-cannes.

WES'S GOOD SHOTS (p. 162)

1. "The French Dispatch" (French press kit) p. 13.
2. Interview with Robert Yeoman, October 2023.
3. Interview with Robert Yeoman, October 2023.
4. Interview with Robert Yeoman, January 2024.
5. Interview with Robert Yeoman, January 2024.
6. Interview with Robert Yeoman, January 2024.
7. Interview with Robert Yeoman, January 2024.
8. "The French Dispatch" (French press kit) p. 15.
9. "The French Dispatch" (French press kit) p. 15.
10. Interview with Robert Yeoman, January 2024.
11. Interview with Martin Scali, October 2023.
12. Interview with Martin Scali, October 2023.
13. Interview with Martin Scali, October 2023.

CASTELLO CAVALCANTI (p. 166)

1. Interview with Darius Khondji, December 2023.
2. Interview with Darius Khondji, December 2023.
3. Interview with Darius Khondji, December 2023.

THE GRAND BUDAPEST HOTEL (p. 173)

1. Matt Zoller Seitz, *The Grand Budapest Hotel* (Abrams, 2015), 72.
2. Scott Foundas, "Wes Anderson Talks about His 'Grand' Influences," *Variety*, February 7, 2014, https://variety.com/2014/film/markets-festivals/wes-anderson-talks-about-his-grand-influences-1201091911.
3. Seitz, The Grand Budapest Hotel (Abrams, 2015), 72.
4. Danny Miller, "Tony Revolori Gives a Star-Making Performance in Wes Anderson's Grand Budapest Hotel," Cinefiled, March 7, 2014, https://www.cinephiled.com/interview-tony-revolori-gives-star-making-performance-wes-andersons-grand-budapest-hotel.
5. Interview with Robert Yeoman, December 2023.
6. Seitz, *The Grand Budapest Hotel* (Abrams, 2015), 89.
7. Interview with Patricia Colin, October 2023.
8. Interview with Patricia Colin, October 2023.
9. Interview with Robert Yeoman, October 2023.
10. Interview with Robert Yeoman, October 2023.
11. Interview with Robert Yeoman, October 2023.

THE VINTAGE LOOK (p. 190)

1. Interview with Turlo Griffin, November 2023.
2. Interview with Turlo Griffin, November 2023.
3. Interview with Turlo Griffin, November 2023.
4. Interview with Turlo Griffin, November 2023.
5. Interview with Erica Dorn, October 2023.
6. Interview with Erica Dorn, October 2023.
7. Interview with Erica Dorn, October 2023.
8. Interview with Erica Dorn, October 2023.
9. Interview with Patricia Colon, October 2023.
10. Interview with Patricia Colon, October 2023.
11. Interview with Patricia Colon, October 2023.
12. Interview with Patricia Colon, October 2023.
13. Interview with Patricia Colon, October 2023.
14. Interview with Simon Weisse, September 2023.
15. Interview with Simon Weisse, September 2023.
16. Interview with Simon Weisse, September 2023.
17. Interview with Simon Weisse, September 2023.
18. Interview with Stéphane Cressend, October 2023.
19. Interview with Stéphane Cressend, October 2023.
20. Interview with Stéphane Cressend, October 2023.
21. Interview with Stéphane Cressend, October 2023.
22. Interview with Stéphane Cressend, October 2023.
23. Interview with Stéphane Cressend, October 2023.

ISLE OF DOGS (p. 199)

1. Interview with Andy Gent, October 2023.
2. *La Septième Obsession* (France), special issue 5 dedicated to Wes Anderson, p. 121.
3. Interview with Erica Dorn, October 2023.
4. Interview with Andy Gent, October 2023.
5. Interview with Andy Gent, October 2023.
6. Interview with Andy Gent, October 2023.
7. Interview with Andy Gent, October 2023.
8. Kate Samuelson, "A Conversation with the Team Behind Isle of Dogs' Painstaking Visuals," *Time*, April 10, 2018, https://time.com/5211233/isle-of-dogs-designer-producer-interview.

THE FRENCH DISPATCH (p. 215)

1. Interview with Jeremy Dawson, January 2024.
2. "Tilda Swinton in the Credits of the Wes Anderson Film in Angoulême," *Charente Libre* (France), November 16, 2018.
3. "The French Dispatch" (French press kit), p. 5.
4. Fiona Ipert, "Léa Seydoux: 'Modernity Worries Me Terribly,'" *The Women's Journal* (France), October 28, 2021.
5. Interview with Martin Scali, October 2023.
6. Interview with Stéphane Cressend, October 2023.
7. Interview with Stéphane Cressend, October 2023.
8. Interview with Robert Yeoman, January 2024.
9. Interview with Robert Yeoman, January 2024.
10. Interview with Milena Canonero, October 2023.
11. Interview with Milena Canonero, October 2023.

ALEXANDRE DESPLAT THE METRONOME (p. 238)

1. Interview with Alexandre Desplat, January 2024.
2. Interview with Alexandre Desplat, January 2024.
3. Interview with Alexandre Desplat, January 2024.
4. Interview with Alexandre Desplat, January 2024.

ASTEROID CITY (p. 241)

1. Interview with Wes Anderson, November 2023.
2. "Asteroid City" (French press kit), p. 16.
3. Interview with Wes Anderson, October 2023.
4. Interview with Wes Anderson, October 2023.
5. Interview with Robert Yeoman, January 2024.
6. Interview with Milena Canonero, October 2023.
7. Interview with Milena Canonero, October 2023.
8. Interview with Robert Yeoman, January 2024.
9. Samuel Douhaire, "*Asteroid City*: In Cannes, Wes Anderson in Great Form," *Télérama* (France), May 23, 2023.
10. Peter Bradshaw, "*Asteroid City* Review—Wes Anderson's 1950s Sci-fi Is an Exhilarating Triumph of Pure Style," *The Guardian*, May 23, 2023.
11. Sandra Onana, "Cannes Film Festival: *Asteroid City* by Wes Anderson, Desert of Déjà-vu," *Libération* (France), May 23, 2023.
12. David Fear, "Wes Anderson's 'Asteroid City' has sharply divided Cannes", *Rolling Stone*, May 24, 2023.
13. Interview with Alexandre Desplat, January 2024.

AT THE THEATER THIS EVENING (p. 254)

1. Interview with Wes Anderson, October 2023.
2. "The Wonderful Story of Henry Sugar" (French press kit), p. 5.

COLLECTION ROALD DAHL (p. 257)

1. Interview with Wes Anderson, October 2023.
2. "The Wonderful Story of Henry Sugar" (French press kit), p. 6.
3. Gregg Goldstein, "*Asteroid City*'s Rupert Friend: 'Maybe I've got the scars and the Bruises now' to play James Bond," *Variety*, May 19, 2023.
4. William Mullally, "Benedict Cumberbatch Talks Pushing Himself, Working with Wes Anderson," *Arab News*, October 20, 2023.
5. Interview with Robert Yeoman, January 2024.
6. Interview with Robert Yeoman, January 2024.
7. Sarah Shachat, "The Sets Move as Much as the Actors in Wes Anderson's 'The Wonderful Story of Henry Sugar,'" IndieWire, October 6, 2023.

THE WES INFLUENCE (p. 264)

1. Remarks by Wes Anderson during the inauguration of the permanent Wes Anderson space at the Cinema & Miniature Museum in Lyon, October 15, 2023.
2. Interview with Lena Weisse, October 2023.
3. Wally Koval, *Accidentally Wes Anderson* (Voracious, 2021), Preface.

BIBLIOGRAPHY

Atkins, Annie. *Designing Graphic Props for Filmmaking* (Phaidon, 2020).

Koval, Wally. *Accidentally Wes Anderson* (Orion Publishing/Interart/EPA (French edition), 2020).

The Making of Fantastic Mr. Fox (Rizzoli, 2009).

Nathan, Ian. *Wes Anderson: La filmographie intégrale d'un réalisateur de génie* [*Wes Anderson: The Complete Filmography of a Director of Genius*] (Gallimard, 2020).

Seitz, Matt Zoller. *The Wes Anderson Collection* (Abrams, 2013).

Seitz, Matt Zoller. *The Grand Budapest Hotel* (Abrams, 2015; Akileos, 2018 [French edition]).

Seitz, Matt Zoller. *Isle of Dogs* (Abrams, 2018).

Seitz, Matt Zoller. *The French Dispatch* (Abrams, 2023).

Wes Anderson, special issue of *La Septième Obsession* [*The Seventh Obsession*], number 5, 2021.

Wes in Town: Un tournage à Angoulême [*Wes in Town: Filming in Angoulême*] (Makisapa, 2021).

Wes Anderson shows shots from *Aboard the Darjeeling Limited*.

INDEX

D

E

F

In the Cygnus car of the famous British Belmond Pullman train.

M

N

O

P

Q

R

Wes Anderson checks the frame on *Moonrise Kingdom*.

ACKNOWLEDGMENTS

Thanks to Nicolas Schaller, co-author of *Steven Spielberg All the Films*, who put me in touch with Laurence Lehoux, a passionate and caring editor.

Thanks to Christelle Fucilli, iconographer, coordinator, first reader, for her patience, good advice, and accessibility, the strong link in the making of this book; to the proofreaders Fanny Delahaye and Valérie Nigdélian for their meticulousness; to graphic designer Lucie Polard and art director Clotilde Roussin for their creativity.

My particular gratitude goes to:

Thierry Frémaux for his enthusiasm when I asked him to write the preface while he was in the midst of preparing for the Cannes 2024 festival;

Matthieu Rey and Cédric Landemaine, the dynamic duo of press attachés who helped me initiate contacts with Wes Anderson's entourage;

Simon Weisse, in charge of miniatures in the director's films, who was the first to get back to me and who opened many doors;

Robert Yeoman, the director's faithful cinematographer, without whom this book would not be what it is, packed with information and some previously unpublished shots;

Andy Gent (puppet master) and Turlo Griffin (conceptual artist and illustrator), for their detailed insights and infectious passion;

Erica Dorn (chief graphic designer), Stéphane Cressend (set supervisor), Patricia Colin (chief lighting designer), and Martin Scali (second unit director), talented members of Wes Anderson's unofficial "French team," whom I called upon extensively and who were unfailingly supportive;

Alexandre Desplat, whose talent lies not only in his scores but also in his words, where poetry vies with passion (I would also like to take this opportunity to pay tribute to the journalist Thierry Jousse, who acted as intermediary);

Director of photography Darius Khondji, for his kind humility and accessibility;

Producer Jeremy Dawson, who took the time to get back to me despite the preproduction schedule of Wes Anderson's twelfth feature film;

Julien Dumont and Lena Weisse, director and communications manager, respectively, of the Musée Cinéma et Miniature de Lyon, for their invaluable assistance;

Jim Jourdane, co-author of the book *Wes in Town: Un tournage à Angoulême*, for his enthusiasm;

Nicolas Tellop, deputy editor-in-chief of *La Septième Obsession*, for his responsiveness.

I would particularly like to thank my four guardian angels, Laure, Louis, Clémence, and Paul, who endured my mood swings and impatience while encouraging me during the absorbing process of the writing of this book;

And, of course, Wes Anderson himself, for his composition, momentum, sophistication, humor, melancholy, and humanity.

Next two page spreads:
Wes Anderson in the middle of the desert (*Aboard the Darjeeling Limited*) and rubble (*The French Dispatch*, with Willem Dafoe, left).

PHOTO CREDITS

© Laura Wilson 8, 16, 18, 19, 24, 28 (top), 71, 109, 110, 112 (top), 112 (bottom), 114-115, 194 (bottom), 196-197
© Robert Yeoman 91, 162, 195 (top), 274, 284-285
© Roger Do Minh 9, 10 (bottom), 12-13, 14-15, 36, 163, 164, 268-269, 286-287
© Andy Gent 139 (top), 139 (bottom), 139 (middle), 209
© Michael Taylor Indian Paintbrush—Searchlight Pictures 175
© Nicolas Receveur pour Belmond Train 267, 277
© Wes Anderson 42
© Van Redin 43

Musee Cinema & Miniature (Lyon, France)

© Roger Do Minh / Musee Cinema & Miniature 192, 265

Aurimages

© 20th Century Fox / BBQ_DFY 201, 202, 204, 205 (bottom)
© 20th Century Fox / Everett Collection 62 (top), 140-141, 198, 203, 205 (top), 205 (middle), 206 207, 208 (top), 208 (bottom)
© AF archive / Mary Evans 177 (top)
© American Empirical Pictures / BBQ_DFY 100, 166, 168 (top), 168 (bottom), 169 (top)
© Capital Picture / KCS 234-235
© Channel 5 / AF archive / Mary Evans 53
© Columbia Pictures / AF archive / Mary Evans 25 (top), 32-33
© Columbia Pictures / Everett Collection 20, 30-31
© Columbia Pictures / Mary Evans 29
© Columbia Pictures / The Kobal Collection / Shutterstock 25 (bottom)
© Embassy / The Kobal Collection / Shutterstock 95
© Eon Productions / Everett Collection 191
© Everett Collection 35, 69, 94 (top), 179 (top)
© F.C. Produzioni / PECF / Everett Collection 92, 93
© Focus Features / Pop. 87 Productions / BBQ_DFY 73, 96-97, 169 (bottom), 190, 240, 244, 245, 246-247, 248, 249 (top), 249 (bottom), 252
© Focus Features / Pop. 87 Productions / Capital Picture / KCS 170, 243, 250, 253 (top), 262
© Fox Searchlight / AF archive / Mary Evans 57 (bottom), 117, 125, 129, 130, 131, 143 (bottom), 259
© Fox Searchlight / Mary Evans 104, 107, 127 (top), 128
© Fox Searchlight / BBQ_DFY 165, 182-183
© Fox Searchlight / Everett Collection 98 (top), 98 (bottom), 99 (bottom), 108, 111 (top), 113, 116 (top), 116 (bottom), 122, 127 (bottom), 132, 133, 137, 172, 176, 177 (bottom), 179 (bottom), 184, 185, 186-187, 188-189, 193 (top), 193 (bottom), 236 (top)
© Fox Searchlight / MoviesCom 111 (bottom)
© Fox Searchlight / The Kobal Collection / Shutterstock 57 (top), 142 (top), 161 (bottom), 178
© Indian Paintbrush / AF archive / Mary Evans 154 (top), 160 (top)
© Indian Paintbrush / BBQ_DFY 77
© Indian Paintbrush / Everett Collection 147, 149 (top), 149 (bottom), 152 (bottom), 153 (bottom), 154 (middle), 157
© Indian Paintbrush / SunsetBox / AllPix / Aurimages 155
© Indian Paintbrush / Zuma Press 152 (top)
© Les Films du Carrosse / Everett Collection 232
© Netflix / BBQ_DFY 28 (bottom), 160 (bottom), 253 (bottom), 256 (bottom left), 256 (bottom right), 256 (top left), 256 (top right), 260 (bottom), 261 (top), 261 (bottom), 263
© Netflix / Everett Collection 194 (top)
© Orion Pictures / Everett Collection 52
© RKO / The Kobal Collection / Shutterstock 64 (bottom)
© Searchlight Pictures / AF archive / Mary Evans 102, 103
© Searchlight Pictures / BBQ_DFY 118, 120-121, 171, 214, 225 (top), 230, 260 (top)
© Searchlight Pictures / Everett Collection 195 (bottom), 218 (bottom), 219, 228 (top)
© The Swimming Company / The Kobal Collection / Shutterstock 255
© Touchstone Pictures / AF archive / Mary Evans 44, 45, 46 (bottom), 50-51, 233
© Touchstone Pictures / Everett Collection 46 (top), 48 (bottom), 48 (top), 49, 56 (top), 56 (bottom), 61 (top), 61 (bottom), 64 (top), 65, 66-67, 68, 72, 78, 81, 82, 83, 85 (bottom), 86, 88-89, 90, 142 (bottom), 143 (top), 161 (top), 237 (top), 237 (bottom), 254
© Touchstone Pictures / Mary Evans / Aurimages 63, 270, 281
© Touchstone Pictures / The Kobal Collection / Shutterstock 38, 41, 58, 70, 85 (top), 236 (bottom)
© Touchstone Pictures / Zuma Press 10 (top), 84, 87 (top), 87 (bottom), 99 (top)

Prod DB

© 20th Century Fox—American Empirical Pictures—Indian Paintbrush Scott Rudin Productions—Studio Babelsberg / DR, 54-55, 138, 211, 212-213, 217, 218 (top), 220-221, 222, 223, 224, 225 (bottom), 226-227, 228 (bottom), 231, 251 (bottom)
© 20th Century Fox—American Empirical Pictures / DR 134, 135
© American Empirical Pictures—Indian Paintbrush—Scott Rudin Productions / DR, 150-151, 154 (bottom), 156, 158-159
© Focus Features—Indian Paintbrush—American Empirical Pictures, 210, 251 (top)
© Touchstone Pictures / DR 47, 74-75

Bridgeman Art Library

© Monica Fritz, All rights reserved 2023 94 (bottom)
© Mary Evans 180 (bottom)

Getty Images

© Martyn Goodacre 6
© Stefania D'Alessandro 37
© Vera Anderson 136
© 2016 Anthony Harvey 238
© 2023 Stephane Cardinale—Corbis 264

Hemis.fr

© parkerphotography / Alamy Stock Photo 126 (top)
© Jeff Gilbert / Alamy Stock Photo 126 (bottom)

Library of Congress

© Library Prints and Photographs Division of Congress 180 (top), 181

DR

Kenneth C. Zikel 23, 119, 148 et 153 (top)

Every effort has been made to find the copyright rights holders of the elements cited in this work. The publisher undertakes to correct unintentional errors or omissions in future reprintings.

ABOUT THE AUTHOR

CHRISTOPHE NARBONNE
has been a film journalist for almost thirty years (twenty-three of which he spent with *Première* magazine as a columnist), as well as a cinema consultant (film presentations, video bonus content). He loves Alfred Hitchcock as well as Kool and the Gang, sports, and comics. He published his first novel, *Noir sur Blanc* (Assyelle), in 2022.

Translation by Caroline Higgitt and Paul Ratcliffe by arrangement with Jackie Dobbyne of Jacaranda Publishing Services Limited

Cover design by Katie Benezra

Original title: Wes Anderson, *La Totale*
Published by Éditions E/P/A—Hachette Livre, 2024

Black Dog & Leventhal Publishers
Hachette Book Group
1290 Avenue of the Americas
New York, NY 10104
www.blackdogandleventhal.com

BlackDogandLeventhal @BDLev

First English-language edition: September 2025

Published by Black Dog & Leventhal Publishers, an imprint of Hachette Book Group, Inc. The Black Dog & Leventhal Publishers name and logo are trademarks of Hachette Book Group, Inc.

Additional copyright/credits information is on page 283.

LCCN: 2024930302

ISBNs: 978-0-7624-8864-3 (hardcover), 978-0-7624-8865-0 (ebook)

Printed in China

10 9 8 7 6 5 4 3 2 1